C000192910

The Labour Party, War and Relations, 1945–2006

Questions of war were not central to the founding of the Labour Party, yet questions of war – specifically, under what circumstances the party would support the dispatch of British military forces to fight abroad – have divided and damaged the party throughout its history more deeply than any other single issue.

The Labour Party, War and International Relations, 1945–2006 opens by identifying and examining the factors that have influenced the party's thinking about war, before considering the post-1945 Cold War context and analysing a range of cases: the Korean War; the party's response to the 1956 Suez crisis; the Wilson governments' approach to the Vietnam War; Labour's response to the 1982 invasion of the Falkland Islands; the crisis over the August 1990 Iraqi invasion of Kuwait, culminating in the 1991 war; the wars of the 1990s over Bosnia and Kosovo; and the case for war in Iraq developed by the Blair government during 2002–03.

This is a timely book that both illuminates approaches to past wars and helps us understand the basis of current military commitments. As such it will be of great interest to students across courses in Politics, History, and War Studies.

Mark Phythian is Professor of Politics at the University of Leicester, UK

The Labour Party, War and International Relations, 1945–2006

Mark Phythian

Routledge
Taylor & Francis Group

LONDON AND NEW YORK

First published 2007
by Routledge
2 Park Square, Milton Park, Abingdon, Oxon, OX14 4RN

Simultaneously published in the USA and Canada
by Routledge
270 Madison Avenue, New York, NY 10016

Routledge is an imprint of the Taylor & Francis Group, an informa business

© 2007 Mark Phythian

Typeset in Times New Roman
by Taylor & Francis
Printed and bound in Great Britain by
TJ International Ltd, Padstow, Cornwall

British Library Cataloguing in Publication Data
A catalogue record for this book is available from the British Library

Library of Congress Cataloging in Publication Data
A catalog record for this book has been requested

ISBN 13: 978-0-415-39911-1 (hbk)
ISBN 13: 978-0-415-39912-8 (pbk)
ISBN 13: 978-0-203-93899-7 (ebk)

For Di

Contents

Preface

Questions of war were not central to the founding of the Labour Party, yet questions of war – specifically, under what circumstances the party would support the dispatch of British military forces to fight abroad – have arguably divided and damaged the party throughout its history more deeply than any other single issue. While the historian Michael Howard has written of the liberal dilemma generated by the question of war,[1] it has also created an acute and specific Labour variant that the party has never been able to fully resolve, and that this book sets out to explore.

Its focus is the period since 1945. Nevertheless, it opens with an overview of key events during the previous 40 years that helped give form to the party's approach to the question of war. It goes on to identify and examine the factors that influenced the party's thinking about war, and considers how far we can talk about a distinctive Labour Party approach. The chapters that follow are not intended to provide a blow-by-blow account of the wars under discussion. Their course is considered in relation to the way in which they illuminate the principles that have shaped the party's attitudes. Chapter 2 examines the Cold War context and the debates and divisions that the process of taking sides in the Cold War generated. This process determined the framework within which decisions over war were taken in subsequent years. In particular, Cold War alliance with the US brought with it various costs arising from pressure to deploy British troops in support of wider US/Western objectives which, for a party whose *raison d'être* lay in social reform and economic redistribution, represented clear opportunity costs. The most divisive case arose over British involvement in the Korean War and the associated rearmament programme, the subject of Chapter 3. This chapter goes on to examine the party's response to the 1956 Suez crisis, which solidified its reputation as an upholder of the authority of the United Nations, an organisation that party members had earlier played a key role in creating.

Chapter 4 deals with the war in Vietnam during the 1964–70 governments of Harold Wilson, the only war covered in this book in which Britain did not play a substantial military role. Nevertheless, the Wilson governments faced acute pressure from the US to commit even a token contingent of troops – famously, President Johnson told Wilson he would settle for the Black Watch, as even a few pipers would provide the desired appearance of internationalisation[2] – but resisted. Yet Wilson was criticised at the time and thereafter for supporting the US war in Vietnam. From the vantage point of the early twenty-first century, where Wilson's handling of the Vietnam issue can be considered in the context of the Blair government's commitment of British troops in support of a US war in Iraq, it is time for a reassessment.

Chapter 5 deals with the party's response to the April 1982 Argentinian invasion of the Falkland Islands, and the divisions generated by the questions of whether and at what point it would be right to go to war to recover them. Chapter 6 deals with the crisis over the August 1990 Iraqi invasion of Kuwait, culminating in the 1991 war to remove Iraq. This occurred during the very early stages of the transition from a Cold War to a post-Cold War world, and can be considered either the final significant war of that earlier era, or the first of the new, post-Cold War era. Chaper 7 deals with the very different kinds of war that emerged in this post-Cold War world as the decade progressed, and focuses on the position of the Labour Party in relation to the wars over Bosnia and Kosovo. The party's approach to the Kosovo war was markedly different to its approach to the earlier Balkan wars. By 1999 it had returned to office under a new leader, Tony Blair, who had re-styled the party and demonstrated a willingness to commit British forces to war situations that put him at odds with elements of the Labour tradition outlined in Chapter 1. This became more pronounced during 2002–03 as Blair prepared the party and country for war in Iraq alongside the US, the subject of Chapter 8. Ultimately, the experience of the Iraq war, and the manner in which the case was made, would damage the party and hasten the end of Blair's premiership. His post-2003 thinking on the question of war and his response to the July 2006 Israeli war inside Lebanon are considered in the Conclusion, which also considers the Blair approach in the context of the wider Labour tradition relating to questions of war.

I would like to thank a number of people who have helped in the preparation of this book. Research for it was undertaken in the Labour History Archive and Study Centre, Manchester; the National Archives, Kew; the US National Archives, College Park, Maryland; Warwick University Library; the Modern Records Centre, University of Warwick; and the Bodleian Library. I would like to thank the staff of all of the above for their help, and particulary Darren Treadwell at the Labour History Archive and Study Centre. In addition, the book has benefited from discussions with the Rt. Hon. Tony Benn, Tam Dalyell, Lord Hurd of Westwell, the Rt. Hon. Sir Gerald Kaufman, MP, Lord Kinnock of Bedwellty, Lord Owen of the City of Plymouth, and the Rt. Hon. Clare Short, MP. I am grateful to all of them for taking the time to discuss the issues covered in this book with me and for their helpful insights. I would also like to thank John Dumbrell for loaning me documents from his own research into the foreign policy of the

Johnson Administration, Jim Pfiffner, with whom I have worked on the question of the case for war in Iraq, and Paul Rogers. I am particularly grateful to Craig Fowlie at Routledge for his interest and support throughout the project and to Jo Calvert, Nick Comber and Natalja Mortensen for guiding the manuscript through the production process. Thanks also to those members of the History & Governance Research Institute at the University of Wolverhampton whose efforts have made it such a success. Finally, thanks to my parents, to James and Hayley, and to Diane Evans for 'looking after me', and to whom the book is dedicated.

1   The Labour Party and the question of war

The Labour Party is a moral crusade or it is nothing.

Harold Wilson, 1964[1]

Labour is about altruism. The philosophy of democratic socialism is based on a moral view of life, and that must shine through everything we do. We start from moral principles and go out to devise practical policies to implement them. If there is no morality it is not worth having ... on this I would not shift an inch.

John Smith, July 1992[2]

Britain has always been a country willing to lift its eyes to the far horizon and judge its actions by their immediate impact not only on ourselves but on world events and history. The decisions that we take are of momentous import for the world and its order and stability. Let us ensure that those decisions are the right ones, for we shall live with their consequences.

Tony Blair, May 1995[3]

The Labour Party and the question of war, 1900–1945

In February 1900 the Labour Representation Committee was formed as a vehicle to advance the interests of the trade union movement. It returned two members of parliament at that year's general election, increasing its representation to 29 in the election of 1906. Immediately thereafter it changed its name to the Labour Party. On 12th February 1906, the newly elected MPs met in committee room 12 of the House of Commons for the party's inaugural meeting, electing Keir Hardie as Chairman by a single vote on a second ballot. They met again the following day to agree the priorities,

upon which the party propose to draft Bills or Motions: trades disputes; women's suffrage; canals nationalisation; unemployed amendment act; compensation act; steam enginemen's boiler bill; mines – employment of boys; women's local government; mines regulations; miners' eight hours; taxation of land values; child feeding; old age pensions; housing; shops bill.[4]

Issues of foreign policy or war and peace were absent.

Eight years later, however, the outbreak of the First World War would create the most serious divisions within the party to date. As a member of the Second International the party was expected to oppose the war but, particularly after the German assault on neutral Belgium, a majority of the parliamentary party came to favour a declaration of war on Germany. Chairman Ramsay MacDonald, believing that Britain should remain neutral, resigned, to be replaced by Arthur Henderson on the eve of the declaration of war. He was not the only prominent figure in the party to oppose the war. Keir Hardie took his opposition to audiences in England and Wales, where he was met with outright hostility and accused of harbouring pro-German sympathies.[5] Nevertheless, the prominence of some of those who opposed the war could not obscure the fact that a vast majority of the party responded to the patriotic fervour it unleashed by wholeheartedly supporting the war effort, with some aware of the risk of a party considered unpatriotic being punished by the voters at the end of what many expected to be a short war.

The war obliged the Labour Party to give sustained consideration to questions of war and peace for the first time. The January 1916 party conference established a committee to consider post-war issues, and a special party conference held at the end of the following year adopted a Statement of War Aims. This called for the creation of a League of Nations and included a wide-ranging statement on the need to make the world safe for democracy, which contained the essence of what would come to be recognised as core Labour values and principles in relation to questions of war and peace:

> Whatever may have been the causes for which the war was begun, the fundamental purpose of the British labour movement in supporting the continuance of the struggle is that the world may henceforth be made safe for democracy.
>
> Of all the war aims, none is so important to the peoples of the world as that there shall be henceforth on earth no more war. Whoever triumphs, the people will have lost unless some effective method of preventing war can be found.
>
> As a means to this end, the British labour movement relies very largely upon the complete democratisation of all countries; on the frank abandonment of every form of Imperialism; on the suppression of secret diplomacy, and on the placing of foreign policy, just as much as home policy, under the control of popularly elected Legislatures; on the absolute responsibility of the Foreign Minister of each country to its Legislature; on such concerted action as may be possible for the universal abolition of compulsory military service in all countries, the common limitation of the costly armaments by which all peoples are burdened, and the entire abolition of profit-making armament firms, whose pecuniary interest lies always in war scares and rivalry in preparation for war.[6]

While the Labour Party has never been a pacifist party *per se*, as this clearly suggests, an instinctive pacifism, ingrained "deep in Labour's psyche"[7] grew out of the experience of 1914–18, rooted in the fact that:

> Although most workers were swept along at first by the tide of khaki chauvinism, once that war was over the conviction grew that these lonely pacifist spirits who had opposed the war throughout, had been right. The case was, indeed, unanswerable: millions had died for little real purpose, politicians and generals alike had betrayed the trust put in them, and only the armourers had thrived. The betrayal of the common man – the common soldier – by his 'natural leaders' shattered a social compact which previous industrial and socialist agitation had, by comparison, hardly dented. The betrayal was simply too great to be emotionally accommodated. Something instinctively sacred to British socialists had been violated. The cry went up – it echoes down the years – never, never, ever again.[8]

The principles outlined in the Statement of War Aims were reflected in postwar criticism of the terms imposed on Germany by the Treaty of Versailles and the allied intervention in post-revolutionary Russia. At the same time Labour's commitment to disarmament became a defining feature of the party throughout the following decade, culminating in the League of Nations' agreement to the convening of a world disarmament conference in 1932, presided over by Arthur Henderson.

Although initially disappointed at the form the League of Nations had taken, Henderson moved the party towards support for this instrument intended to ensure the avoidance of future wars. However, the League was seen essentially as an instrument designed to prevent rather than respond militarily to wars. "That the League might be called upon to intervene in an already erupted conflict", one historian has noted, "remained a possibility mentioned by no one within the party".[9] Hence, there was a considerable degree of naivety or innocence underpinning Labour's international policy that "realists" like Hugh Dalton warned against,[10] and which was to be severely challenged by events in Spain.

The Spanish Civil War, partly because it was fought against the backdrop of fascism in Germany and Italy threatening the peace of Europe, was viewed by many of the Left as having a significance that transcended the borders of Spain. Over 2,500 Britons volunteered to fight on the Republican side against Franco's Nationalists, and at least 500 were killed whilst doing so.[11] The debate over whether Britain should intervene in the conflict took place in the context of the interventions in support of Franco's forces by Hitler and Mussolini – the former airlifting Franco's Army of Africa from Morocco in July 1936 – and, from September 1936, the Soviet Union's decision to arm Republican forces. Although Clement Attlee had immediately offered the Republic "all practicable support",[12] the British government's policy of non-intervention enjoyed majority public support, so much so that in September 1936, Philip Noel-Baker warned Attlee, "there is probably a good deal of public opinion in favour of 'non-intervention', and ... for the Labour movement to take the lead in this matter means going against a pretty strong tide".[13]

Support for intervention grew on the Left as the war went on, particularly after the April 1937 bombing of Guernica and the March 1938 bombing of Barcelona. However, it was never strong enough to overcome three major hurdles. First, the National Government's large parliamentary majority (249 after the 1935 general election) kept it well insulated from interventionist pressure and allowed it to continue with a non-interventionist policy that was umbilically linked to its wider appeasement policy. Second, the Labour Party had been seriously weakened by the events of 1931, and the war in Spain was the occasion for yet further rather than fewer divisions. Finally, calls to assist Republican forces or intervene on the Republican side sat uneasily alongside the party's continued opposition to British rearmament.

The Spanish Civil War acted as a catalyst in accelerating the decline of the strong influence that pacifism had exerted on the Labour Party since the end of the First World War, a process that could be traced back to Ernest Bevin's attack on party leader George Lansbury at the 1935 party conference. Events in Spain obliged pacifists to re-consider whether there might be circumstances in which war was justified, and even necessary. Nevertheless, even though at the outbreak of war the Labour Party had declared its support for the Republic, its leadership effectively accepted Foreign Secretary Anthony Eden's arguments for non-intervention, based on the need to work to avoid a wider European war against Germany and Italy. A policy of non-intervention was confirmed at the September 1936 TUC Congress, although the subsequent party annual conference in Edinburgh adopted a resolution calling for the abandonment of non-intervention if it was shown to have been ineffective.[14] Deputy Leader Arthur Greenwood was forced to concede that as a policy, non-intervention represented a "very bad second best".[15] This shift was confirmed by the 1937 annual conference, although the practical consequences were limited to fundraising campaigns by the likes of the Spain Campaign Committee and the various charities that grew out of or were linked to the party.[16] As Tom Buchanan has argued, the trade unions, "defined their internationalism in bureaucratic terms, relating directly to specified organisations in other countries, perceiving their responsibility to foreign trade unionists and their families in humanitarian terms".[17] This was a major reason why rank and file party members were so frustrated and ultimately disappointed by the party's approach to the war. They did not accept that principle had been adequately translated into practice. Konni Zilliacus would reflect that: "Labour's behaviour over Spain was the greatest mistake of the Labour Party since the war, and denoted not only a political but a moral and intellectual failure on the part of its leaders".[18] However, the leadership's caution was informed by the potential electoral consequences of involving Britain in a war arising from a cause that did not pose an immediate threat to British interests, and which would alienate the Catholic vote, recognised as central to Labour's continued electoral recovery.

With regard to the threat posed by Germany, by 1937 the Labour Party had begun to overcome divisions arising from the memories and lessons of the First World War. The debates of the 1930s were to be resolved in favour of those who recognised the threat posed by Hitler, bringing Labour's opposition to the annual Service Estimates to an end. As Hugh Dalton had warned during that year's annual conference in Bournemouth, as things stood; "a British Labour Government, coming to power tomorrow, would be in danger of humiliations, intimidations and acts of foreign intervention in our national affairs, which it is not tolerable for Englishmen to con-template".[19] Hence, by September 1939 Labour was far more united on the question of war than it had been in 1914, its reaction to the declaration of war described as "one of relief".[20] It was a war against Nazism, not the German people, one that had been increasingly accepted as inevitable, and even necessary.

During the war itself, the threat posed by Hitler, given solid expression by the German bombing of British cities, engendered a shift in thinking about foreign policy, with the survival of the sovereign British state assum-ing primacy over all other international considerations. The party's wartime statement, *Labour, the War and the Peace* explained that the party, "unre-servedly supports the Allied war of resistance to Nazi aggression because, though loathing war, it regards this war as a lesser evil than the slavery which finally would be the only alternative".[21] Foreign policy was no longer governed by abstract principles; now it was about the hard politics of defence, security and national survival. Writing in his memoirs Clement Attlee remarked that it was fair to say that, "until 1935 the Parliamentary Labour Party had given little or no serious attention to defence pro-blems".[22] Following the First World War, there were "no potentially hostile Powers of any military strength, while at the League of Nations all the emphasis was on disarmament".[23] Partnership in the wartime coalition meant that for the first time Attlee and his senior colleagues had their "minds focused on the national interest in a world dominated by power politics".[24] As Neil Kinnock put it: "By the end of the Second World War the pacifist element in the Labour movement, although clearly recognisable, was not influential. Those who had counselled early intervention against fascism were regarded to be the people of the longer-dated wisdom".[25] However, the experience of the First World War, the debates of the 1930s, and the divisions over the Spanish Civil War, did bequeath a legacy to post-1945 generations in the form of what Kinnock has termed, "a retained reservation about the use of force [which] continued to characterise the Labour Party and made it distinctive from Conservatives and, to the extent that it mattered at the time, Liberals".[26]

The Labour Party's values and the question of war

The remainder of this chapter identifies and considers the component parts of this "retained reservation about the use of force". Implicitly, it also raises the question of whether and how far we can speak, as Neil Kinnock suggests, of a "distinctive" Labour approach. Writing in 1937, Clement Attlee had suggested that such a distinction was inherent in the very notion of a Labour Party:

> It must be perfectly clear that the Labour Party rejects altogether the theory that foreign policy is something that must be kept out of party politics. It does not agree that there is some policy to be pursued by this country irrespective of what party is in power, a policy which is national and so transcends party differences. There is a deep difference of opinion between the Labour Party and the capitalist parties on foreign as well as on home policy, because the two cannot be separated.[27]

This begs the wider question of whether under Labour governments there ever was, or should have been, a distinctively "socialist" foreign policy, related to the expectation that Labour, in office, would "make a difference".[28] In practice, any party that can simultaneously accommodate such diverse leading figures as Ernest Bevin and George Lansbury, Aneurin Bevan and Hugh Gaitskell, Tony Benn and Denis Healey, is a broad church inevitably given to compromise on matters of principle. Nevertheless, we can identify certain values and currents that have shaped the approaches the party has taken to the question of war since 1945.

The single most important of these has been the party's *insistence on the primacy of the United Nations (UN) in conflict resolution* and hence an unwavering *commitment to international law*. Indeed, strong support for the UN is a central Labour tradition, in part a consequence of the contribution of the Attlee government to its founding. Clare Short has suggested that this amounts to an, "emotional and romantic attachment" to the UN that other political parties do not share.[29] Across the next 50 years Labour Members of Parliament (MPs) would often reflect on the impact its establishment had on them personally and their expectations of it. For example, in a debate during the 1990–91 Iraq crisis, Michael Foot reflected that:

> I am almost the only hon. Member who was here when the charter was voted upon in the Parliament of 1945. I went to San Francisco as a journalist and saw what happened, and I was proud that the Labour party that I supported, and its leader Clem Attlee, played a foremost part in shaping that charter and learning from the experience of the 1930s.[30]

Similarly, in the same debate, Tony Benn explained: "I believe in the UN ... I felt – like every member of my generation – that it represented the alternative to war".[31] Stan Orme recalled how:

At the end of 1945, I was a young airman stationed in the middle east and awaiting demobilisation, along with millions of other service men who had served throughout the second world war. I looked forward to a different Britain and to a different world from that which existed when we entered the 1939 war. Over the next 40 years, I fought and worked for a United Nations that would be a world force for peace and sanity.[32]

For this generation, the UN was all that stood between world order and anarchy, and there was a determination to ensure it worked and therefore succeeded where the League of Nations had failed.[33] Indeed, Tony Benn moved an amendment to the Party's Constitution that saw a commitment to the UN being written into it (Clause IV, point 7), pledging the party

> ... to support the United Nations Organisation and its various agencies and other international organisations for the promotion of peace, the adjustment and settlement of international disputes by conciliation of judicial arbitration, the establishment and defence of human rights, and the improvement of the social and economic standards and conditions of work of the people of the world.

Epitomising this commitment, at the height of the Suez crisis the Labour Party campaigned under the slogan *Law, Not War.* For Neil Kinnock, when faced with potential war situations as party leader, "the critical necessity was to satisfy the requirements of the United Nations Charter", and ensure that, "any military intervention was consistent" with its provisions. For Kinnock, "the intensity of that commitment" could be considered a distinguishing feature.[34]

For many on the Left, opposition to the US intervention in Vietnam during the 1960s was rooted in the fact that it was, to quote Philip Noel-Baker, "a flagrant violation of the Charter" which risked reducing it to, "a scrap of paper, as the Covenant of the League of Nations became in 1939".[35] In the post-Cold War era, another expression of this commitment to the UN Charter was the regularly stated fear that unless the UN grasped the interventionist nettle in a way that Cold War paralysis had prevented it from doing, it would fast become irrelevant to issues of international security.[36]

In contrast, members of the Conservative Party were more likely to adopt an essentially realist view of the UN and its potential, and invest less faith in it, seeing it as being driven by a balance of Security Council (UNSC) members' interests as much as by any commitment to particular values. A classic expression of this view was provided by former Conservative Prime Minister Edward Heath in April 1993, shortly after the Srebrenica massacre:

> What is the United Nations? It is the five members of the Security Council. The right hon. Member for Copeland [Jack Cunningham] is surprised that other countries do not carry out actions to support the

resolutions. Those countries do not take action because they take no part in the Security Council and are not interested, or they find that their own interests are affected to their disadvantage. There is no need to be surprised at that. The right hon. Gentleman said that the resolutions must be enforced, but how do we enforce them? How do we force other countries not to do deals under the counter? It is a practical matter which must be dealt with by the United Nations.

The United Nations always acts after the event. It has no means of pre-empting the dangers that the world faces today. It has no intelligence service of any sort and it does not know what is going to happen. It has no information service, no means of assessing risks in actions that can be taken and no military staff to advise the Secretary General. It has absolutely nothing. If it is to perform any worthwhile service in this new world, it must have all those things and be properly organised; otherwise, it is just a matter of a discussion in the Security Council and the pressure exerted by its individual members.[37]

Prior to 1999 this historical commitment to working through the UN meant that it was Conservative governments that were the more likely to express concern that by doing so they would not be able to proceed on their desired course because they might attract a UNSC veto. As then Foreign Secretary Douglas Hurd argued immediately after the 1990 Iraqi invasion of Kuwait:

It cannot be right to put the choice entirely and wholly within the machinery of the United Nations. We know that machinery. We know that it includes vetoes and – [Interruption.] That reaction suggests that some hon. Members have not seriously considered the matter. We cannot leave open the possibility that necessary action against the aggressor would be blocked by such means. If we were to leave open that possibility, we would leave open the possibility that he [Saddam Hussein] might go away rejoicing in possession of Kuwait. The House has undertaken and said that the first priority must be to prevent that from happening.[38]

In practice, Labour's insistence on the primacy of the UN resulted in the evolution of a distinctively restrictionist approach to military interventions. The restrictionist approach insisted that for the good of all military force should only be deployed in strict accordance with the UN Charter, either in self-defence, a right enshrined in Article 51 of the Charter,[39] or arising from a resolution of the UNSC. Moreover, the clear expectation was that every effort would be made to comply with Article 2 of the Charter, specifically its provisions that: "all Members shall settle their international disputes by peaceful means in such a manner that international peace and security, and justice, are not endangered"; and "all Members shall refrain in their international relations from the threat or use of force against the territorial integrity or political independence of any state, or in any other manner inconsistent with the Purposes of the United Nations".[40]

This approach had the benefit of satisfying fundamental just war conditions of legitimate authority, right intention, just cause, last resort and, because any action would conform strictly to the terms of UNSC resolutions, proportional means.[41] In theory this left little room for ambiguity, although in practice arguments about the precise meaning of and authority vested in specific UNSC resolutions have meant otherwise. The restrictionist approach also emphasised the fact that Article 51 does not afford states a blank cheque in response to aggression; it merely affords them the right to make an initial response which should be reported to the UN in advance of a UN response. For example, during the 1982 Falklands conflict, Labour leader Michael Foot reminded the Parliamentary Labour Party (PLP) that,

> under Article 51 there had to be reports to the Security Council and the Secretary General on all acts of self-defence that were taken. There was no carte blanche for complete freedom of action by the Government and this was a very crucial point. We had to be careful that our own Government did not violate Article 51.[42]

This refusal to contemplate the use of force outside the UN framework and insistence on a strict adherence to the terms of Article 51 is rooted in a history of past abuses of humanitarian justifications for military intervention. The Second World War was the defining event in twentieth-century British history, the post-mortem over the policy of the 1930s protracted, the lessons felt sharply. In this context, the memory of Hitler's presentation of his invasion of Czechoslovakia as being a response to the persecution of the German minority was omnipresent in the post-1945 period.[43] For the Left, post-1945 US military interventions also served as a reminder of the risk of abuse of the humanitarian justification. The fact that a number of Labour backbenchers viewed the US military intervention in Vietnam as being a breach of the UN Charter has already been mentioned. In addition, under Neil Kinnock's leadership, the party opposed the Reagan Administration's interventionism in Central America, arguing that:

> claims made by the United States administration that it needs to intervene in Central America in order to stem Soviet-Cuban aggression is but a new name for an old claim – stemming from the Monroe Doctrine – its self-assumed right to dominate the Central American and Caribbean areas.[44]

Reagan Administration justifications for the October 1983 invasion of Grenada were many and shifting (Fidel Castro listed them among the "19 lies" told by the US over the invasion[45]), but the first were humanitarian in character and dismissed as "dishonest" by Shadow Foreign Secretary Denis Healey, who characterised the invasion as a violation of the UN Charter. "If Governments arrogate to themselves the right to change the Governments of other sovereign states", Healey warned, "there can be no peace in this world in perhaps the most dangerous age which the human race has ever known".[46]

The adoption of a restrictionist posture was also rooted in two related Labour traditions: first, Labour's historic *suspicion of power politics and secret diplomacy,* traceable back to its critique of the origins of the First World War, but still being deployed by Labour critics of government policy in the post-1945 era[47] and, second, Labour's *tradition of anti-colonialism.*[48] Hence, the principle that the bar had to be set high so as to guard against the risk of abuse was established as a consequence of the lessons of the 1930s, and reinforced throughout the Cold War period.

A further defining value has been a pronounced preference in favour of diplomacy over the resort to military force as a means of resolving conflicts, to the extent that *the resort to war is a last resort.* This approach was consistent with just war doctrine and reflected the conclusions drawn from the experience of the First World War and the important strain of pacifism that ran through the party. It is captured well in Michael Foot's 1991 eve-of-war advice that, "we should not think twice, but four, five or more times to try to find a different way out".[49] Indeed, considerations of last resort were present in Tony Blair's 1999 Doctrine of the International Community speech outlining the five questions that should be considered in determining the circumstances under which military intervention is permissible:

> First, are we sure of our case? War is an imperfect instrument for righting humanitarian distress; but armed force is sometimes the only means of dealing with dictators. Second, have we exhausted all diplomatic options? We should always give peace every chance, as we have in the case of Kosovo. Third, on the basis of a practical assessment of the situation, are there military operations we can sensibly and prudently undertake? Fourth, are we prepared for the long term? In the past we talked too much of exit strategies. But having made a commitment we cannot simply walk away once the fight is over; better to stay with moderate numbers of troops than return for repeat performances with large numbers. And finally, do we have national interests involved?[50]

However, there is a clear problem with the question of last resort; namely, how to recognise whether it has been arrived at. In a sense, this is less likely to be an issue in cases with a clear national interest/national security dimension, as in such cases insistence on last resort is likely to be seen as a first cousin of appeasement. Nevertheless, last resort is an inherently controversial judgement, because it is inherently difficult to define. In particular, the wars of 1991 and 2003 against Iraq were opposed by sections of the Labour Party on the grounds that all diplomatic options had not been exhausted. While there were those who believed that this was also the case in the 1982 Falklands war, there was something of a different dynamic at work, and many in the PLP knew, or at least suspected, that the window within which any diplomatic solution could be agreed would expire soon after the British naval task force grouped off the Islands. With regard to last resort, the key question is: how long is too long? Just war theorists urge that the requirement not be taken literally given that, "as popularly conceived, it is almost impossible to ascertain when the last resort has been reached because non-violent alternatives are always available, at least theoretically".[51] However, this does not, of itself, help in answering the question.

Easy deployment of the appeasement analogy by political opponents, or those looking to close off wider debate about potential options in a crisis situation, has made rational debate around last resort problematic. As Tam Dalyell complained to Edward Heath during a December 1990 debate on the Iraq-Kuwait crisis: "part of the difficulty is the confusion which equates dialogue with appeasement, when dialogue and appeasement are very different matters", to which Heath replied:

> The hon. Gentleman is absolutely right, and I am afraid that 'appeasement' is used as a weapon against those who want to have what the hon. Gentleman calls dialogue, simply to whip up public feeling. Most of those who use it were not even alive in the 1930s, when it happened, and have never studied what the problems of appeasement were.[52]

Closely related to this consideration are the application of what might be termed *the moral calculus*, a belief in the importance of setting a moral example and belief in Britain's "moral responsibility",[53] and *opposition to dictatorial rule* and its corollary, *the spread of democratic governance* – a source of considerable intra-party dissonance over Iraq.

All of these considerations combine to constitute Labour's *internationalism* – an at times rather vague notion that could, for example, be invoked by pacifists and rearmers simultaneously in the 1930s, but which suggests an extension of the party's socialist and social democratic commitment to equality to the international arena, and has served to distinguish Labour foreign policy from that of the Conservative Party. Conservatives have been more likely to invoke the national interest than internationalism as a basis for foreign policy and, particularly, approaches to the question of war. Nevertheless, at times Labour politicians have attempted to portray principles founded on internationalism as being synonymous with the national interest in order to generate public support for military commitments, as with Robin Cook's 1995 insistence that: "we do have a national interest at stake in the Balkans. That national interest is in upholding the principle that borders must not be changed by force".[54]

This again raises the question posed in 1936 by events in Spain of whether there is an appropriate balance to be struck between the pursuit of values (framed as internationalism or cosmopolitanism) and interests (framed as national interests or communitariansim) in determining responses to questions of war. In turn, this raises the question of consistency, which carries within it the seed of suspicion of ulterior motive. There have been defences of inconsistency in military interventions,[55] but historically Labour has tended, in part due to its tradition of anti-colonialism and in part because of its suspicion of US motives for intervening overseas (discussed below), to be highly sensitive to the risk of abuse that is contained within arguments for accepting greater selectivity. The events of the 1990s would make this a source of considerable intra-party division. For example, Tony Benn in part based his opposition to the 1999 NATO war over Kosovo on the grounds that he did:

> not accept for one moment the reason given by Ministers for the war. They say that it is a war for humanitarian purposes. Can anyone name any war in history fought for humanitarian purposes? Would the Red Cross have done better with stealth bombers and cruise missiles? Of course not. War is about power, for the control of countries and resources. The other humanitarian crises that have been mentioned are informative – the Kurds, the Palestinians and the people of East Timor. The British Government are still arming the Indonesian Government when they are repressing the people of East Timor. What is the basis of that? I am not asking the Government to go to war with Indonesia, but do they have to go on arming the oppressors? Those arguments create doubts about the credibility of the operation.[56]

As noted above, a further factor that needs to be considered is a deep-rooted *suspicion of US motives* in undertaking military interventions. On the Left of the party this has reflected a more general antipathy towards the US, dating from the Cold War choices of the late 1940s and impact of the Korean War and rearmament in the 1950s, and confirmed by the experience of the Vietnam War. Suspicion of the US was a defining feature of the Bevanite Left during the 1950s, just as a strident Atlanticism did much to define Gaitskellism, and while Bevan himself supported the establishment of NATO, his concerns over the US would re-surface during the Korean War.[57] On balance, the special relationship with the US has been as much a source of difficulty for the right wing of the party as it has a source of anxiety for the left. For Gerald Kaufman:

> One of the great problems always for Britain – it's an even bigger problem now that there is only one superpower – is what do you do about the United States? . . . It may well have very bad leadership, and on the whole the United States has had very bad leadership, but whether the leadership is good or bad it's a big problem for a country like Britain. Do you go against it?[58]

US military interventions had the capacity to embarrass the Atlanticists within the party throughout the Cold War period. For example, in the wake of the failed April 1961 Bay of Pigs invasion of Cuba, Kennedy confidant Arthur Schlesinger Jr was dispatched to take stock of West European reaction, recording how:

> Hugh Gaitskell was rueful but philosophical. "It was a great blow," he said. "The right wing of the Labour Party has been basing a good deal of its argument on the claim that things had changed in America. Cuba has made great trouble for us. We shall now have to move toward the left for a bit in order to maintain our position within the Party." But he asked what he could do to help, suggested people to whom I should talk and even made an appointment himself for me to see the editor of the Daily Herald. Denis Healey, the "shadow" Foreign Secretary, was somewhat more bitter. "I've staked my whole political career on the ability of the Americans to act sensibly," he said. He felt badly let down by the Administration but again was perfectly ready to listen to an account of how things had actually happened. Farther to the left, Dick Crossman said, "You really have got off very lightly. If this had taken place under Eisenhower, there would have been mass meetings in Trafalgar Square, Dulles would have been burned in effigy, and the Labour Party would have damned you in the most unequivocal terms. But because enough faith still remains in Kennedy, there has been very little popular outcry, and the Labour Party resolutions have been the bare minimum. You've got away with it this time. But one more mistake like this, and you will really be through."[59]

Prior to 2002–03, this "US problem" was most acutely felt during the Wilson governments, with regard to the US expectation that Britain would continue to bear the burden of a global role, with all of the opportunity costs that this involved, and the pressure to commit ground forces to Vietnam. As Anthony Crosland complained to Richard Neustadt in July 1965:

> We once policed the world alone; maybe that's your fate now. Why should we keep you from being left alone? Why we if not the others who were 'great' before the war – France, Germany, Italy, Japan. We gain no strength and find ourselves no place by keeping up pretenses, even if at your expense.[60]

If Atlanticist elements within the Party had been embarrassed by earlier US military interventions, the Vietnam War tested the outer limits of their tolerance. By July 1966 George Brown was complaining to Barbara Castle: "You are left-wing and I am supposed to be right-wing, but I've been sickened by what we have had to do to defend America – what I've had to say at the dispatch box".[61] By 1967 both Brown and Harold Wilson were arguing in Cabinet that the alternative to seeking membership of the European Economic Community (EEC) was an undesirable closer alignment in foreign affairs with the US. Referring to Vietnam, Brown told his colleagues that the government: "had to a substantial extent felt bound to follow the policies of the United States; and it would be contrary to the views of a large number of the Government's supporters to be forced to continue in this position". Wilson suggested that if it were not to pursue EEC membership, the logic of its international position could mean that Britain, "might be forced into closer association with United States policy in the Far East" – a clear allusion to the possible commitment of ground forces.[62]

A final influence on Labour's approach to questions of war derives from the fact that a number of prominent Labour figures of the post-1945 period served in the armed forces during the Second World War, and that this *direct personal experience of war,* of either being directly under fire, being required to kill others, or seeing friends killed in action, had a direct bearing on their approach to questions of war and peace thereafter.[63] The most high-profile of these include Denis Healey, who served as Military Landing Officer to the British assault brigade at the 1944 Anzio landings,[64] and David Ennals, who fought in Normandy on D-Day. Clearly, in the years immediately following 1945 the numbers who could draw on this direct experience were greatest. To take a few additional examples, Tony Benn served in the RAF in Africa and the Middle East, and lost his elder brother, Michael, also in the RAF, in a training accident in June 1944.[65] Eric Heffer joined the RAF; Tam Dalyell, Stan Orme, and a number of others were called up or volunteered. These MPs would at times claim that their wartime experiences gave them a special insight into matters of strategy or tactics.[66] Whether or not this was so, the experience certainly shaped their approach to the question of war. For example, towards the end of his life, in a debate following the 1990 Iraqi invasion of Kuwait, Eric Heffer told the House of Commons:

> Some of us spent a long time in the forces in the last war. Some of us had very distinguished records, while others of us had not so distinguished records. That does not matter, because we all bear in mind that we lost many of our friends. I shall never forget them. It is emotional for me because I remember them now. They included youngsters with whom I went to school. I have lived on borrowed time, like all of us who were in the forces. I think also of the civilians who were killed. Look what happened to our cities – London, Liverpool, Coventry and Belfast. We should remember the destruction that occurred and the killing of thousands and thousands of innocent civilians.[67]

The experience of serving in the Second World War could also be drawn upon in advocating a firm approach to collective security, as with the Sheffield Labour MP A.E.P. Duffy during the same crisis:

Perhaps I can take just a few seconds to tell the House that I did my first canvassing for the Labour party when I was 12 years old at the behest of my headmaster. I canvassed for the League of Nations and for what was then Labour party policy – collective security. Ten years later, I was a casualty of war and for many years was 100 per cent disabled. I am still 30 per cent disabled. I am sorry to have to say that because I know that the House does not really want to listen to it, but I must say it to leave the House in no doubt that I do not address the issues of war and peace lightly. By God, I know and I reflect on the missed opportunities of the 1930s. I do not want collective security to fail again. That is the big issue for me. Saddam must not be given any ground for believing that he can undermine international order, that there is any weakening in our resolve or that this country and our allies will not go through with what they have threatened for so many months. What is certain is that no future challenge can even be credibly approached by the United Nations unless the present challenge is overcome.[68]

Equally, the experience of living through the German bombing of British cities during the Second World War could be called upon to explain an opposition to the bombing of targets in or close to civilian centres, on the basis that it was not only immoral but also counter-productive. This was a feature of Labour opposition to the wars over Vietnam, Kosovo and Iraq. For example, in July 1966 in the wake of Harold Wilson's dissociation from the US bombing of oil installations close to Hanoi and Haiphong, Stan Newens described how:

> I remember as a child visiting London during the blitz. That memory makes me wonder how anybody can believe that human beings will respond to the bombing of their capital city by running away and being prepared to negotiate. The only thing that will happen is that they will harden themselves to stand up and fight. If anyone after the bombing of London in 1940 had proposed negotiations with the Germans, he would have stood the risk of being lynched.[69]

The *national and domestic political contexts* are also important to understanding the positions the Labour Party ultimately adopted regarding questions of war. With regard to the national context, Clare Short makes the point that:

> there is a distinctive social democratic outlook on foreign policy and I think the Labour Party belongs in the social democratic tradition, but if you are going to compare and contrast Labour's history in Britain with the social democrats of Scandinavia, although you will find a majority of the people in the party with similar values, Britain has got this

imperial history and Security Council membership and bravado, so you probably get power distorting the sincere values that would be in the party.[70]

A range of domestic political considerations can also influence positions taken, for example, with regard to Harold Wilson's wafer-thin 1964–66 parliamentary majority, or Neil Kinnock's efforts to re-establish the party's electoral credibility on issues of foreign and defence policy in the wake of the 1983 election campaign.[71] After all, the Labour Party's primary aim has been to achieve and exercise power in pursuit of a reformist and re-distributive domestic agenda.

Linked to this is the fact that at times of war or international crisis Opposition carries with it additional risks and responsibilities. The risk of appearing unpatriotic, especially if and when British forces are committed to battle, and risk of consequent electoral punishment, dictates that outright opposition to war is very much the exception rather than the rule. In the post-1945 period it has been restricted to just one case, that of Suez in 1956. However, at times of war the Labour Party in Opposition (like the Conservative Party) has generally been quick to emphasise that its support should not be taken as constituting a "blank cheque" for the government of the day. To reinforce this point, in Opposition the party has tended to consciously carve out for itself positions on specific wars that, while generally supportive, are distinctive, as in, for example, the 1982 Falklands and 1991 Iraq wars.

As noted above, the Conservative Party has been the more comfortable in openly declaring that its foreign policy was firmly rooted in the national interest. While the Labour Party's guiding principles as to the causes and just nature of war draw overwhelmingly on the experiences of the First World War, Spanish Civil War, and drift towards war with Nazi Germany, through which it lived, the guiding principles of Conservatives additionally draw on cases of 19th diplomacy, emphasise the concept of the balance of power, and frame questions of war and peace in terms of a realist-idealist dichotomy, beginning with Castlereagh's role at the 1814–15 Congress of Vienna, the nature of the settlement reached there being seen as rooted in realism rather than idealism.[72] In this, Conservatives do not eschew idealism, but they have tended to place a greater emphasis on balancing it with the language of realism, usually expressed in terms of the "national interest". Former Conservative Foreign Secretary Douglas Hurd's perspective is that:

> the policy maker has also to know the limits of idealism. What 'is' needs to be grasped and understood before he turns to what 'ought to be' ... The idealist tends to believe in a just and peaceful world as if it was a palace descended from heaven. He mourns over every broken pane and every room fouled by violence or hatred. He longs for the

application of universal principles which could, he believes, make the palace whole and clean.[73]

How far does Labour's internationalism distinguish it from the realist strand that informs the Conservative approach? It may be argued that this is a theoretical difference that does not translate into great differences in practice. Nevertheless, it is worth offering examples that illustrate what are almost instinctive differences in approach to questions of war. The first concerns the centrality of the national interest in assessing each case. While Tony Marlow may not be considered the best representative of the mainstream of the Conservative Party, he does provide a clear articulation of this concern, in this case in relation to a possible military response to the 1990 Iraqi invasion of Kuwait:

> We have heard a lot about Britain's aims, but what about our interests? . . . There is a temptation to look upon these events and foreign policy as a moral issue. I hope that my country's foreign policy is moral, and that moral arguments can be used to sustain it. However, foreign policy is always dictated not by moral issues but by national interests, for the very good reason that different people have different moral outlooks . . . What is it about Saddam Hussein that may make it proper to contemplate an offensive war against him? His evil has been compared with that of Hitler. Many speakers in today's debate seem to have returned to 1939, saying that we were threatened then by a major country in Germany and had to stand up and fight against it. The present situation is not like that. As other right hon. and hon. Members have said, Iraq is a long way away. We are not the major player in this issue. We must consider our interests, so any comparison with Hitler does not ring true.[74]

A second difference is quite Hobbesian in tone and emphasises the imperfectability of man within which framework one does one's best while at the same time not compromising the national interest, as in Douglas Hurd's winding-up speech at the end of the two-day debate in September 1990 following Iraq's invasion of Kuwait:

> We all share the hope of a better world order, and we all know that that has ceased to be a platitude and a hope so distant that we just talk about it and nothing happens . . . Some people, particularly Opposition Members, talk of this development in terms of great aspirations and the brotherhood of man. I see it in more traditional, Tory terms, a concert of nations, and so does the right hon. Member for Leeds, East [Denis Healey], who is a good Tory under the skin. I see it in Tory terms as an increasingly effective concert of nations acting *in sensible self interest* for the preservation and extension of international order.[75]

And again, during the war in Bosnia:

> Some speak as though there were some system of international order which already exists, some glass palace of peace which has already been built and which is being shattered by what is happening in Bosnia or in west Africa or the former Soviet Union, where similar horrors are occurring. But there is no such thing. There is no new international order. Man's cruelty to man continues; the tragedies multiply. What does happen is that people try to avert the tragedies, try to prevent them and, when they occur, try to reduce them. Some of those efforts succeed. They have succeeded in Namibia, they have succeeded in Mozambique, and they have partly succeeded in Cambodia. Some fail, such as in Somalia and Rwanda. Bosnia now hangs in the balance, unfortunately tilting the wrong way. On many occasions, Britain does not and should not take part; we cannot be even a part policeman everywhere. But sometimes it is right to join in the effort, as we did in Rwanda and as we are doing in Angola and in Bosnia. I am sure that it is right that we should do so for as long as that is possible, but I think that we should use the possibility of withdrawal to secure that minimum of agreement on the ground that would enable us to continue.[76]

While the dominant restrictionist approach survived a number of challenges during the Cold War years, it faced a more serious challenge in the post-Cold War environment of the 1990s, where it conflicted with the ideas that came to dominate a debate as to whether and in what circumstances military force should be deployed in response to situations of humanitarian crisis. The experience of Bosnia, where there was a limited intervention that came to be viewed by many across the political spectrum as being a case of too little too late, was central to this development, but so too were the experiences of genocidal slaughter in Rwanda and Burundi, from which the international community stood aside. Hence, by the turn of the century it was becoming increasingly recognised that there existed a right of intervention in circumstances of "supreme humanitarian emergency", and efforts were undertaken to define the precise conditions under which such humanitarian military intervention ought to be undertaken.[77] In this context, the war over Kosovo was the occasion for an extensive debate on the Left and within the Labour Party about the proper relationship between state sovereignty and universal human rights. Those who had served as Labour MPs for longest, and hence supported the restrictionist approach for longest, were amongst the least likely to be carried along with the new, more permissive, interventionist tide. For them, the Labour tradition, with its emphasis on the exclusive authority of the UN, the risk of abuse, and suspicion of US motives, combined with Labour's historic commitment to anti-colonialism in determining their rejection of interventionist arguments. As Tony Benn told the House of Commons at the beginning of the Kosovo War:

I have been in the Labour party for 57 or 58 years and have been a Labour candidate 17 times in parliamentary elections, and I never thought that I would be asked by my party to vote for a war against the charter of the United Nations, in a way that could make the situation that confronts the world far more serious. I hope that the House will accept that for me to go into that Lobby tonight will be one of the most difficult things that I have done, but it is something that is absolutely essential if we are to stand true to the values on which the Labour party rests, of internationalism, peace and the peaceful settlement of disputes.[78]

Some, however, such as Ken Livingstone, did swim with the interventionist tide.[79] In general, those who entered parliament in the post-Cold War, post-Iraq War 1992 and 1997 general elections were the most likely to be carried with it. While it can be exaggerated, there clearly was a generational dimension to this divide.

Under the leadership of Tony Blair the principle that states had a *right* to intervene in such cases was rapidly supplanted by a more distinctly liberal-cosmopolitan approach to the use of military force. This was rooted in the natural law concept that all individuals have key inalienable rights, and that where these are being abused by states, outside actors have what amounts to a *duty*, rather than merely a right, to intervene militarily. From the earliest days of his leadership, Blair spoke in terms of *duty*, as when he asked Prime Minister John Major:

After the appalling events in Srebrenica and Zepa, does the Prime Minister agree, first, that rather than talk of withdrawal, having designated safe areas and encouraged people to enter them, it is our duty to pursue all practical means to uphold the United Nations mandate and prevent further ethnic cleansing; secondly, that we should use UNPROFOR to open up the supply road to Sarajevo; thirdly, that we must impress on our American colleagues the absolute necessity of practical support for our actions rather than just rhetoric; and, finally, that, as threat after threat has been made to the Bosnian Serbs but not carried out, over the next few days we must work out our bottom line and this time stick to it, otherwise the consequences for the United Nations and for the resolution of conflicts everywhere will be lasting and disastrous?[80]

Notably, in his reply, Major did not go so far as to agree that Britain had what amounted to a duty. In general, Conservative MPs were less likely to support intervention on grounds of duty, and wanted this to be joined by a national interest defence.[81] Indeed, when Blair spoke in Chicago in 1999 on the "doctrine of the international community", it could almost be seen as a direct rebuttal of Foreign Secretary Douglas Hurd's assertion during the Bosnia War that, "there is no such thing as 'the international community'", itself an echo of Margaret Thatcher's claim that there was no such thing as "society".[82]

Implicit in Blair's approach was the idea that sovereignty is not an absolute value, but an instrumental one. Explicit was the notion that this duty of intervention arose in part as a consequence of globalisation, albeit in an ill-defined way.[83] This became the dominant paradigm in assessing the legitimacy of military intervention at the turn of the century, supplanting Labour's traditional commitment to restrictionism, though creating new divisions in the process. However, such a liberal-cosmopolitan approach significantly lowered the threshold at which it was deemed legitimate to use military force, heightening the risk of abuse that had driven the earlier insistence on restrictionism. This is significant because, in practice, foreign policy is conducted on the basis of a combination of principle and pragmatism, interests as well as values. This remains the case with regard to humanitarian military intervention. As Jim Whitman reminds us: "The political calculations of intervening states are never suspended for humanitarian reasons; they are a determining factor, just as they are when intervention is used to secure the non-humanitarian interests of those states".[84]

The risk of abuse was heightened further by the post-11th September 2001 (9/11) shift in US defence posture towards pre-emptive defence. In just war theory pre-emptive war (or anticipatory defence) has usually been regarded as highly problematic, as the war threshold is lowered to a level that positively invites abuse.[85] This shift carried with it the risk that a case for pre-emptive military attack could be made in what were, objectively, preventive circumstances, where there was no imminent threat to justify military intervention. This risk was realised with regard to Iraq in 2003. In advocating military intervention in Iraq, justified to the public in pre-emptive terms that turned out to be false, Blair compromised much of the Labour tradition regarding war. The impact of his decision to support the US without securing a legitimating resolution from the UNSC was to seriously undermine a key component of the Labour tradition. In future, Labour Party figures would be unable to invoke this tradition as Michael Foot did in 1990 in relation to the Iraqi invasion of Kuwait, when he told the House of Commons:

> The Labour party has no need to be apologetic about these matters. On several occasions, Conservative Governments have refused to support the United Nations charter; indeed, they have acted in flagrant defiance of the charter, as they did in 1956. I do not say that our record is spotless, but it is a good deal better than that of Conservative Governments. We have done our best to try to sustain the charter of the United Nations.[86]

2 Taking sides in the Cold War

The question of the Party's attitude towards issues of war and peace in this period is inextricably bound up with wider questions about its perceptions of both the US and the Soviet Union, and the related question of its attitude towards atomic and then nuclear weapons. The Labour Party was always a broad church, but these issues exposed a fault line that was to wrack the Party from the 1950s to the 1980s. By the time Harold Wilson took office in 1964 this fault line had developed into a chasm that Wilson had to somehow bridge in order to hold the Party, and with it the government, together. For Wilson, as for Attlee before him, the issues at its core not only affected foreign policy; in the choices they imposed they also dictated the limits of the possible in domestic policy.

As the Second World War ended, Britain was still a world power. Its military forces were spread across much of the globe, and accepted the surrender of German forces in Europe, Italian forces in Abyssinia, and Japanese forces in French Indo-China and the Dutch East Indies. However, this high visibility masked a very different emerging reality of decline. In particular, Britain's relative decline vis-à-vis the US during the Second World War was marked. Militarily it was no match for the US by any measure of conventional armaments. Moreover, the US possessed the atomic bomb, which transformed notions of power in international politics. To take a few indicators, at the end of the war Britain, the world's leading naval power prior to the war, could boast 14 battleships, 52 aircraft carriers, 64 cruisers, 368 destroyers and 122 submarines. The US now had 25 battleships, 99 aircraft carriers, 74 cruisers, 850 destroyers and 242 submarines.[1] The post-war reconstruction of Western Europe exposed the economic dimension of decline. During the 1950s France and West Germany's growth rates were, respectively, double and treble those of Britain. During the same period, the armed forces of both France and West Germany came to exceed those of Britain. As John Young has argued, Britain was condemned to lose its former predominance no matter what it did as other powers industrialised, expanded, and challenged British dominance. Several factors that account for the decline – technological developments, growing Asian nationalism, and shifting patterns of industrial production – were evident before the

Second World War. However, the war acted as a catalyst and affected Britain's ability to mount a response.[2] Whatever role Britain was going to play in the post-war world, it would be markedly different to the pre-war one. The only badges of distinction it held on to were its "special relationship" with the US and intention to retain a presence in strategically significant imperial locations such as the Gulf states, East Africa, Singapore and Cyprus. Labour's Cold War foreign policy would be geared towards ensuring the retention of the prestige that these brought, and through this prestige influence, even at substantial cost.

Notwithstanding Attlee's wartime exposure to power politics, his pre-war commitment to the principles underpinning the League of Nations was transferred to the emerging UN. Indeed, from his earliest days in office until early 1947, the degree of faith that Attlee placed in the UN, together with his proposals for imperial retreat or retrenchment, placed him at odds with his Foreign Secretary, Ernest Bevin. This faith was abundantly – and to officials, alarmingly – evident in the weeks prior to the result of the 1945 election being announced, while Attlee was attending the Potsdam conference alongside Churchill. From there he replied to a memo from Anthony Eden expressing great concern over Soviet intentions in the eastern Mediterranean and Middle East by telling Eden that, in his view:

> The concept of the special interest of Great Britain in the strategic areas and the acceptance of responsibility for them involves us in a continuing heavy burden of defence expenditure ... I am afraid of us undertaking responsibilities which we shall be a little [*sic*] fitted to undertake in the economic conditions of the post-war period. If we really believe and intend to operate a world organisation for peace we ought, I think, to get away from old conceptions. In my view the only realistic policy is that of placing all these strategic areas under international control, not the control of one or two powers, but of the United Nations.[3]

As Smith and Zametica have observed, this must have "struck Eden as absurdly naïve – as internationalist outpourings of the worst kind".[4] Eden would not have been alone, especially in light of Attlee's clear sympathy for the Soviet predicament over Black Sea access, even going so far as to compare this with Britain's hold on Gibraltar.[5] Attlee's approach was also firmly at odds with prevailing attitudes in the Foreign Office (FO). For example, Gladwyn Jebb, then head of the FO's Economic and Reconstruction Department, was alarmed by Attlee's usage of the term "power politics" which, in the Labour vocabulary carried clear and negative connotations. "What", asked Jebb "is meant by 'power politics'"?

> I should myself like to think that this term refers to a *misuse* of power in the conduct of foreign policy. If this is so, the term could apply, for instance, to Hitler's attempt to dominate Europe. But until such a time

as the Great Nations are prepared voluntarily to renounce their sovereignty, or at any rate some essential part of it, until such a time in fact as a World State has been created, international politics can only be an expression of power. Marshal Stalin said this in so many words during the present talks in Potsdam; and however much we may deplore it it is impossible to contest the truth of his observation.[6]

It is difficult to overstate the degree of faith the Labour Party invested in the newly formed UN, seen as an antidote to the power politics that had led to earlier wars. For Labour, it offered an opportunity to re-establish as paramount in world affairs the internationalist principles of the inter-war years, while learning from the mistakes of the time to produce a genuinely internationalist approach to foreign policy which would help to secure the continuation of Anglo-US-Soviet co-operation. Speaking at the opening session of the General Assembly in London in January 1946, Attlee declared that the UN:

> must become the overriding factor in foreign policy. After the First World War there was a tendency to regard the League of Nations as something outside the ordinary range of foreign policy. Governments continued on the old lines, pursuing individual aims and following the path of power politics, not understanding that the world has passed into a new epoch. In just such a spirit in times past in these islands great nobles and their retainers used to practise private war in disregard of the authority of the central government. The time came when private armies were abolished, when the rule of law was established throughout the length and breadth of this island. What has been done in Britain and in other countries on a small stage has now to be effected throughout the whole world.[7]

Attlee's thinking on the post-war order survived Potsdam, to be laid out in a September 1945 memorandum. This argued that the British empire could, "only be defended by its membership of the United Nations Organisation", and that if, "the new organisation is a reality, it does not matter who holds Cyrenaica or Somalia or controls the Suez Canal".[8] However, the first stirrings of military unease at Attlee's suggestions began to emerge, with Alan-brooke, the Chief of the Imperial General Staff, confiding to his diary that: "We were ... shaken by Attlee's new Cabinet paper in which apparently the security of the Middle East must rest in the power of the United Nations!!"[9] In fact, opposition to this perspective was widespread. Underpinning Attlee's worldview at this time was a somewhat less pessimistic assessment of Soviet intentions than that held by the leadership of the Conservative Party, the senior civil service, the military, and even elements of his own Cabinet, most notably his Foreign Secretary, Ernest Bevin.[10]

In Cabinet, Bevin commanded the foreign policy arena and was rarely challenged. There were no specialist Cabinet ministerial or official committees covering foreign policy issues that could promote debate on foreign policy options.[11] As a result, Bevin's pronounced antipathy towards communism and individual Soviet leaders (at the September 1945 Council of Foreign Ministers meeting in London he publicly compared Molotov to Hitler) would heavily influence the ultimate direction of foreign policy under Attlee. But for a last-minute change of mind by Attlee, it would have been Hugh Dalton who became the Labour Foreign Secretary, with Bevin occupying the Treasury. Ultimately, however, Attlee's desire to separate Bevin from Herbert Morrison, towards whom Bevin exhibited a keen antipathy (although they shared the same distrust and generally low opinion of the Soviet Union), denied Dalton the one post he most keenly wanted, but which his Germanophobia would ultimately disqualify him from holding.[12] As Chancellor and Foreign Secretary the two would clash frequently. Whereas Dalton saw overseas expenditure as an area of potential savings, Bevin was instinctively committed to defending Britain's imperial presence in the Middle East and beyond. In part, this division reflected the representation of departmental interest, but went much deeper. Burke Trend considered Dalton the, "most left-wing member of the Big Five",[13] while Bevin possessed an anti-communism rooted in his own pre-war trade union experiences. With regard to Bevin Harold Wilson diagnosed, "a congenital attitude veering from deep suspicion to ill-concealed hatred of the Russians".[14] There is also little doubt that Bevin, characterised by one labour historian as having "strong views but in some key areas no great reserves of knowledge",[15] was influenced in his outlook by the world view of senior FO officials.[16] The FO certainly saw the potential in Bevin; the permanent Under-Secretary Sir Alec Cadogan wrote at the time of Bevin's appointment:

> I think we may do better with Bevin than with any other of the Labourites. I think he's broadminded and sensible, honest and courageous. But whether he's an inspired Foreign Minister or not I don't know. He's the heavyweight of the Cabinet and will get his own way with them, so if he can be put on the right line, that may be all right.[17]

Nevertheless, while it is appropriate to note the importance to Bevin of his FO advisers, and the continuity in these from Churchill's wartime government, this should not lead to the conclusion that Bevin's views on foreign policy were exclusively moulded by the FO. As John Saville has noted, Bevin, "did not have to be converted to the traditional ways of Foreign Office thinking for they were already part of his political and emotional perceptions: the belief in the great power thesis; the acceptance of British imperialist rule wherever that was possible; a lack of realism in international economic affairs; and a comprehensive and all-embracing hostility towards the Soviet Union and all its works".[18]

For Bevin, the advice emanating from the FO reinforced that of the Chiefs of Staff. In turn, both of these reinforced his own biases and put him at odds with Attlee, as in his protest over Attlee's reluctance to maintain pre-war commitments to Greece and Turkey. In March 1946 Attlee confided to Dalton that he was:

> pressing on the Chiefs of Staff and the Defence Committee a large view of his own, which aims at considerable disengagement from areas where there is a risk of us clashing with the Russians. This would mean giving up any attempt to keep open the passage through the Mediterranean in war-time, and to pull out from all the Middle East, including Egypt, and, of course, from Greece. We should then constitute a line of defence across Africa from Lagos to Kenya and concentrate a large part of our forces in the latter. We should face the prospect of going round the Cape in wartime and, the future attitude of India being somewhat uncertain, we should concentrate a great part of the Commonwealth defence, including many industries, in Australia. We should thus put a wide glacis of desert and Arabs between ourselves and the Russians. This is a very bold and interesting idea and I am inclined to favour it.[19]

As late as December 1946, Attlee was demonstrating a guarded optimism about future co-operation with the Soviet Union, advising Bevin that, "it is difficult to tell how far Russian policy is dictated by expansion and how far by fear of attack by the US and ourselves. Fantastic as this is, it may very well be the real grounds of Russian policy. What we consider merely defence may seem to them preparation for an attack".[20] In this assessment, Attlee was some distance from Bevin's firm belief in the Soviet Union's inherently aggressive intent – an assessment that ascribed a high priority to the role of ideology in Soviet behaviour, whereas Attlee ascribed the higher priority to traditional Russian foreign policy aims. In January 1947 this ideological prism led Bevin to warn Attlee, in the starkest terms to date, that his approach would lead to; "Munich all over again, only on a world scale, with Greece, Turkey and Persia as the first victims in place of Czechoslovakia ... If we speak to Stalin as you propose, he is as likely to respect their independence as Hitler was to respect Czechoslovakia's".[21]

Attlee's more internationalist brand of foreign policy by now faced concerted opposition from all sides, leaving him increasingly isolated – opposed by the FO, his own Foreign Secretary, elements of his own Cabinet, the military, and the Conservative opposition – and in mid-January he moved to accept the dominant view, although holding out over the need to withdraw from Greece and Palestine.[22] Montgomery, at that point Chief of the Imperial General Staff, claimed later that Attlee only did so because the Chiefs warned him of their intention to resign *en masse* if he sought to insist on his own preferred approach to the Middle East and the defence of the Empire more generally.[23] Others have cast doubt on this claim, partly because Montgomery was out of the country at the time and so could not have orchestrated a mass resignation, and have instead suggested that Attlee conceded because the only other way forward in light of such concerted opposition would have been a direct appeal to Cabinet, a course of action he chose not to pursue.[24] Either way, it is clear that key figures in the 1945 Labour government, not least the Prime Minister himself, came much later than their officials and senior military figures to a belief in an ideologically motivated, inherently aggressive Soviet Union.[25]

Meanwhile, throughout the period from 1945 until the announcement of the Marshall Plan, there was also a vigorous debate within the Labour Party over how closely Britain should be aligned with the foreign policy of the US. Just as with the Soviet Union, so with the US the end of the Second World War saw the overriding common interest that bound the wartime allies together give way, and separate national interests reassert themselves. Hence, in the immediate post-war period there was no great commonality of interests between Britain and the US. Indeed, the sources of difference were the more obvious. During 1946 and 1947 Foreign Secrtary Ernest Bevin would have to work hard at convincing the US that there were shared interests. Paradoxically, alignment with the US would require Attlee's government to undertake actions and share burdens that ran counter to the national interest that had motivated the approach in the first place. Within the alignment, Britain's interests would become increasingly marginal, with the Attlee government obliged to subsume them to wider, essentially US-mandated, demands. Britain was to pay a heavy price in the Attlee years and beyond for this approach. It was designed to maintain influence, but brought with it obligation without power.

Writing in the late 1980s, Jim Callaghan recalled a feeling at the time that:

> In 1945 America and Britain together formed the most powerful and influential combination in the world. Anglo-American joint decisions would shape the future of the immediate post-war world. I do not remember that I consciously reasoned to myself in this way. There was no need to do so. The facts were self-evident.[26]

Even so, the early post-war years witnessed demonstrations of American power that can only have reinforced the emerging sense amongst senior Labour figures of the centrality of realpolitik to state survival. Key amongst these were the prompt, unsentimental and wholly unexpected termination of the Lend-Lease agreement in 1945,[27] leading to the December 1945 decision to "mortgage the empire" by accepting a £3.75 billion US loan at commercial rates. As Jim Callaghan recalled:

> The debate on the American loan and its consequences had an unsettling effect, for it shook many settled convictions and prejudices. Until then, if questioned, I would have been in no doubt that Britain was a great power – one of the big three who had won the war ... [placing] us in a different category from France, which had surrendered, or Germany, Japan and Italy which we had defeated. I had no doubt that to hold a British passport entitled the user to special consideration when he travelled

abroad as a citizen of the world's largest empire, of which London was the centre. And I was suddenly mortified to discover that our economy was in such bad shape that we must borrow from the United States on terms which demonstrated our weakness.[28]

Harold Wilson too recalled his shock that: "Britain was in pawn, at the very time that Attlee was fighting to exert some influence on the post-war European settlement", and that the "only solution was to negotiate a huge American loan, the repayment and servicing of which placed a burden on Britain's balance of payments right into the twenty-first century".[29] Later the equally abrupt ending of co-operation on atomic weapons would constitute a further jolt. Nevertheless, a combination of Bevin's authority in the Party, the latitude he was granted by Attlee,[30] and his pronounced Atlanticist and stridently anti-communist world view, combined to exert an influence that was decisive in tying Britain so closely to the US.

Inevitably though, the emergence of a Cold War alignment in foreign policy generated dissent within the Party. As early as March 1947, following an hour-long address by Bevin to a meeting of the PLP, six MPs voted against a motion that the PLP "endorses the Foreign Policy of His Majesty's Government".[31] Also that year over 100 Labour MPs signed a motion condemning Churchill's "iron curtain" speech in Fulton, Missouri, although Attlee resisted Tom Driberg's invitation to condemn the speech in Parliament. That year's annual conference debate on foreign policy featured a high proportion of voices critical of the Attlee government for not living up to campaign pledges on relations with the Soviet Union.[32] Some, like Hugh Dalton, shared these concerns in private but chose not to voice them publicly. This disputation carried over into the Richard Crossman-drafted, and unprecedented, amendment to the 1946 King's Speech calling for a review of the Party's foreign policy[33] (in response to which Attlee again underlined the centrality of the UN to Labour's international policy[34]), the December 1946 "Spelthorne" letter from the Spelthorne Divisional Labour Party accusing the leadership of choosing to "line-up with American imperialism", and into the pages of *Tribune* more generally.

Tribune was the vital instrument via which the Keep Left group of Labour backbenchers, prominent within which were Richard Crossman, Michael Foot and Ian Mikardo (the authors of the original *Keep Left* pamphlet), maintained its advocacy of a Third Force future for Britain, one that avoided close alignments with either the US or Soviet Union. As early as April 1944, Aneurin Bevan was using its pages to argue that:

No progressive foreign policy is to be expected from America either under a Democratic or a Republican Administration ... But if America gives us headaches, Russia gives us heartaches ... the only solution likely to lay the foundations for peace and prosperity ... is an organic confederation of the Western European nations.[35]

With the end of the war the idea of a Third Force was held to hold the key to avoiding a future atomic conflict between East and West, and would be at the forefront of opposition to Bevin's foreign policy.

Those within the party advocating closer relations with the Soviet Union became fewer and increasingly marginal as it stamped its authority on eastern Europe, at the same time leaving no doubt as to its hostility towards the Attlee government and Bevin in particular. Keep Left's early belief that the Soviet Union would be supportive of an independent socialist Europe was thus exposed as false. In the pages of *Tribune* Soviet animosity was attributed to the fear of having to, "face a competition for international attraction from a country which is neither capitalist and reactionary, nor Bolshevik, but the champion and pathfinder of democratic socialism".[36]

In this context, Keep Left's April 1947 manifesto, calling on Britain to organise a European Third Force and thereby distance itself from US foreign policy while adopting a less confrontational approach with the Soviet Union, was rapidly undermined by events,[37] and challenged via the immediate riposte of Denis Healey's pro-Bevin tract, *Cards on the Table*. By the time of the June 1947 foreign affairs debate, a month after *Cards on the Table* was published, the FO's Pierson Dixon could observe with some satisfaction that, "the whole House was soberly anti-Russian".[38] Beyond the Keep Left group, there remained isolated critics such as Sydney Silverman and William Warbey (later, leading backbench critics of Harold Wilson's Vietnam policy), and mavericks such as Tom Driberg.[39] A small band of further backbench critics were labelled "fellow-travellers" and so neutralised. It was a label not without foundation in some cases, for example, when applied to John Platts-Mills, who described the 1948 coup in Czechoslovakia as "a great victory for the workers",[40] or Leslie Solley,[41] but particularly harsh in the case of Konni Zilliacus, especially given his support of Tito and later portrayal in a Soviet show trial as an agent of British intelligence, a trial that resulted in the conviction and hanging of the accused.[42] A former official at the League of Nations, he paid the price of being a foreign policy expert in an environment where there was no room for nuance, and little toleration of deviation from the official line. At the 1949 annual conference, the resolution confirming the expulsion of Zilliacus and Solley was easily passed, by 4,721,000 votes to 714,000. It would take the resignation of Bevan over the opportunity costs of the Korean War and rearmament to re-legitimise parliamentary opposition to the government's Cold War foreign policy.

Bevin too had once toyed with the idea of moving towards the creation of a "third force", led by Britain but taking in Western Europe, the African colonies, and utilising Britain's presence in the Middle East. By the time of the Marshall Plan, however, he had abandoned any hope of Britain acting independently of the US. For Bevin, the reality was that Britain badly needed US economic assistance, and so could hardly aspire to help fund, much less lead, a revival of Western Europe. Moreover, he was convinced of the need for US support for the defence of Western Europe. Maintaining the US commitment to this was at the heart of Labour's foreign policy. Responses to US requests for Cold War support (material or financial) would henceforth always involve a calculation of the likely impact of a negative response on the US commitment to Western Europe. This meant that it would be a brave Labour politician who would turn down a US request, especially in the context of Labour's wartime schooling in the pursuit of the national interest and defence of the state, and of the decades-long effort, going back to the first MacDonald government, to prove to the entire electorate that Labour, the representative of the working class, could be trusted to safeguard the national interest just as effectively as any of the other parties.

As with the general thrust of foreign policy, there is also evidence that Attlee had to be influenced by Bevin in his commitment to the atomic bomb programme. The 1946 McMahon Act had the effect of cutting Britain out of the atomic loop, despite its earlier contribution to the Manhattan Project, necessitating a decision on whether to pursue an independent British atomic bomb. Bevin was absent at the start of the October 1946 Cabinet committee meeting which discussed facilitating this by releasing the funds required to improve the supply of fissile material. In his absence Hugh Dalton and Chancellor Stafford Cripps opposed the plan on cost grounds, in particular in terms of the opportunity cost in relation to Labour's housing programme. Bevin arrived just as the paper was about to be withdrawn, to tell the meeting:

> We've *got* to have this ... I don't mind for myself, but I don't want any other Foreign Secretary of this country to be talked at, or to, by the Secretary of State in the United States as I just have, in my discussions with Mr Byrnes. We've got to have this thing over here ... We've got to have the bloody Union Jack on top of it.[43]

Indeed, it has been argued that deterring the Soviet Union was very much a subsidiary concern in British thinking on nuclear weapons, and that "the prize sought was the maintenance, even extension, of British standing with the United States"[44] – that is, that the British nuclear deterrent, with all of its opportunity cost implications, was aimed not at the Soviet Union, but at maintaining a status Britain could not otherwise retain in the post-war world. As Morgan put it:

> Britain's nuclear weapons programme, whether a deterrent or not, was the logical outcome of Britain's assertive and highly self-conscious foreign policy during the post-war years. Bevin's Union Jack waving over the bomb was a symbol of a wider independence ... Attlee's decision to develop British nuclear weapons was taken solely to bolster the nation's

political power, and with no knowledge of the military or scientific consequences.[45]

This is also clearly evident from the extent to which British politicians later sought to dissuade the US from considering permitting West Germany to acquire nuclear weapons, or any input into the use of them. In scribbling his "Thoughts on Foreign Policy" just prior to the 1964 election, future Foreign Secretary Patrick Gordon Walker emphasised the need to avoid, "a US alliance with Germany over our heads", and prevent the appearance of, "a European nuclear weapon".[46] A Germany with nuclear weapons or input into European nuclear defence decisions would signal the sidelining of Britain as a major power and lead to a fundamental shift in transatlantic power relations. Given that the nuclear weapons issue would come to represent one of the clearest indicators of Britain's dependence on the US it is ironic that the atomic bomb was initially conceived as a means of asserting British independence from the US in foreign and defence policy. Attlee recalled that:

> If we had decided not to have it, we would have put ourselves entirely in the hands of the Americans. That would have been a risk a British government should not take ... at the time nobody could be sure that the Americans would not revert to isolationism ... There was no NATO then.[47]

Attlee would subsequently speak of "that stupid McMahon Act", and how it illustrated the way in which the US had become, "inclined to think that they were the big boys and we were the small boys; we had to show them they didn't know everything".[48] To that extent, as Sassoon argues, the bomb served as, "a screen against reality, a phallic symbol concealing an underlying inadequacy; the empire had no clothes but, thanks to the bomb, no one could see its emaciated limbs, let alone its empty stomach".[49]

Just as the decision to develop a British atomic bomb was taken in secret by the Attlee cabinet – the wider Labour Party and general public did not learn of it until it was revealed by Churchill in 1952 at the time of weapons testing off the Australian coast – so too was the later decision to allow the US to station atomic weapons and the aircraft to deliver them in the UK. The agreement to host US atomic weapons may have been an informal decision, but it was one that had far-reaching consequences. It served to corrode British independence in foreign and defence policy-making in a Cold War context and generated the fear, first exposed in the context of the Korean War, that the US could drag Britain into a war in defence of US-defined interests not necessarily shared by its partner, and that this could now involve a pre-emptive or retaliatory Soviet atomic strike on US bases in the UK.

At the same time, by 1947 a series of events had persuaded US policy-makers of the important role that Britain still had to play in the emerging Cold War world. Ironically, it was the British admission of its inability to fund a continued role in Greece, followed by the proclamation of the Truman Doctrine, that offered the US definitive proof that a strong Britain with a continued overseas presence was an important component of the post-war order. The Truman Doctrine itself was couched in stark, almost apocalyptic, terms, contributing to the accelerating polarisation between East and West. In the FO Gladwyn Jebb was highly critical, considering it doctrinaire and inflammatory, but within the Cabinet it was received with "warm enthusiasm".[50] It should have marked the end of persistent fears of an American return to its pre-war isolationism, certainly in combination with the permanent stationing of US forces in Germany and the creation of NATO. However, right up to the end of the 1960s Labour leaders would continue to express the fear that resisting US policy preferences might result in a weakening of the US commitment to the defence of Western Europe. This was a fear that US administrations would play on (especially though the invocation of Congress' independence from the executive branch), but how real it ever was is an open question.

The economic corollary of the Truman Doctrine was the Marshall Plan. The role of the Plan in cementing Cold War divisions remains controversial, as does the linked question of whether the Plan was from the outset intended to exclude the Soviet Union and its allies.[51] For some, although the tone of its presentation may have been,

> mild and non-ideological, its implications were anything but ... the Plan was not merely a reactive move designed to prevent economic chaos; instead, it was the most dedicated effort yet to reduce Communist influence in Europe and was intended to affect not only the most obvious countries like France and Italy, but also the smaller states under Soviet control.[52]

For others, such a view ignores the question of Soviet agency in the origins of the Cold War. Whichever, it is clear that Bevin did his utmost to ensure that the Soviet Union would not be a party to the Marshall Plan. In part, this reflected Bevin's concern that Soviet involvement would affect the amount of US aid flowing to the UK.[53] His view of the Soviet Union as a competitor for Marshall aid allocations helped cement Bevin's Cold War attachment to the US and resulted in yet further distancing from the USSR. At a June 1947 Paris meeting with Soviet ministers, Bevin, according to his own account to his Cabinet colleagues, "aimed at the outset ... on thrashing out the differences of principle between us, making that the breaking point".[54] The Paris meeting duly broke up without the Soviet Union feeling able to accept the terms proposed, and with the Cold War about to fully dawn.

Nevertheless, the fact of Marshall aid – Britain was to be the principal recipient of the US$12 billion earmarked for Western Europe under the Plan – converted a number of former critics, such as Crossman, and disarmed others. In January 1948, Crossman, in confessional mode, told the House of Commons:

I will be frank. My own views about America have changed a great deal in the last six months. Many members have had a similar experience. I could not have believed six months ago that a plan of this sort would have been worked out in this detail with as few political conditions. It is an amazing tribute to Mr Marshall's personality that he has disciplined all the forces against him in America itself and has at least got this policy presented to Congress in a form as acceptable as it is to Western Europe.[55]

This helps explain why, when the House of Commons debated British entry into NATO in May 1949 only three Labour MPs (Emrys Hughes, Silverman and Warbey) spoke against the idea, and none voted against it. However, a relationship intended to allow Britain to maintain global influence and its independence very soon began to erode that independence, so much so that one historian has suggested that, "one might ask if American or Soviet actions contributed more to Britain's decline since 1945".[56] NATO entry tends to be regarded as the crowning achievement of Bevin's tenure as Foreign Secretary, with all preceding actions leading to this ultimate triumph. However, there is no escaping the fact that Bevin set British foreign policy on an ultimately unsustainable basis, in part a consequence of his fondness for the empire, in part a consequence of his personal anti-communism and acceptance of the necessity of a US commitment to European defence with its wider, global, implications. It was a legacy that not only resulted in divisions which helped keep the Party from power for 13 years, it also haunted the Wilson government, which reluctantly and in the face of considerable resistance began to confront aspects of this legacy in its second term.

Cold War considerations helped shape all others, displacing areas of pre-war preoccupation. One of these was the question of relations with Franco's Spain. Although Spain was excluded from membership of the UN at its founding and the Attlee government joined with the US and France in 1946 in calling for the "peaceful withdrawal" of Franco and an end to his regime, the emergence of the Cold War both reduced its significance as an issue and was a powerful disincentive for further action. While deploring the nature of the regime in place in Madrid (but recognising its impeccable anti-communist credentials) there was no question of military intervention to remove it, especially as Spain became an increasingly important trading partner. As Tom Buchanan concludes:

> Compared to the massive tasks that faced Bevin and his colleagues in reconstructing the post-war world, Spain was, sadly, a trivial concern. The Labour government's inactivity is easy to chastise with hindsight, but it is more difficult to identify an active policy that would have brought constructive results. There was no direct prospect of direct allied military intervention once the war in Europe had finished, while

economic sanctions would only have hurt the already impoverished Spanish people.[57]

The emergence of the Cold War also impacted on how a number of leading Labour Party figures came to view the international system. They did so in a manner consistent with the emerging US academic science of international relations. Ironically, this analysis was essentially rooted in study of the same nineteenth-century diplomatic history that underpinned much Conservative thinking about international politics. It was antithetical to any notion of a "socialist" foreign policy. By the mid-late 1950s, this new science would be largely supplanted as the cutting edge theorising about international security by the rise of the technocratic language of nuclear strategy, itself built on the foundations of Realist analyses of the strategic environment. Denis Healey in particular immersed himself in these debates on behalf of the Party, in a period when attitudes towards nuclear weapons became a key expression of the Party's attitude towards questions of war and peace more generally.

Healey was to play a central role in the foreign and defence policy debates of the post-War period, articulating (and indeed, doing much to develop) the premises on which a Gaitskellite approach to foreign policy were based. From 1945 until he entered Parliament, he had served as the Labour Party's International Secretary, tasked with rebuilding relations with continental socialist parties and acting as a bridge between the government and the wider party on foreign policy issues. Whether Healey's role was to help construct policy or merely give form to policy positions is unclear. At one point in his memoirs he talks of his role as being to "explain the Government's foreign policy to the Party and the world".[58] At another, he characterises it as being "to act as its interpreter" in relation to the early events in the emerging Cold War.[59] In either case, Healey was granted considerable latitude, if only because:

> No one in the Government would talk much in public, or even to me in private, about the underlying principles and objectives of their policy, as distinct from justifying their position on particular issues. So I had to learn for myself, from observation, both about the nature of foreign policy as such, and about Britain's specific problems in the postwar world and how the Government planned to deal with them.[60]

Healey had made his first visit to the US in September 1949. Leaving behind a bombed-out London where rationing was still in force, Healey was impressed by his experiences of Detroit, "the sort of industrial city I had seen so often in American films", and Washington, "another world again, of spacious avenues flanked by dazzling white buildings".[61] Like Lincoln Steffens in reverse, he had seen the future, previously only available through the cinema, and for him it worked. This marked the first of a series of annual lecture trips by Healey to the US, which stretched across the 15 years until he became Wilson's Defence Secretary. As he later wrote, this first visit, "gave me a love for the country and its people which has survived many political disappointments; my love only deepened as I travelled the continent more widely and my knowledge increased".[62]

These experiences and observations helped guide Healey to a stridently Realist view of world politics, wherein, "the basic unit in world affairs was the state" and where a, "common ideology was no more likely than class solidarity to override the realities of national feeling",[63] and which was at odds with more traditional Labour Party thinking on the subject. Healey became convinced that in this international anarchy, "order could not be maintained by law alone" and neither "could treaty obligations by themselves guarantee how governments would behave in a crisis".[64] The key influences here were Reinhold Niebuhr and, in particular, Hans Morgenthau. A product of Frankfurt and Munich universities who fled Nazi Germany for the US in 1937,[65] Morgenthau published both of his seminal works in the first four years of Healey's tenure as International Secretary. His first book, *Scientific Man Versus Power Politics*, published in 1946, marked him out as the pre-eminent modern exponent of a Hobbesian view of human nature, and the author most concerned with applying it to the canvas of contemporary international politics, a reputation confirmed by *Politics Among Nations* published two years later. For Morgenthau:

> Continuity in foreign policy is not a matter of choice but a necessity; for it derives from factors which no government is able to control but which it can neglect only at the risk of failure ... the question of war and peace is decided in consideration of these permanent factors, regardless of the form of government ... and its domestic policies. Nations are 'peace-loving' under certain conditions and are warlike under others.[66]

Power was central to Morgenthau's conception of international politics, though as Kenneth Waltz went on to point out, it was unclear whether the source of Morgenthau's pessimistic outlook arose from his assumptions about human nature, or arose out of the "international anarchy" of global politics – in effect whether the pursuit of power was an end in itself or a means to an end:

> We have here two ideas: first, that struggles for preference arise in competitive situations and force is introduced in the absence of an authority that can limit the means used by the competitors; second, that struggles for power arise because men are born seekers of power ... One who accepts the second idea will define national interest in terms of power, because men naturally seek power. One who accepts the first idea will also define national interest in terms of power, but this time because under certain conditions power is the means necessary to secure the ends of states. In the one instance, power is an end; in the other, an instrument.[67]

Regardless of whether Healey ever felt the need to resolve this dilemma, Morgenthau's ideas seem to have had a considerable influence on his writings of the period, and Healey, in turn, exercised a considerable influence over Labour thinking about the question of war into the 1990s. The influence of Realism on Healey is clear from the title of his contribution to *New Fabian Essays*, "Power Politics and the Labour Party".[68] Also clear was his debt to Hobbes, whose *Leviathan* he considered "a better handbook for foreign policy than *Fabian Essays*".[69] For Healey a preference for a woolly utopianism rather than eagerness to confront the realities of power politics was an unfortunate but defining trait of Labour's approach to foreign policy. Moreover, the Party had erred in assuming that "power politics" was a "specific evil" rather than "a generic characteristic of politics as such". On this reading, the lesson of the failure of the League of Nations was not necessarily that it exposed the weaknesses of the League as a mechanism, but that it exposed the self-interest of states. Given the faith that Labour leaders had invested in the League, this implied a certain naivety on their part. Healey's analysis was standard Realist fare focused on the nation-state, "political entities, not moral entities; with interests and desires, not rights and duties". Their relations were determined, "primarily by their power to pursue their interests".[70] Given all of this and considering Britain's straitened post-War circumstances, Healey's analysis led him to outline three guiding principles of British foreign policy:

> Britain's influence on world affairs in the immediate future will depend more than ever on her material power to help a friend or harm an enemy. Britain's fundamental interest in unity with the United States will remain supreme. And an understanding of power politics will be more than ever necessary to a successful socialist foreign policy.[71]

In this context, Healey and the wing of the Party whose outlook he articulated, saw neutralism or Keep Left's talk of a Third Way as an opting out of a struggle in which Britain had a burden-sharing responsibility. As he wrote in the 1955 pamphlet "Neutralism":

> Refusal to commit oneself in the struggle against Communist expansion in fact means an abdication of responsibility to play an active role in progressing beyond power politics towards an international society ... the neutralist is not prepared to co-operate fully in any activity with the states which have already taken their position against Communist expansion unless the Communist states are also involved.[72]

Hence, two essentially different understandings of the nature of the Labour Party's foreign policy emerged on the left and right wings of the party between the mid-1940s and mid-1950s – and, indeed, may be regarded as doing much to define those wings.[73] The divisions that these created in the era of the Gaitskell-Bevan rivalry were deep and lasted well beyond the 13 years during which they relegated the party to an opposition role. For example, from the right wing of the party Roy Mason struggled to conceal his bitterness when he recalled, over 30 years after the events he described, how:

> There were many on the Left who saw the NATO alliance as a capitalist and militarist conspiracy, people who were wilfully blind to the aggressive nature of Soviet Communism and whose hatred of the Americans went beyond all reason. They seemed to me little better than the appeasers who had given Hitler a free run in the Thirties. And in their eagerness to defy party policy and undermine the leadership of Hugh Gaitskell, they were going a fair way towards making Labour unelectable.[74]

Healey's influence was significant, and extended to Hugh Gaitskell (Morgan goes so far as to call Healey the "main intellectual influence on Gaitskell"[75]), as is evident in Gaitskell's 1956 volume, *The Challenge of Co-existence*, which rejected ingrained Labour Party suspicion of balances of power, and instead argued that:

> For my part I have never looked on the balance of power as an evil thing which is itself the cause of war. The balance of power is simply an attempt to ensure that no one power or group of powers occupies such a dominating position that the temptation to indulge in aggressive war against others is overwhelming. If the balance is there, runs the doctrine, then it will provide a deterrent against attack.[76]

Hence, the post-Second World War foreign policy trajectory of the Labour Party involved a shift from the pressures to mould a foreign policy founded on principles of socialist internationalism to one that accepted the logic of Cold War balance of power alliances and high levels of defence spending, and which included a secret commitment to a British atomic bomb programme. A Party which, under the influence of writers like Angell and Hobson, had initially "rejected traditional foreign policy whereby sovereign states competed aggressively to enhance their own national interest",[77] and now become a key partner in a Cold War alliance which involved it in precisely such a competition. For a Party whose roots could be traced back to a non-conformist anti-militarism and which, in 1927, had established diplomatic relations with the Soviet Union (and re-established them in 1929 after the Conservatives had severed them), this represented a shift that a significant minority were either suspicious of or resisted. The Party's earlier internationalism still found concrete expression in its support for the newly established UN, but its Cold War alliance role meant there was a constant tension between the party's internationalist inheritance on the one hand and the imperatives of Cold War realpolitik on the other. Nevertheless, a commitment to the principles of international law as represented by the UN, an updating of the enthusiasm for the League of Nations that had done so much to give definition to the Party's foreign policy in its early years, remained a cornerstone of Labour's Cold War foreign policy. It would be tested in the decades to come.

3 The Labour Party and war in the 1950s
Korea and Suez

Korea and the question of rearmament

In February 1949, Ernest Bevin had established the Permanent Under-Secretary's Committee within the FO to "consider long-term questions of foreign policy and to make recommendations".[1] Throughout 1949, a number of papers emerged, several of which focused on the centrality of the relationship with the US. A paper in March confirmed that, "in the face of implacable Soviet hostility and in view of our economic dependence on the United States ... the immediate problem is to define the nature of our relationship with the United States".[2] A second paper, "Anglo-American Relations: Present and Future", set out the key assumption underpinning the relationship, that Britain was, "the principal partner and ally on whom the United States of America can rely".[3] Britain had to continually justify this assumption, lest the US look for a more reliable pivot in the form of France or even Germany, or even worse, realise the omnipresent fear of Labour policy-makers and retreat from the defence of Europe. These scenarios could be avoided, the paper advised, if Britain, "can show enough strength of national will and retain enough initiative to maintain her position as a leading world power, and, as such, influence United States policy".[4] A further paper from April 1950 listed Britain's overseas objectives as being:

1. To maintain the British position as a world power;
2. To maintain the Commonwealth structure;
3. To maintain a special relationship with the United States;
4. To consolidate the whole 'Western' democratic system;
5. To resist Soviet Communism;
6. To ensure that the Middle East and Asia were stable, prosperous and friendly.[5]

As one commentator has observed, this prioritisation suggests that concerns over prestige and status were greater than concerns over security.[6] This should come as no surprise, as former Ambassador to the US Sir Oliver Franks wrote in the mid-1950s, it was part of the "habit and furniture" of the British mind to regard the country as a "Great Power".[7] Such was the state of official thinking when, on 25th June 1950, the communist North invaded South Korea, offering the UK its best opportunity to date to demonstrate to the US its capacity to fulfil its role as "principal partner and ally".

The same day, the UNSC adopted Resolution 82 which determined that the invasion constituted a breach of the peace, called for the immediate cessation of hostilities and withdrawal of North Korea to the 38th parallel, and called upon all member states to "render every assistance" to the UN in the execution of the resolution.[8] It was passed by nine votes to nil, with only Yugoslavia abstaining, a feat rendered possible by the Soviet Union's boycott of the UNSC over its refusal to recognise mainland communist China as the legitimate body to represent that country on the Council. Two days later, as North Korean tanks rolled through the South Korean capital, and again in the absence of Soviet representative Jacob Malik, the UNSC passed Resolution 83, which noted the appeal from South Korea for the UN to take immediate and effective steps to secure peace and security, and recommended that member states furnish such assistance as necessary to, "repel the armed attack and to restore international peace and security in the area", by seven votes to one, with just Yugoslavia opposing. This sanctioned what President Truman agreed was a "police action". "We are not at war", he told reporters on 29th June. Nevertheless, this case represented the first time that, "a world organisation had voted to use armed force to stop armed force".[9]

In response to the invasion, the Attlee government moved swiftly in support of the UN resolutions, putting the Pacific Fleet under US command,[10] support commended by Winston Churchill who offered Attlee his party's backing in carrying out "what seems his inescapable duty".[11] There was little dissent from the government's own backbenches during the House of Commons debate of 5th July, possibly because the PLP had been warned on the morning of the debate that, "the whole world would be 'listening' to what was being said: History was in fact in the making",[12] but also because British naval forces had already been engaged in attacks by air and sea, with a British frigate coming under attack from North Korean Yak aircraft. Nevertheless, concerns within the party over the legality of the response, the earliest post-1945 illustration of the party's strict restrictionist approach to the use of military force, obliged Attlee to launch a concerted defence of its legal basis.

There were three dimensions to concerns about the legality of the response. The first concerned the absence of the Soviet representative. Attlee explained that:

> If a member of the Security Council, and in particular a permanent member, chooses to refrain from exercising its right of voting, not by failing to vote when present, but by refraining from attending the meeting at all, that member must be regarded as having deliberately abstained from voting.[13]

Second, there was the question of whether China was correctly represented, a question complicated by the Attlee government's recognition of the People's Government as the *de jure* government of China. Third, there was the fact that South Korea was not itself a member of the UN, and that Article 51 of the UN Charter spoke explicitly of how:

> nothing in the present Charter shall impair the inherent right of individual or collective self-defence if an armed attack occurs against a *member* of the United Nations, until the Security Council has taken the measures necessary to maintain international peace and security.[14]

Attlee explained that the purpose of Article 51 was, "not to create a new right but merely to make it clear that an inherent right vested in every State is not prejudiced".[15] He expressed the hope that Parliament would, "not spend very much time on these legal subtleties", and instead concentrate on the central reality: "If the United Nations is not to go the way of the League of Nations, the members must be prepared to act when the need arises. If the peoples wish to avoid another world war they must support their Governments in asserting the rule of law".[16]

The limited dissent that was voiced from the left of the party, for example, by Emrys Hughes, focused on concerns that support would be taken by the government as a "blank cheque" – a recurring theme in decades to come. Tom Driberg warned that the war would only remain within the legal paradigm set out by Attlee so long as UN forces did not carry the war past the 38th parallel. Driberg also raised another question that was to recur in years to come, concerning the nature of the regime that British forces were being asked to defend. In the Korean case the question was how far Britain should be expected to go to defend a government as authoritarian and corrupt as that of Syngman Rhee. Attlee had anticipated this in arguing that it was impermissible to invade a state just because a government fell below western standards, telling the House that he, "never knew that an excuse for assaulting someone peacefully pursuing his way was that his character was not very good".[17]

While the collective Cabinet view was one of "unconditional support" for the US, there was significant dissent from both Cripps and Bevan, partly over the lack of American consultation.[18] Nevertheless, Kenneth Younger, FO Minister of State, at the time deputising for the hospitalised Bevin, called Britain's backing "an almost instinctive reflex".[19] At the same time the FO's propaganda arm, the Information Research Department, was mobilised to convince the British public of the importance of supporting a country about which it knew little and whose people the British chargé d'affaires in Seoul had termed, "the thievingest people and the greatest 'gimme' exponents of all time".[20] For some in the Labour Party, and in the FO, the question of the necessary response was linked inextricably to memories of Munich and appeasement. The general view at the time was that the, "attack was certainly launched with Soviet knowledge and almost certainly Soviet instigation",[21] an analysis we now know to be flawed.[22] In this context, the UN had to assert its power and so distinguish itself from the League of Nations which had failed to challenge Japan in the Far East or Italy in Africa.[23] For example, at a party rally in Manchester a week after the invasion, Herbert Morrison departed from his prepared text to tell his audience that:

> only by showing that the free democracies will take a stand can we hope to convince disturbers of the peace that aggression does not pay ... By accepting this fresh challenge I have every hope that a world war can be averted. That is the only way to preserve the peace. Otherwise we shall slip along the slippery slope that led to the war of 1939; a war that could have been prevented if the nations of the world had had the courage to act in earlier years.[24]

Believing initially that it could limit its physical contribution to that of the Pacific Fleet, the Attlee government gave its support so as to consolidate the special relationship and also to secure some influence over the US in the conduct of the war, given the risk of it expanding to involve China.[25] While in the early stages of the conflict the Chiefs of Staff knew little of US plans, they soon found themselves dealing with US requests for the commitment of British ground forces. Now it was the turn of the military chiefs to sound a warning note, telling Attlee that the commitment of land or air forces would be "militarily unsound".[26] Indeed, at a Defence Committee meeting just three days after the invasion of the South, the First Sea Lord, Lord Fraser of North Cape, told the politicians that the Chiefs of Staff, "doubted whether in fact action by sea and air forces alone could restore the situation in Korea, but so far as the United Kingdom were concerned no land or air forces could be made available".[27]

Clear British interests informed this approach. Diverting forces from Malaya would cause difficulties there, while involvement in a conflict that could involve China and lead to a Chinese assault on Hong Kong would risk drawing Britain into a war with China for which it was hopelessly ill-equipped. The Chiefs' opposition to the dispatch of British land forces was reiterated at the Cabinet meetings of 4th and 6th July, by which time the FO's Sir Pierson Dixon had added his warning that sending land forces could prove unpopular domestically. He also raised the spectre of a US decision to use atomic weapons, and the need to obtain an assurance that these would not be used without consultation with the UK.[28] Hence, the initial British naval contribution was intended to demonstrate British solidarity with the US and the UN. It was not perceived as being primarily a fighting force, nor was it conceived as the first part of a wider British military commitment. Both the Attlee government and the military chiefs hoped that this alone would be a sufficient contribution from the "principal partner and ally".

However, during July the US applied further pressure on the UK to deepen its commitment. In particular, a unilateral US approach to the UN Secretary-General resulting in an appeal to member states for additional forces presented the Attlee government with a dilemma. Now the government's commitment to the UN, its need to demonstrate its continued importance to the US, and its continued belief in its world role, were pitted against the realities of an already stretched military commitment, the implications of increased military expenditure on its core domestic programme, and the clear advice of the Chiefs of Staff. In discussing how to respond to the Secretary-General's request, Kenneth Younger came up with the ingenious idea of playing the "Malaya card" and arguing that:

> we need send no further help since our forces were fully occupied in Malaya in a resistance to aggression closely similar to the situation in Korea and that to prevent a similar occurrence in Hong Kong we were forced to maintain a strong defence there.[29]

Nevertheless, US pressure would prove irresistible. On 20th July General Omar Bradley had outlined the importance of land reinforcements at an Anglo-US meeting in Washington, leaving Ambassador Oliver Franks of the view that, "we shall now be expected to respond with at any rate a token force".[30] In presenting the US case to Younger, Franks went on to (over-)emphasise Britain's importance to the US in a manner reminiscent of Churchill's more emotive wartime speeches:

> underneath the thoughts and emotions engendered at times by difficulties and disagreements between us and them there is a steady and unquestioning assumption that we are the only dependable ally and partner. This derives from our position in the world over past decades, our partnership with them in two world wars and their judgement of the British character. The Americans in Korea will be in a tough spot for a long time. They look round for their partner. The United States Administration know that our economy is only just recovering to sustain our commitments. They know we have these commitments all over the world. They know that in many of them, especially in the Far East, we are taking a heavy load in the same struggle. Nevertheless, the United States Administration faces and shares the expectation of the American people that we shall show we are with them on the ground in Korea.[31]

The US expected the Attlee government to make sacrifices at home and, Franks warned, the US reaction to a negative decision by the Attlee government would be "deep and prolonged" and would "seriously impair the long term relationship".[32]

In this context, and while maintaining their insistence that forces should not be diverted from Malaya or Hong Kong, the Chiefs of Staff came to accept that the political advantages of meeting the US request outweighed the military disadvantages. Hence, a month after the North Korean invasion, with Bevin incapacitated through illness, under pressure from the US, with Sir Oliver Franks reinforcing the US line, and the Conservatives positioned to exploit any political space between London and Washington, Attlee convinced his Cabinet to approve the commitment of two infantry battalions, to be taken from Hong Kong. This agreement would subsequently be met by further US demands, this time that they shoulder their share of the global anti-communist policing burden at the heart of Containment and increase defence spending, just as the US was itself doing. At each turn, British credibility and the future of the special relationship was said to be at stake. Still, there was unease within the Cabinet. As early as August 1950, Hugh Dalton was recording that, "the war in Korea has begun to upset people. The fear of a Third World War is becoming very real and widespread".[33] More openly, Bevan was warning the Cabinet that:

> Our foreign policy had hitherto been based on the view that the best method of defence against Russian imperialism was to improve the social and economic conditions of the countries now threatened by Communist encroachment. The United States government seemed now to be abandoning this social and political defence in favour of a military defence.[34]

Bevan warned his Cabinet colleagues that this shift was misjudged and that Britain would be "ill-advised to follow it".

However, the Munich analogy remained a powerful one for a generation that had witnessed the rise of Hitler and failure of leading powers to check it before 1939. Outwardly, the Cabinet appeared united, *Tribune* invoked the spectre of Munich in supporting the commitment of British forces, and opposition on the Labour benches was initially very limited. The Party conference in October supported the commitment, and Bevan, whose principal defining characteristics on questions of war and the Cold War world were inconsistency and unpredictability, spoke in support. However, the wider public was hardly enthusiastic and the commitment failed to generate a "rally effect" – an increase in popular support for the government arising from its involvement in the conflict as, for example, occurred with the 1982 Falklands war.[35]

By November 1950 the situation seemed even less propitious than it had in the summer. China had entered the war. MacArthur's advance into North Korea had altered the context of the original Labour commitment, representing a challenge to the restrictionist basis of support, and Britain's influence on US strategy was simply non-existent. Reporting back on discussions in New York in October 1950, Bevin advised Attlee that Britain would only retain its influence on the US as long as it remained "unobtrusive".[36] The dilemma for Bevin and Attlee was that to have attempted to influence US strategy would have been to compromise the political benefits they expected to accrue from the initial, and speedy, agreement to provide ground troops. Now, however, British interests in the region, hitherto separate from the conflict on the Korean peninsula, were potentially threatened, the cross-party consensus was being eroded, by-election defeats had reduced the government's majority to a slender margin, and the left wing of the Party was becoming increasingly restive at the apparent autonomy enjoyed by MacArthur, the lack of political will in Washington to rein him in, and the absence of any British influence. Hence, there were limits beyond which British support could not be guaranteed and these seemed to be within sight at the end of 1950, resulting in Attlee's December 1950 visit to Washington.

This arose out of President Truman's November 1950 press conference remark that there had "always been active consideration" of the use of the atomic bomb in the ongoing Korean conflict,[37] and that any decision on the use of the atomic bomb was the responsibility of the commander in the field. It was a remark made just weeks after Chinese entry into the war and clearly directed at that involvement. Hugh Dalton immediately wrote to Attlee warning that: "The latest events, so full of the gravest possibilities – including Truman's statement today on the atomic bomb – have convinced me that *you ought to fly out to Washington at once* – to confer with Truman".[38] Cabinet discussion reflected a general sense of alarm over Truman's comments. "The responsibility for deciding on the use of the atomic bomb would have to be defined", the Cabinet were told:

> A decision of this importance could not be left to commanders in the field or even to the United States government alone. All nations which had contributed to the United Nations forces in Korea should be consulted and there should be unanimity among them before a decision was taken to use the bomb.[39]

In Washington Attlee met with Truman, Secretary of State Dean Acheson, and senior US military figures, and in his autobiography provided an upbeat, if vague, account of the talks.[40] On his return he told the Cabinet he was "entirely satisfied" after Truman had told him he, "regarded the atomic bomb as in a sense a joint possession of the United States, the United Kingdom and Canada, and that he would not authorise its use without prior consultation ... save in an extreme emergency".[41]

Dean Acheson's account of the meeting, however, was quite different, and demonstrated that it was not at all clear that Truman could deliver on this apparent commitment, least of all constitutionally. From Acheson's perspective, the talks with the "Job's comforter" Attlee did not go well.[42] When Attlee discussed MacArthur, reflecting the domestic British feeling that he had far too great a degree of latitude, Truman, according to Acheson's account, concluded the discussion by telling Attlee that the US, "would stay in Korea and fight. If we had support from others, fine; if not, we would stay on anyway".[43] Acheson's most difficult moment came on the last day of the conference, when Truman and Attlee retired to Truman's study alone: "They had, said the President cheerfully, been discussing the atomic weapon and agreed that neither of us would use these weapons without prior consultation with the other. No one spoke".[44] Acheson pointed out that, constitutionally he could not agree to this. The relevant section of the communiqué already under preparation was hastily redrafted to read:

> The President stated that it was his hope that world conditions would never call for the use of the atomic bomb. The President told the Prime Minister that it was also his desire to keep the Prime Minister at all times informed of developments which might bring about a change in the situation.[45]

Despite the upbeat assessments that Attlee brought back from Washington with him, the visit was, at best, only a qualified success.[46] The lesson that should have been drawn related to Britain's *lack* of influence over US use of its own atomic weapons. It was an outcome that was to have a lasting impact on Labour's foreign policy. Nevertheless, it became almost an article of faith amongst Gaitskellite Atlanticists that Attlee's influence had helped to introduce a degree of caution into US behaviour.[47] For them, as for Attlee, the significance of the talks lay in the fact that, "the United Kingdom was lifted out of 'the European queue' and we were treated as partners, unequal no doubt in power but still equal in counsel".[48] They also shared the view that Attlee expressed to Bevin, that the "United States Government implicitly and on occasion explicitly assumed that we are their principal ally and that we must be prepared in the last resort to continue the struggle together and alone".[49]

By the end of the year, the course of the war was causing concern amongst MPs and across constituency parties. Hugh Dalton recorded a conversation with Jim Callaghan where he confided in Dalton that:

> he found many of his party members, particularly the older ones, very unhappy about our present international policy. They didn't want war with Russia, were now not at all sure that we ought to have gone into Korea, were upset by the atrocity stories there, had been still more upset by Truman on the Atom Bomb, thought Attlee hadn't been strong or outspoken enough at Washington, and generally feared that we had become a satellite of the USA and had lost our independence and were being dragged into war. For the first time he didn't feel he carried most of the meeting with him. Tony [Crosland] has said just this and more to me about a delegate meeting in his constituency. It's clear that dissatisfaction and concern are growing rather fast in the Party.[50]

Equally, it was clear by this time that British advice on the diplomatic or military conduct of the war was largely unwelcome. By January 1951, Kenneth Younger was writing in his diary that this, "may be the moment at which to assert our independence of the USA in foreign policy in that the Americans have clearly reached a frame of mind in which they count upon us always to 'go along' with them, no matter what our misgivings. We have got to stop this rot if we ever want to have real influence upon them".[51] More significantly still, Hugh Gaitskell both privately doubted Britain's ability to influence the US in Korea, and also recognised that supporting the US could well have disastrous consequences for wider British interests. He even doubted the degree of control he was able to exert as Chancellor over the defence budget. However, none of these private concerns were reflected in his staunch public support and were instead restricted to his diary. As he observed there in an entry for 10th January 1951:

> so long as the Chinese are advancing they are not likely to be ready to talk, and if we are actually thrown out of Korea pressure on America for some retaliatory action on China will be very, very strong. They talk of a limited war but we all feel that there is no such thing, and the worst of it is that the Chinese would probably retaliate, if blockade is organised against them or if the Americans bomb them, by occupying Hong Kong and moving south through Indo-China to Malaya. I fear too that a young Nationalist movement with such enormous numbers may be too difficult to restrain in any case.
>
> The awful dilemma is that if we cannot restrain the Americans then we have to go in with them in China, which nobody wants, or desert them. If we desert them obviously it may have very serious consequences in their participating in European defence. The immediate issue is whether or not in UNO China shall be declared an aggressor, but even if we get over this hurdle I am afraid there will be others to come later on.
>
> It is not surprising in these circumstances that there is now developing something like a panic about our Defence programme. It is to be accelerated. We do not yet know by how much, nor what this will involve, but inevitably the atmosphere becomes more and more like 1940.[52]

Initially, the rearmament programme which arose from involvement in Korea had been broadly welcomed by the Party. Previous critics of the government's foreign policy, such as Crossman from the Keep Left wing, spoke publicly in its defence:

> The prime object of this rearmament plan is to meet the situation presented by the precedent of Korea. Up to Korea the Communists in the Kremlin have done everything short of war. In the case of Korea a secondhand war was started. What we have to do now is, by next

summer, to have sufficient strength so that no further experiments of this sort can be undertaken.[53]

The precise scale of the rearmament programme was unveiled in January 1951, by which time the Labour government had committed Britain to a higher level of defence spending per head of population than was the case in the US.[54] For a Party in which pacifism had been an important founding element, and in which Arthur Henderson's early work in the field of disarmament had become a key reference point, this was bound to be increasingly controversial as the initial shock of June 1950 receded (and less than eight months after his speech in favour of rearmament, Crossman himself was supporting the resignations of Bevan, Wilson and John Freeman), even disregarding its impact on the government's social programme. By January 1951 backbench dissent was clearly growing. At a 31st January meeting of the PLP, Herbert Morrison felt obliged to make, "a strong appeal to all Members to remain united at the present time and not to precipitate a difficult parliamentary situation by either putting down or signing awkward motions".[55] In early 1951 Sydney Silverman and Fred Messer were rebuked for inviting party members to a "Peace Through Socialism" conference, designed to generate support for a shift in government foreign policy away from support for the US and towards a "third force" position. There was no concealing the rapidly rising discontent.

In 1951 the defence budget was increased by over 50%, up to almost 10% of GDP (from where a rise to approximately 14% was envisaged). At the same time, the Ministry of Food announced a reduction in the weekly meat ration from 10d to 8d per week – enough to buy approximately four ounces.[56] As a consequence of rearmament, by mid-1951, what had been a modest surplus of £307 million in 1950 had been transformed into a £369 million deficit, by year's end it stood at £521 million, the optimism of that year's Festival of Britain sucked dry. On 3rd September 1951, the butter, bacon and cheese rations were all cut.[57] In a November 1951 draft memorandum for the parliamentary committee of the PLP, Gaitskell noted that the initial American approach regarding Britain's rearmament, "was accompanied by vague promises of substantial aid. For example, I remember that the general impression we were given was that the Americans would take care of us if the balance of payments went wrong".[58] In practice, this simply did not happen.

The prioritising of the global security role over the domestic agenda was again confirmed in Gaitskell's April 1951 budget, his first and only and the immediate cause of the Cabinet resignations of Aneurin Bevan, Harold Wilson and John Freeman. The focus of protest was the introduction of charges for false teeth and glasses, an issue on which Gaitskell refused various attempted compromises that would have staved off the resignations, and which were met with consternation on the Tribunite Left.[59] Wilson himself recalled that it was the "squandering of our resources" through the rearmament programme that caused him to resign, and that therefore the reasons for his resignation had a different emphasis from those of Bevan.[60] The divide between Bevan and Gaitskell that this exposed has tended to be portrayed as one arising from domestic politics – variously couched in terms of consolidation versus advance, reformism versus socialism, pragmatism versus realism,[61] or simply of differences in political styles or backgrounds.[62] However, this is clearly not the case. At issue was the acceptance of the erosion of commitments central to the domestic reform agenda in order to pay for the demands of Cold War foreign policy. As Kenneth O. Morgan has noted, Gaitskell, the Chancellor of the Exchequer, used primarily political arguments in support of his position, to the extent that, "his commitment to the American alliance overrode his economic judgement".[63]

The resignations brought further into the open and gave full form to the fault line that separated the Atlanticist leadership from the emerging Bevanite Left. Gaitskell's biographer notes the irony, that:

> Gaitskell – supporting a rearmament package for an anti-communist war in south-east Asia – emerged as the Labour government loyalist; while Bevan – supporting the idea of a free health service and opposing an over-ambitious rearmament package which squandered much of the post-war recovery in export trade – emerged as the government rebel and splitter.[64]

For Gaitskell, the relationship with the US was of paramount importance, everything else secondary to it. Even a sympathetic biographer, Brian Brivati, concedes that Gaitskell's Atlanticist beliefs, "were based on a deep sense of patriotism and a great affection for America and Americans; occasionally it is difficult to separate the two, but the patriotism *tended* to come first".[65] As Gaitskell confided to a journalist in 1952, "there is only one thing we have to do in the next few years, and that is to keep the Labour Party behind the Anglo-American alliance".[66]

The issue did expose the inconsistency at the heart of Bevan's stance on foreign and defence policy. Previously supportive in Cabinet of NATO and Britain's own atomic bomb, seemingly ambivalent over rearmament, what propelled him towards this stand on this issue? There is no doubt that a degree of personal antipathy towards Gaitskell played its part, an antipathy returned by Gaitskell in at least equal measure. This was a consequence of personal ambition thwarted – Gaitskell succeeded Cripps at the Treasury after being an MP for just five years, a post that Bevan himself had coveted. To then use that position to take funding away from his own creation, the National Health Service, and divert it to a military programme that Bevan could demonstrate at least a partial track record in opposing, was too much for the combustible Welshman to bear. Hence, the split was as much political as personal. Bevan also thought Gaitskell too "wildly pro-American and anti-Russian", and believed it was this pro-Americanism that was leading such "rootless men" to dismantle the welfare state.[67] If the Vietnam War is sometimes represented as presenting the Johnson Administration with a choice between guns and butter,[68] then Korea and rearmament similarly presented the Attlee government with a choice between guns and dental health. It chose guns. It never recovered from the political and social implications of the Korean commitment and associated rearmament programme, although, of course, these had not been apparent at the time of the initial offer of limited, naval, support. That April, the Bevanite movement was born at a meeting attended by Bevan, Wilson, Crossman, Foot, Barbara Castle, Mikardo, Jennie Lee, Driberg, and seven other MPs. Attlee called the general election for October 1951, and a divided Labour Party was defeated. The government of Churchill that replaced it agreed with the Bevanites that the cost of the proposed rearmament programme was too much to bear, and consequently scaled it back. Throughout 1952 the PLP expressed its concern at the conduct of the war, and intra-party division over Korea, extending to the wider question of British proximity to the US in foreign policy, was evident.[69] Once out of office, the Left kept up a running commentary on the stalemate in Korea through the pages of *Tribune*, before the war drew to a close in 1953. Gaitskell himself acknowledged a rise in anti-Americanism as a consequence, which he partly attributed to envy, but also to people's fear that the US would drag Britain into another war, one which even Gaitskell worried might well, "engulf and destroy Britain and Europe while very probably leaving the territory of America physically untouched".[70] The fault line that would give definition to the Labour Party for the next generation had been created.

The Suez crisis

Next to Munich, in the twentieth century the Suez debacle divided the British public more deeply than any other foreign policy issue. It also marked the first important post-war foreign policy issue over which Labour and Conservative front benches were polarised and locked in bitter debate, and remains the only occasion on which they openly opposed each other over the deployment of British troops in a combat role. It was a debacle that was far from inevitable, arising from a situation that had a striking parallel in events just five years earlier in Iran, at the time of the Attlee government.

There, in March 1951 Prime Minister Mossadegh had announced his intention of nationalising the assets of the Anglo-Iranian Oil Company, in which the British government was the majority shareholder, and which included the world's largest oil refinery at Abadan, an island on the Shatt al Arab waterway. While the US preference was for the nationalisation to be accepted, negotiations based on acceptance of the principle of nationalisation in return for compensation and an understanding on the supply of oil got nowhere, and Foreign Secretary Herbert Morrison despatched paratroopers and extra naval cover to the eastern Mediterranean and reinforced air bases in Iraq in readiness to use force if required.[71] Morrison, who, in a stiff field, stands out as one of the poorer foreign secretaries of the post-war era (Harold Wilson believed he "made a fool of himself at the Foreign Office"[72]), seemed unwilling to deal personally with the crisis, preferring to busy himself with preparations for the Festival of Britain and ensuring that his ministerial responsibilities did not unduly affect his travel schedule.[73] By the time of his return from a period of foreign touring in September the Attorney General, Sir Frank Soskice, had given his view that Britain had "no right at all" in international law to intervene by force outside the framework of the UN.[74] Additionally, Attlee informed the Cabinet that the Truman Administration had declined to support any British military action over the impasse. Attlee was himself opposed to military action in these circumstances, and wanted to seek a negotiated solution via the UN. Morrison's reaction was to denounce the UN and argue for a military intervention, despite the absence of US support.[75] While the FO assessment was that the British public would probably support armed intervention without UN sanction, and while Opposition leader Winston Churchill had offered Attlee his support for military intervention, the party's commitment to the UN and international law prevailed, although the significance attached to the US response at a time of financial vulnerability should not be underestimated. In any case, in the context of Britain's contemporaneous military commitment in Korea alongside other existing commitments, not to mention the divisive rearmament debate, to add to these burdens by virtue of such an expedition was an irresponsible suggestion.

Nevertheless, Morrison argued that the use of force would enhance British prestige. Aside from Shinwell's support at Defence, Morrison was isolated in Cabinet where the Attorney General made it plain that Morrison's argument had little to recommend it in international law, under which force could only be used as a last resort to save lives. The case was duly referred to the UN. Just days later, and without a hint of irony, Morrison referred to Abadan in his speech to the Labour Party Conference, telling delegates that:

> As long as I am Foreign Secretary I will not be ... party to a war which is not necessary and can possibly be avoided. I do not accuse the average Conservative of being a war-monger and thirsting for the shedding of blood ... But it is their temperament; it is the background of their mental outlook... if the country wants peace it had better vote for the people who can be most surely relied upon to preserve peace.[76]

Shortly afterwards, during the 1951 general election campaign, Gaitskell, a member of the Ministerial Committee on Persia formed by Attlee to oversee the situation, spoke of the "central issue" in the crisis as being:

> about the use of force – when it is and when it is not justified ... We have never doubted that it would be justifiable to use force to protect

the lives of British citizens if they were threatened by a serious outbreak of rioting and disturbance. We would have sent our troops in to rescue them and bring them out ... Should we, however, have used force to protect British property or to compel the Persians to allow the British employees of the company to remain? I do not think there is much doubt that this has been in the mind of many Conservatives all along. Indeed, Mr Churchill's recent attack on Mr Attlee makes it quite clear. I can understand this point of view though I do not share it. The argument runs like this: 'The Persian government have repudiated an important contract. They have been taken to the Hague court which made an interim recommendation which they at once flouted. They have rejected the reasonable offers we have made. They have stolen British property and expelled British citizens. We will not tolerate it. We have the power and we will use it.' It is all very tempting, but also very dangerous. Had we followed this course, we should have run the grave risk of war with Persia, with the possibility of wider and far more serious consequences. We should have been acting on our own without the backing of the Security Council before whom we should no doubt have been arraigned as aggressors ... surely the right course is to do as we have done and bring the whole matter to the Security Council.[77]

Five years later, in the case of Suez, Conservative Prime Minister Sir Anthony Eden was faced with a similar challenge and similar options, but reacted very differently, insisting that he was standing up to an aggressive Third World Arab leader who had acted in defiance of international law, and deceiving Parliament in the process.

By now Labour leader, Hugh Gaitskell's front bench in 1956 has been described as presenting, "the most pro-Israeli image of any British party in the eight years since the creation of that state".[78] Gaitskell himself had made a cause of advocating a more responsive approach to Israeli requests for arms, particularly with regard to the debate over whether or not to supply the Centurion tank. Concern over Israel's security was certainly a factor in Gaitskell's negative assessment of Nasser, confirmed by Egypt's 1955 arms deal with Czechoslovakia. On the night of Nasser's 26th July 1956 speech announcing his takeover of the Suez Canal Company to help finance the Aswan Dam project from which the Americans had just announced their withdrawal, Gaitskell was attending a reception at 10 Downing Street. His initial reaction, as recorded in his diary, was to tell Eden and Foreign Secretary Selwyn Lloyd that, "they ought to act quickly whatever they did and that, as far as Great Britain was concerned, public opinion would almost certainly be behind them".[79] In a sense, this was one of the lessons he had drawn from the Abadan crisis, as had Morrison, who wrote in his memoirs of how it had taught that, "if military action was to be politically effective it should be quick".[80] Gaitskell's only piece of advice was that the government "must get America into line". At this stage he did not expect this to prove particularly difficult as, "after all, the Americans had themselves precipitated this by their decision to withdraw all financial assistance for the Aswan Dam".[81]

In his diary, Gaitskell observed that nobody in the PLP seemed to object to his condemnation of Nasser in Parliament on Friday 27th July, the implication being that he would continue to take the same line. Then, however, he had limited himself to nothing stronger than the fact that Labour, "deeply deplore this high-handed and totally unjustifiable step by the Egyptian Government",[82] not even mentioning Nasser by name. During the 2nd August Suez debate Eden's account of Nasser's seizure of the Canal was much more restrained than Gaitskell's response, possibly a consequence of Gaitskell's concern that his speech should not seem either unpatriotic or irresponsible.[83] Gaitskell presented his own objections to Nasser's actions as being threefold. First, while not objecting to nationalisation *per se*, this was different as it gave Nasser control over "an international waterway of immense importance to the whole of the rest of the world".[84] Second, the manner in which it was seized was objectionable and, third, there was Nasser himself:

> We cannot forget that Colonel Nasser has repeatedly boasted of his intention to create an Arab empire from the Atlantic to the Persian Gulf. The French Prime Minister, M. Mollet, the other day quoted a speech of Colonel Nasser's and rightly said that it could remind us only of one thing – of the speeches of Hitler before the war ... I have no doubt myself that the reason why Colonel Nasser acted in the way that he did, aggressively, brusquely, suddenly, was precisely because he wanted to raise his prestige in the rest of the Middle East. He wanted to show the rest of the Arab world – "See what I can do." He wanted to challenge the West and to win ... It is all very familiar. It is exactly the same that we encountered from Mussolini and Hitler in those years before the war.[85]

This gave rise to a further concern; Nasser's potential to destabilise the region and the potential threat he posed to the state of Israel.[86] There was little evidence of the intellectual trajectory of Labour foreign policy thinking in the speech to this point. Long-standing commitments to decolonisation, support for nationalist movements in the Third World, not to mention nationalisation, all conflicted with Gaitskell's national interest defence and demonisation of Nasser, justified by reference to the appeasement of the 1930s. However, he concluded by reflecting on the possible use of force, which could not be excluded, but emphasising the necessity of working through the UN. He reminded MPs of how, "for many years in British policy, we have steadfastly avoided any international action which would be in breach of international law or, indeed, contrary to the public opinion of the world". However, whether with the words that followed Gaitskell was ruling out military action, or merely insisting on US support for such a course, is unclear. "We must not", Gaitskell warned, "allow ourselves to get into a position where we might be denounced in the Security Council as aggressors or where the majority of the Assembly were against us".[87]

Robert Rhodes James, present in the House, recalled:

> It was strong meat, and one had to be there to appreciate how strong it was in its delivery ... His hostility to Nasser was expressed with much fervour and eloquence; his qualifications were notably more *sotto voce*. It was in this way that he seriously misled Eden, the House of Commons, the press and public opinion.[88]

Nor was Gaitskell alone on the Labour benches in his approach to the issue, some were in general agreement with him over the use of force, some went even further. Denis Healey argued that if Nasser were to interfere with transit through the Canal there was, "no doubt that this House, and, indeed, world opinion outside Britain, would fully support forceful action by this country, in conjunction with its Allies *or even alone*".[89] Towards the end of a speech in which he had stressed the centrality of the UN, Herbert Morrison nevertheless foresaw the possibility that the Eden government might have to operate outside it:

> I say to the United Nations that if it wishes – as we would wish it – to become the great moral authority of the world and the great decisive instrument, it must stop dodging vital international issues. If our Government and France and, if possible, the United States should come to the conclusion that in the circumstances the use of force would be justified, then I think that it is up to each hon. Member of this House to tell the Government whether we would support them or whether we would not. For my own part, in principle, if, after an elaborate and proper consideration, the Government and our friends come to that conclusion, I think that in the circumstances of this particular case it might well be the duty of hon. Members, including myself, to say that we would give them support.[90]

Hence, action outside the UN but in partnership with the US would be acceptable. In the House of Lords, Attlee made a more measured speech, emphasising the need to work through the UN, warning that "nothing would be worse than for us to plunge into this business on our own", that Nasser was "a thoroughly objectionable type of dictator", and offering his party's support to the government "in whatever action is necessary, provided that we act within the sphere of International Law".[91] Nevertheless, even he came to think that once the military operation had been commenced it should have been seen through, on the basis that: "If you've broken the eggs you should make the omelette".[92]

A number of questions arise. To what extent did Gaitskell's position shift between July/August and September onwards? If it did, how can we account for this shift? Finally, did Gaitskell's initially supportive stance encourage Eden along a path he might otherwise not have chosen? These are controversial questions, partly made so by biographers of Gaitskell seeking to minimise the fact or extent of Gaitskell's shift and biographers of Eden emphasising it. For Eden biographer D. R. Thorpe, after their exchange in Downing Street:

> Eden mistakenly interpreted Gaitskell's positive response as a tacit sign there would be bipartisan support. He did not expect a blank cheque, but on the other hand he did not foresee the bitterness and animosity that would unfold as British troops went into action.[93]

For Gaitskell biographer Brian Brivati, on the other hand, "the evidence suggests that in fact he was entirely consistent in his beliefs, though fluctuating occasionally in emphasis".[94] Similarly, Gaitskell biographer Philip Williams insists that "Gaitskell's views did not shift",[95] and that it was the Conservative press and enemies within the Labour Party who, "later propagated the myth that he had supported Eden's policy of using force", only to shift his ground under pressure from Labour MPs.[96]

However, there is considerable evidence of pressure from within the parliamentary party, at least some of which had a direct bearing on Gaitskell's approach to the question and resulted in him modifying his original position as articulated on 26th July. A key piece of evidence on this is to be found in Gaitskell's diary entry for the period. The entry covering the period 31st July – 3rd August was dictated on 2nd and 3rd August, after his 2nd August speech, over which Gaitskell admitted to being, "a little embarrassed by far too much praise from the Tories, including Waterhouse and other members of the Suez group".[97] This records a meeting with Kenneth Younger while he was working on his speech, and Younger offering, "some valuable help as to what exactly I should say on the United Nations, and as it turned out these paragraphs suggested to me by him were immensely important".[98] Furthermore, Douglas Jay credits John Hynd and himself with persuading Gaitskell to refer to the UN in his speech, recalling that: "Gaitskell at first thought this unnecessary, and had unfortunately been induced by his sympathies with Israel, and a visit from the Israeli Ambassador, to include some words in his speech about Hitler and Mussolini. But he agreed to our suggestion".[99]

Hence, at least three people approached Gaitskell over the UN component of his speech. Additionally, on 1st August Gaitskell had met with the Foreign Affairs Steering Group (Tony Benn, William Warbey, John Hynd, Denis Healey, Kenneth Younger and Alf Robens) "partly in order to smooth them down and make them feel that they had been consulted".[100] Gaitskell was unimpressed with Benn, Warbey and Hynd who, he felt, "rush to the defence of any eastern country and ... completely ... ignore the fact that Nasser is a dictator".[101] In particular, he felt that Benn had "extraordinarily poor judgment" and was "the last person in the world I would go to for advice on policy".[102] Nevertheless, it represented another indication of the party's concern at the tone of Gaitskell's remarks. He would also have been aware of a degree of backbench dismay at his 2nd August speech. One of these backbenchers, Tony Benn, recalled it thus:

> Gaitskell made a speech of bitter denunciation of Nasser. He followed the Prime Minister in an emergency debate and was wildly cheered by the Tories and heard in near silence by his own Party. I felt so sick as I listened that I wanted to shout 'shame'. I very nearly did buttonhole him afterwards and say that his speech had made me want to vomit.
>
> Gaitskell's speech had only one saving grace. It ended with a phrase declaring that as a signatory of the UN Charter, Britain was bound not to use force without its authority. But the dominating impression of the whole speech was that British prestige and influence required really tough action.[103]

Moreover, pressure may have also been applied by Bevan. Initially, he too had been very critical of Nasser, so much so that his article on Suez for the 3rd August issue of *Tribune* was somewhat out of line with the leading article. That weekend, however, Bevan attended a dinner party along with Jennie Lee, Ian Mikardo and Leslie Hale as guests of John Mackie, later to become a junior minister in the 1964 Wilson government. Mikardo credits the guests with helping transform Bevan's position (originally that, "Nasser's a thug and he needs to be taught a lesson") to the extent that:

> Three days after our dinner-party he was arguing the very case we had put to him, even using some of Leslie Hale's phraseology, and Gaitskell followed him. From that point Labour's anti-Suez campaign, 'Law, not War', took on a stronger impetus and a sharper edge.[104]

Certainly, during August there is evidence of Gaitskell responding to backbench Labour concern, for example in sanctioning a letter by Jay and Healey to *The Times* in which they outlined the circumstances in which they felt the use of force would be justified.[105] Still, this showed that there were circumstances under which the use of force could be supported by Labour, and the party, along with the Liberals, did not object to the call up of reservists.

To his biographer Philip Williams, Gaitskell recognised the British national interest in the Canal, or at least the passage of oil and British ships through it (a distinction emphasised by Denis Healey at the time[106]), deplored Nasser's method in seizing the Canal and, "never believed in the Third World right or wrong, or approved of ambitious military dictators just because their skins were dark".[107] For Eden biographer Robert Rhodes James, there was, during August, "a step backwards from the fervour of the 2 August speech", but one that fell well short of a *volte-face*.[108] Still, Williams concedes that a key variable in this situation was the attitude of the US. Gaitskell clearly did not oppose the use of force *per se*, but as the situation unfolded into a large-scale military operation in defiance of the US, Commonwealth and UN, oppose it he did, and to great effect. Harold Wilson would recall Gaitskell's speeches on Suez as:

> models of construction, moving in their oratory and utterly consistent. He strongly rejected Egypt's claim to have the right to prevent free passage through the Canal, but was equally vigorous in opposing the British Government's decision to seek to force the Canal by an invasion. When it began, and right through the period of the fighting, his speeches ranked as the greatest of his life.[109]

Hence, after the summer recess Gaitskell's approach was no longer as equivocal as it had been in early August. The question of the role of the UN became central, and he rightly attracted much praise for his firm and articulate opposition to Eden's military adventurism and deceit of Parliament in the weeks that followed. In his speech to the House of Commons of 12th September, Eden had studiously avoided any commitment to work through the UN in resolving the dispute, though he was careful to say that he did not rule out such a course. He also made use of the 1930s' appeasement analogy that Gaitskell had invited, but lent it added weight by invoking his own direct experience of the era, arguing that:

> Of course, there are those who say that we should not be justified and are not justified in reacting vigorously unless Colonel Nasser commits some further act of aggression. That was the argument used in the 1930s to justify every concession that was made to the dictators. It has not been my experience that dictators are deflected from their purpose because others affect to ignore it. This reluctance to face reality led to the subjugation of Europe and to the Second World War. We must not help to reproduce, step by step, the history of the 'thirties. We have to prove ourselves wiser this time, and to check aggression by the pressure of international opinion, if possible; but, if not, by other means before it has grown to monstrous proportions.[110]

Gaitskell now argued that the use of force in the absence of any further provocative action on the part of Nasser would set a dangerous precedent, thereby undermining the UN and whole basis of international law and directly challenging a number of Labour's core foreign policy values. If Eden were to go ahead, "ignoring the Charter of the United Nations and taking the law into our own hands, we are reverting to international anarchy. We are asserting the view that each nation decides in its own right what it is going to do, and we are saying that only power counts".[111]

Such an approach would undermine what he regarded as the onward march towards the development of a "world authority", which was necessary to prevent a relapse into international anarchy. At the same time, Gaitskell emphasised that he did not rule out the use of force, if authorised by the UN. In this case there could be no other justification for force. Article 51 of the UN Charter did not apply, as it had in Korea, because an act of nationalisation of a national asset could not be equated with an aggressive act of military force. He concluded that:

> Every motive – self-respect, self-interest, our responsibility for world leadership, our membership of the Commonwealth, our alliances – all these things point to the same conclusion: that we should stand by our pledges to the United Nations honestly and fairly and, by our restraint and our patience, set an example to the world.[112]

On 31st October British aircraft began bombing four Egyptian airfields, an attack which carried on into the following day. The confrontation in the House of Commons that day, where Gaitskell was assisted by clinical interventions from the likes of Bevan and Sidney Silverman, was described by veteran *Times* reporter Iverach McDonald as, "quite the most shattering experience I've ever sat through … the divisions, the uproar, the emotion were much worse than at the time of Munich".[113] While Gaitskell was quick to point out that, "millions of British people are profoundly shocked and ashamed that British aircraft should be bombing Egypt, not in self-defence, not in collective defence, but in clear defiance of the United Nations Charter",[114] Silverman highlighted the fact that in the absence of a declaration of war British forces were being obliged to commit illegal acts, and could expect no protection if captured by Egyptian forces. Eden was unable to summon up any kind of convincing response to Gaitskell and Bevan's further requests for clarification as to the status of the conflict and of British service men involved in it. Amidst scenes of near-anarchy, the Speaker had little option but to suspend the sitting. When it resumed Eden conceded that there had been no declaration of war, likening the situation to that of June 1950, a poor comparison, as Silverman pointed out, given that North Korea was not recognised by the UN and hence there could not have been a declaration of war. More significantly, perhaps, the response to the North Korean invasion had been co-ordinated under UN auspices, following legitimating votes in the UNSC. Now, six years later, Britain had committed military force against a fellow member of the UN. If not war, "what are we at with Egypt then", Silverman asked, "at peace?"[115] Eden's answer was that Britain was in a state of "armed conflict" with Egypt, although he could not answer Gaitskell's question as to, "exactly what is the difference between war and armed conflict?"[116]

There was no precedent for the division between the Labour and Conservative parties on this issue. Never before had the Labour Party collectively opposed a British military commitment as it was actually underway. The notion that politics had to stop at the water's edge and that national unity overrode all other considerations while British troops were in action, regardless of the circumstances, was demolished forever by Suez. Instead, Tony Benn warned the government that:

> in the discharge of our solemn obligations and our duty the Opposition will fight this action in the country – everywhere – because it is wrong and because we have faith in the instinctive sense of decency and fair play of the British people. We shall hound the Government down, and then we shall have the terrible task of trying to rebuild the credit of this country which the Government have so wantonly thrown away.[117]

The fact that Eden's deception of Parliament – and it was on a breathtaking scale – had extended to Gaitskell himself added a measure of wounded pride. Had the 5th November landing at Port Said by British and French paratroopers been planned in consultation with the US and with its approval, and had Gaitskell thereby been included from its inception, it is worth asking whether his commitment to the UN would have been as non-negotiable and whether he may have behaved differently.[118] This was essentially Michael Foot's argument, that Gaitskell was, "gratified to find his criticism of the British Government coinciding so closely with that which came from Washington", and that, "it was probably the injury to the Anglo-American alliance which gave the spur to his passion".[119] Nevertheless, in his televised address at the height of the crisis, Gaitskell was able to contrast his and his party's tradition of support for the UN with the flagrant violation of the UN Charter by Eden: "What are the consequences?", he asked. "We have violated the Charter of the United Nations. In doing so, we have betrayed all that Great Britain has stood for in world affairs. Since the war, at least, we have supported every stand against aggression". Gaitskell concluded: "This is not a Labour Party matter – it touches the whole nation – all those who care for the rule of law in international affairs".[120]

Suez was a defining political event for a generation of British politicians. It spawned various legacies, but one was to reinforce in Labour MPs who were in the House at the time and future MPs who protested outside it, such as Gerald Kaufman, a strict restrictionist approach to the use of military force. Suez was an act of aggression, but also an enormous deceit perpetrated by a government that deliberately mis-sold a war to the British public. The capacity for governments to commit force on the basis of such a deceit was instrumental in confirming the Labour Party's reluctance to support the use of force unless deployed in support of resolutions passed by the UNSC. Indeed, over 40 years later, Tony Benn, who worked closely with Hugh Gaitskell at the culmination of the crisis, would make the experience a reference point in explaining to the House of Commons his opposition to the Blair government's decision to go to war over Kosovo without the explicit sanction of the UN.[121]

4   Harold Wilson, the Labour Party and the Vietnam War

The Vietnam War cast a permanent shadow over the Wilson governments' foreign policy, particularly in relation to the question of whether or not Wilson would commit British troops in support of US forces there. Barbara Castle considered Vietnam to be the cause of more anger amongst Wilson's usual supporters than any other issue.[1] Moreover, this anger was enduring. When asked to list the most shameful acts in the Party's history, a survey of Labour MPs conducted to mark the Party's centenary placed the Wilson government's support for the Vietnam War joint first with Ramsay Mac-Donald's 1931 "betrayal".[2] This shows a poor grasp of the party's history. In reality, Wilson played a limited hand with considerable skill, caught between US pressure, bleak FO analyses of the military outlook on the one hand but advocacy of support on the other, backbench opposition, a wafer-thin parliamentary majority, and an opposition waiting to capitalise on any slip. Wilson consistently declined to meet the US request for the dispatch of British ground forces to Vietnam. As the poll cited above suggests, this achievement was not regarded as such at the time, but inevitably emerges in a more positive light when contrasted with the Blair government's 2002–03 decision to commit British troops to war in Iraq.

As direct US military involvement in Vietnam began to deepen in the first half of 1964, the Johnson Administration launched its "more flags" policy. This attempt to internationalise the war effort on the lines of the Korean War had a number of aims – neutralising potential opposition in Europe and in Congress, steeling the highly questionable resolve of the South Vietnamese forces, and demonstrating a united front to the Hanoi leadership and its international backers.[3] However, the international response was unenthu-siastic. When US Secretary of State Dean Rusk lobbied a meeting of NATO members in May 1964 the best offer he received was for limited non-military support. Although the search for "more flags" would become global in range, taking in Asia, Australasia, Latin America, Africa and Europe, the most important countries to be approached and resist, all the while pro-claiming general support for US aims if not methods, included Japan, West Germany and Britain. As this suggests, a certain nervousness about possible US actions in Vietnam and a desire to distance the UK from US military policy were evident prior to Wilson assuming office. For example, as early as March 1964 James Cable in the FO's South East Asia Department was advising that:

> The moment may be rapidly approaching at which we should urge our views on the US Government, both in order to dissuade them from courses liable to lead to dangerous increases in international tension and also to make clear that we are unwilling to extend our support for their existing policy to embrace hypothetical new policies of this kind. The timing of the approach is a little difficult to judge. Should we make it before the US Government have reached a decision (at the risk of irritating them by displaying premature and perhaps needless alarm) or should we make it when they have reached their decision (at the risk of being too late to exert any influence)?[4]

The in-coming Wilson government would inherit this FO pessimism regarding the US war. Nevertheless, this official nervousness co-existed alongside a Gaitskellite belief in the necessity of adapting British foreign policy to accommodate US priorities. As Patrick Gordon Walker, soon to become Foreign Secretary, wrote in an August 1964 "Thoughts on Foreign Policy" sketch:

> Almost every British policy will react in one way or another upon our relations with USA. We must try to co-ordinate these and build a coherent whole out of them.
>
> If we are dependent upon US for ultimate nuclear protection, we must so arrange our relations with US that our share in the pattern of US alliance is as indispensable as we can make it ...
>
> In some matters we should (in our own interest) shift closer to American ideas. In others we will be further away. In some points we must adapt our ideas to theirs – in exchange for similar concessions by US in matters that greatly concern us.[5]

Given the "more flags" imperative it was inevitable that the US would look to raise the question of a British troop commitment with Wilson at the earliest feasible moment following his victory in the October 1964 general election. This arose at a December 1964 Washington summit, where Johnson raised the question of British troops going to Vietnam, "even if only on a limited – or even a token – basis".[6] While Wilson recalled Johnson raising the question "without excessive enthusiasm",[7] it had clearly been at the fore-front of Johnson's mind just five days earlier when, during an interview with a British newspaper, he asked why Britain had just eight men in South Vietnam (the Thompson advisory mission[8]) when it could easily deploy a military force of two to four hundred? This would ensure that the US was not exposed in a "colonialist position". "We want your flag", Johnson explained.[9] Wilson, however, had to operate in the context of his slim parliamentary majority, the implacable opposition of a small but not insignificant number of backbench MPs (one would not have been an insignificant number in the context of the parliamentary arithmetic of the time), and a tradition of over a decade of consistent Labour support for Vietnamese independence and opposition to French colonialism and US involvement.

Moreover, the FO prognosis of the situation hardly acted as a spur to intervention. In advance of Wilson's December 1964 visit to Washington, the FO had produced a memorandum on Vietnam outlining what it saw as Wilson's limited room for manoeuvre. It warned that the US government was moving towards embarking on a limited offensive against the North. The FO accepted that such a policy was, "likely to be unpopular with significant sections of British public opinion", but considered that alternatives strategies involving diplomacy, "could only lead to a settlement gravely adverse to Western interests and deeply humiliating to the United States". Hence, there was "no option" but for the Wilson government to, "promise diplomatic support for their policy in Viet-Nam".[10] The situation was complicated by three further factors. Although diplomacy looked unlikely to yield a result acceptable to the US, Britain was a co-Chair (alongside the Soviet Union) of the Geneva Conference, a position which carried with it an implicit responsibility to move both parties towards a negotiated settlement. Second, Britain was ultimately reliant on US support over Malaysia. Finally, there was no prospect of a US victory if the present defensive strategy was continued. On the contrary, it was feared that South Vietnam's "willingness to continue the struggle might collapse in a matter of months". Hence, the FO's assessment of the US situation in Vietnam was, at the end of 1964, quite bleak:

> It may be too late for a limited offensive to save South Viet-Nam, but we agree with the US Government that mere continuation of the defensive offers no hope of victory. We also agree that a decision to write off South Viet-Nam, though possibly the lesser of two evils, would have profoundly damaging repercussions on US prestige and the Western position in South East Asia.[11]

Hence, in his meeting with Johnson, Wilson deployed a combination of alibis to explain why Britain could not assist with troops, beginning with the government's economic situation and the economic drain of the East of Suez role, and taking in the confrontation with Indonesia over Malaysia, "Britain's forgotten post 1945 war",[12] in which, by the end of 1964, up to 54,000 British forces personnel were deployed.[13] In effect this was a repeat of Kenneth Younger's attempt to play the "Malaya card" in heading off US pressure for the commitment of British troops to the Korean peninsula in 1950. Better still, as long as peace efforts were regularly attempted, there was the insistence that Britain's role as co-Chair of the Geneva Conference meant it simply could not intervene even if it had the capacity – an argument that became even more important once the confrontation with Indonesia ended in 1966.

Indeed, Patrick Gordon Walker deployed the co-Chair card in reminding Dean Rusk about the importance of maintaining proportionality in the conflict, thereby avoiding unjustified escalations. He told Rusk:

> If at any time more sudden dramatic action was taken by the US Government which was out of proportion to what had provoked it, this would put the UK Government in a difficult position internally and internationally. There would be great pressure upon them to call the 14-Power Conference. Any retaliation which the US Government undertook should therefore be related to the scale of the action against which retaliation was being taken. It should be retaliation such as the US had carried out successfully in Laos. Within this framework ... the UK Government supported the US and would not wish to call the 14-Power Conference without consultation.[14]

It is important to consider Wilson's own understanding of the origins and nature of the Vietnam crisis, in particular the meaning and implications of the 1954 Geneva Accords, something on which Wilson did not himself elaborate in any of his memoirs. At the time they were being negotiated, and as befitted a key figure on the Bevanite Left of the party, Wilson was a vocal critic of US foreign policy in Indochina, telling a meeting in Manchester, for example, that:

> The Government should not further subordinate British policy to America. A settlement in Asia is imperilled by the lunatic fringe in the American Senate who want a holy crusade against Communism. Not a man, not a gun must be sent from Britain to aid French imperialism in Indo-China. Nor must Britain join or encourage an anti-Communist alliance in Asia. Asia is in revolution and Britain must learn to march on the side of the peoples in that revolution and not on the side of their oppressors.[15]

Hence, his sympathies were impeccably anti-imperialist, suggesting an understanding of the nationalist underpinnings of the conflict. Moreover, he clearly supported the 1954 Geneva Accords and was critical of the failure on the part of South Vietnam to hold the promised elections, arguing that: "We are put in an impossible position if steps are not taken to ensure that the agreement is honoured and if it is possible for North Vietnam to point to a failure to carry out the terms of the agreement".[16] However, from the mid-1950s his interest in Indochina and criticisms of US foreign policy subsided. As Opposition leader, he made no comment on the assassination of Diem. However, his pronouncements of the mid-1950s clearly suggest that his analysis of the nature of the Vietnamese conflict was similar to that of his backbench critics of the 1960s, such as that contained, for example, in

William Warbey's 1965 account *Vietnam: The Truth*.[17] Central to this was support for the principle contained in the Geneva Accords that during 1955 consultations between representatives of the two zones would lead to internationally supervised elections in 1956, resulting in a unitary Vietnamese state.

In office, this posed an awkward intellectual problem for Wilson. In logic, his support for the US had to rest on the notion that there was a *de facto* partition of Vietnam into two separate entities, that the South was in effect a state in its own right, and that the North was committing acts of aggression against the South, which therefore had the right of every state to defend itself. Wilson would resolve this dilemma, at least publicly, by announcing in February 1965 that the nature of the conflict in Vietnam had now changed. "A year ago", he told the House of Commons,

> the general supposition was that the fighting in South Vietnam was a spontaneous, so-called nationalist rising on the part of the Viet Cong people. But now there is no attempt at all to deny the responsibility of North Vietnam, who have said that they are fighting a war in South Vietnam. That makes a very big difference, I think, in terms of our analysis of the problem.[18]

Nevertheless, the question of whether the conflict in Vietnam was a civil war remained a very awkward one for Wilson thereafter, as, for example, in this July 1965 attempt to explain the nature of the conflict:

> It is in part, both in origin and character, a civil war, but it is equally a war that most of us feel would not be sustained and could not be intensified but for the participation of North Vietnam in the fighting both with troops and with supplies.[19]

His backbench critics would retain a different perspective, as illustrated by Philip Noel-Baker in April 1967:

> It has always been nonsense to pretend that there are two separate nations in Vietnam. Air Vice-Marshal Ky is from the North. Pham Van Dong, the Prime Minister of the North, comes from the South. Last autumn, Ky caused a Cabinet crisis by trying to pack his Ministry with his Northern friends. The truth is that the Vietnamese are one nation, with the same language, the same religions, and a national history of which they are intensely proud. The basic falsehood on which the policy of US intervention has been built is to treat them as two nations, when in reality they are one.[20]

The deterioration in the situation on the ground in Vietnam in early 1965, culminating in the February 1965 US bombing of North Vietnam, posed further problems for Wilson. In Parliament, he was faced with a motion signed by 50 backbenchers condemning the attack. Sensing the prospect of further escalation, Wilson shared his concerns in a telephone call to Lord Harlech, the British Ambassador to Washington, specifically that:

> alone of the major powers Britain was appearing to keep silent over South Vietnam and appearing to simply tag along in the wake of the Americans. For presentational reasons, therefore, it was highly desirable that the Prime Minister should be seen to be consulting the Americans. He was perfectly prepared to back the Americans in what they had to do in South Vietnam. But it would be easier for him to do this if he were seen to be in discussion with the President of the United States.[21]

Wilson then phoned Johnson on the transatlantic "hotline" to suggest a prime ministerial visit to Washington. In doing so, Wilson's model was clearly Attlee's December 1950 visit to Washington. Johnson does not seem to have been keen to take the call at all, but having done so rejected the idea of a Wilson visit, advising him instead to "keep a normal pulse". As Johnson wasted no time in pointing out, when Attlee flew over to Washington in 1950, Britain had troops in Korea. There were no British troops in Vietnam, and so there would be no flight to Washington:

> As far as my problem in Vietnam we have asked everyone to share it with us. They were willing to share advice but not responsibility ... I won't tell you how to run Malaysia and you don't tell us how to run Vietnam ... If you want to help us some in Vietnam send us some men and send us some folks to deal with these guerrillas. And announce to the press that you are going to help us. Now if you don't feel like doing that, go on with your Malaysian problem ... [22]

Although Wilson sought to pretend otherwise to his backbench critics,[23] Johnson had been deeply unimpressed by his attempted intervention, and was in no hurry to meet with him thereafter.[24] However, backbench pressure on Wilson continued to mount, obliging him to be seen to be doing something. While the government's narrow majority can be interpreted as constraining potential rebels[25] – one act of defiance could set in train a series of events that brought down the government – it is clear that Wilson felt the pressure of backbench opposition and, increasingly as the conflict wore on, extra-parliamentary opposition. In January 1965, 11 public figures and 22 Labour MPs, including William Warbey, signed a letter of protest. Warbey became a particularly persistent critic of Wilson's, highlighting the danger of giving diplomatic support to a US policy which was contrary to the letter and spirit of the Geneva accords, and more than once threatening to resign.[26] Despite the clear backbench pressure, the parliamentary arithmetic compelled Wilson to resist calls for a debate on Vietnam. In March 1965 he confided to West German Chancellor Erhard the pressure he was under to make a statement in the House and that, if forced to do so, "he would try to say as little as possible".[27]

Instead, backbench unrest over the US bombing of North Vietnam was met by Wilson's insistence that it was legitimate because it was directed at disrupting Vietcong supply routes, whereas it would be counter-productive if designed to force Hanoi to the conference table.[28] Criticism that the Wilson government's close association of Britain with US policy in Vietnam was undermining its credibility as a mediator was also a constant. South Vietnamese Prime Minister Air Marshal Ky's mid-1965 statement of his admiration for Adolf Hitler, and stated belief that, "we need four or five Hitler's in Vietnam", did little to dampen the mood on the Labour backbenches.[29] The issue which was of most immediate concern to Labour backbenchers during 1965–66, however, was the intensification of US bombing over North Vietnam.

When it became clear that some form of parliamentary statement was unavoidable, Dean Rusk issued advice on its tone and content, along with a request that Foreign Secretary Michael Stewart be reminded, "personally from me that if he has a political problem at home, so do we, but ours extends to South East Asia". In particular, Rusk requested that any statement by Wilson relate to Britain's responsibilities as co-Chair of the Geneva Conferences, thereby minimising the risk of an appearance of division between, "the two Governments which are carrying the major free world burden in South East Asia". Moreover, Rusk advised:

> Any reference to "hostilities" should make a clear distinction between aggression from the North and United States efforts to assist in meeting that aggression. We would not object if the Prime Minister would wish to remind the House that the United States has made it clear that American forces in Viet Nam could come home if North Viet Nam would leave its neighbours alone.[30]

In the event, Wilson's performance was "greatly appreciated" by Rusk.[31] While Wilson refrained from criticising the US, or even offering advice given the resentment with which it was likely to be met, FO assessments of the US position remained bleak, despite the extension of the war to the North. Indeed, by mid-February 1965, the FO had concluded that "defeating the Viet Cong on the ground in South Viet-Nam is no longer a realistic objective", leaving the US with two options, "raising the stakes or cutting losses". Hence, the Wilson government found itself in a quandary – supporting a US policy that had, in the FO's assessment, no clear goals and little or no chance of military success, but constrained from sharing this assessment for fear of the US response.[32]

Downing Street shared FO analyses of the hopelessness of the US position by this time. A 1st March 1965 minute on Vietnam concluded that, "the Americans cannot win and cannot yet see any way of getting off the hook which will not damage their prestige internationally and the President's position domestically", to which Wilson added, "Yes. I very much agree".[33]

However, as the FO warned, Wilson's silence was, "giving the Russians and Chinese the opportunity of spreading it about that HMG is no more than a lackey of US Government policy and can take no stand on its own without the approval of its dollar masters".[34]

When Wilson met US Ambassador David Bruce later that month he gave a clear indication of the limits to UK support if military escalation was not accompanied by political initiative. The current trend in US Vietnam policy risked placing Wilson, "in an intolerable position" that could well lead to "stories about satellites and the 51st state", he complained to Bruce. He concluded by warning that, "if things went on as they were, they could well lead to the biggest difficulty between Britain and the United States for many years, possibly since Suez".[35]

British concerns were hardly diminished when, shortly thereafter, US Ambassador to South Vietnam, Maxwell Taylor, issued a statement to the effect that "no limit existed to the potential escalation" of the war. At the same time the Pentagon admitted to US use of chemical weapons in Vietnam, further heightening backbench pressure on Wilson.[36] In response, Wilson asked Foreign Secretary Michael Stewart, then in Washington, to "leave the Secretary of State and the President in no doubt at all about the difficulty into which we have been put". Wilson noted stories to the effect that, "instead of planned bombing missions which have themselves escalated far beyond measured tit-for-tat raids, American pilots will range freely selecting their own targets". As a consequence, it was "becoming harder and harder for us" to support the US when "the facts seem to support the jibe that HMG is the tail-end Charlie in an American bomber".[37]

Although widely remembered, and not without some justification, as one of the firmer supporters of the US war effort, Stewart nevertheless delivered this message, before going on to address the National Press Club in equally clear terms: "In the choice of measures everyone responsible should consider not only what is militarily appropriate for the job in hand but the effect on people around the world. What I am, in fact, asking the United States to display is what your Declaration of Independence called 'a decent respect for the opinions of mankind'".[38]

If the British government was becoming increasingly frustrated by the actions of its American ally and the lack of consultation, so Johnson was becoming increasingly frustrated with Wilson and his requests for consultation and attempts to mediate in the absence of a British military commitment. If Wilson felt under pressure over Vietnam then, quite evidently, so too did Johnson. When, in April, Patrick Dean took over as British Ambassador to Washington and presented his credentials to Johnson (alongside the recently appointed ambassadors from Chile and Denmark), Johnson used the opportunity to deliver a mini-lecture on what was expected of an ally. He told the new ambassadors that:

> there was a strong feeling in Congress and in the United States that America's friends should give them more support. He strongly criticised

the attitude of the Labour back bench in Parliament and said that although he was still at all times ready to listen to what his allies had to say, he would not be deterred by purely negative opinion. He was not a murderer, nor did he seek to wage war. The bombing by American aircraft had been carried out against strictly military targets – against steel and concrete as he put it – not even against factories, still less towns. No women or children had been killed and the sole purpose was to prevent the supply of arms to those who were attacking South Viet-Nam.

... In any case, the British were forced to kill quite a few Indonesian infiltrators every day and he made no complaint. He said that his friends and allies should certainly state their views, but they should not stab him in the back or slap him in the face (at this point the President slapped his own face quite vigorously).[39]

Just two days later, Wilson met Johnson in the White House, reiterating, in the context of Australian willingness to commit a battalion to Vietnam, the fact of the "Malaysian burden".[40] He subsequently recorded that thereafter:

Apart from an occasional moment in future years when President Johnson revived the notion of a British military presence in Vietnam, these April talks set out a division of function which he more than once stressed publicly. The American Government would not be deflected from its military task; but, equally, he would give full backing to any British initiative which had any chance of getting peace-talks on the move.[41]

The conflicting pressures he faced were reflected in the energy and time Wilson devoted to exploring the possibility of a diplomatic solution to the Vietnam War. Indeed, 1965 could be said to have been the year of the Wilson Vietnam peace initiative. It was also the year before the general election that saw Wilson achieve his first comfortable parliamentary majority, a time when he could not afford to risk backbench dissent hardening and spreading in response to US escalation. Hence, these peace initiatives have tended to be viewed as being essentially motivated by this consideration.[42] In addition to regular suggestions that the Geneva conference might be reconvened, 1965 saw three discrete though wholly unsuccessful initiatives. The first of these involved Patrick Gordon Walker. Ultimately unable to secure election to Parliament, Gordon Walker had been obliged to give way to Michael Stewart as Foreign Secretary, and in April 1965 Wilson sent him on a fact-finding tour of South-East Asia where he held talks in Saigon, Vientiane, Rangoon, Bangkok, Kuala Lumpur, Pnom Penh, Tokyo and Delhi. However, his mission was doomed as neither Peking nor Hanoi were prepared to let him in.[43]

The second was the Commonwealth mission arising out of the June 1965 Marlborough House Commonwealth conference. This would have comprised four heads of government – of Britain, Nigeria, Ghana and Trinidad – and involved visits to Washington, Saigon, Hanoi, Moscow and Peking. However, the initiative was still-born.[44] As with the Gordon Walker tour, Hanoi and Peking refused to receive it, as did Moscow. Nevertheless, this failure led seamlessly into the third Wilson peace initiative of the year – the July 1965 Harold Davies peace mission.[45] This collapsed when word of the supposedly secret mission was leaked, but, according to Barbara Castle, who saw these initiatives as a response to backbench and Cabinet pressure over Vietnam, Wilson was not overly disappointed as the gesture had been made.[46]

A more substantial effort came with the February 1967 Phase A/Phase B plan. This grew out of a visit to London by Soviet premier Alexei Kosygin and built on proposals outlined in Moscow by Foreign Secretary George Brown the previous November.[47] For Wilson, the Soviet Union's leverage over Hanoi (which, in retrospect, Wilson clearly over-estimated) and his own track record with the Soviet Union and personal relations with Kosygin and Foreign Minister Andrei Gromyko could combine to bring about peace. The initiative coincided with a new peak in dissent within the Party over the war, and came in the wake of the government's defeat at the 1966 Labour Party Conference on Vietnam. Central to it was the idea that in return for a US commitment to an indefinite halt to bombing, North Vietnam could be persuaded to stop infiltrating the South, which would in turn lead to a halt to the US military build-up, from which point the two parties could proceed to negotiations. Like its predecessors, it ultimately came to nothing.

These initiatives were based on a fundamental misconception about the weight of British influence in Washington – part of a general post-1945 self-deception about the moral force Britain carried with it in world affairs and belief that there was substance to Macmillan's Greeks/Romans analogy. In reality, the initiatives were not welcomed in Washington, where they were regarded with "slightly irritated tolerance".[48] Fatally for its prospects, the Phase A/Phase B proposal exposed divisions within the Johnson Administration and led to an eleventh hour intervention which shifted the terms of a possible bombing halt, sabotaged the initiative, and left Wilson and the British government looking somewhat subservient to Washington.[49] By this point, the Wilson government was acting as if it was a licensed peacebroker for the US, when it plainly had no such licence. George Brown subsequently conceded that the Phase A/Phase B plan, "petered out partly, perhaps, because we were too anxious to be intermediaries and didn't check enough with the Americans beforehand".[50] Moreover, Wilson's proximity to the US meant that he had little chance of being accepted by Hanoi as an "honest broker", but there was certainly more substance to the efforts than is suggested by George Brown's biographer, who dismissed them as "little more than vanity diplomacy on Wilson's part".[51] Crucially, though, Johnson never invested much faith in these efforts, neither did he see British efforts as occupying a distinctive place in the expanding catalogue of efforts to mediate, as he made clear in his memoirs:

During the many years we spent searching for a peace formula, I learned that everyone who engaged in such efforts came to think that his own particular approach was the one that would, or should, succeed. Whether they were Poles or Italians, Swedes or Indians, the Secretary General of the United Nations, or journalists, or merely self-appointed peacemakers, they were all convinced that their moves were the only ones that promised success, that their route was the one to take ...

Most of those working so hard to find a peace formula carried no major day-to-day responsibilities in Vietnam or Southeast Asia. This lack enabled them to take a detached, above-the-battle stance. I have no doubt, for example, that the British government's general approach to the war and to finding a peaceful solution would have been considerably different if a brigade of Her Majesty's forces had been stationed just south of the demilitarized zone in Vietnam.[52]

Wilson's December 1965 visit to Washington coincided with demands from 68 Labour MPs for an end to the US bombing of North Vietnam.[53] Parallels with the Korean War were always present for Wilson and were revived by reports that at NATO Defense Secretary McNamara had spoken of, "the near certainty of war with China". It was in this context that during his December meeting with Johnson, Wilson, "repeated that if US aircraft were to bomb Hanoi or Haiphong we should be forced publicly to dissociate from that action".[54] In fact, the Christmas period saw a US bombing pause, although the resumption of US bombing at the end of January 1966 intensified opposition to US policy within the Labour Party (94 MPs signed a telegram supporting Senator William Fulbright in his criticism of Johnson's actions), heightening the problems for Party managers in the run-up to the (still to be announced) general election.[55] Chief Whip Ted Short recalled how he, "tried everything I knew to persuade the organisers not to send this message, though had I been a backbencher, I would have signed it myself".[56] In a bad-tempered debate in the House of Commons, Wilson defended Johnson's resumption of bombing, provocatively telling the House that he, "should have liked to have seen the peace lobby outside the Chinese Embassy demanding that the Chinese Government should use their influence ... on Hanoi ... to make peace".[57]

In the run-up to the March 1966 general election Conservative front bencher Enoch Powell hinted that, if re-elected, the Wilson government had a secret plan to commit US troops to Vietnam, clearly demonstrating the extent to which British support for the American war effort was considered to be an electoral liability.[58] Nevertheless, the result was a three per cent swing to Labour, giving the party a net gain of forty-eight seats, thereby easing Wilson's acute party management dilemma over Vietnam, although at the same time allowing committed rebels the luxury of knowing that they could register their protest without necessarily bringing down the government. Addressing the PLP in mid-June, Wilson reassured Labour MPs that there was no question of Britain sending any troops to Vietnam, no direct or indirect deal or understanding with Washington that linked US economic support to British support for the war, and reiterated that he had made it clear that any bombing of major North Vietnamese population centres such as Hanoi or Haiphong would lead his government to dissociate themselves from it.[59]

That month Johnson sent word to Wilson that this is precisely what he planned to do. When the bombs fell on 28–29th June, Wilson duly issued a statement of dissociation. Wilson subsequently claimed that the FO tried to water down his statement, but he had to tread a fine line, and it is difficult to see how a statement that dissociated the government from the bombing could have been watered down further and still retained its meaning.

The subsequent debate in the House was the most bad-tempered yet, with opposition leader Edward Heath suggesting that the government should be more solidly behind the US, and a succession of Labour backbenchers demanding that it dissociate itself not just from the bombing, but from the entire US policy in Vietnam. Foreign Secretary Michael Stewart sought to deflect attention to Viet Cong conduct, although at no little cost to his reputation:

> The cruelties which follow inescapably from aerial bombardment have received widespread publicity. In a world where there are opportunities for communication of facts and of knowledge, it is inevitable and right that that should be so, and the cruelties which follow inevitably from aerial bombardment have a terrible and spectacular nature about them which particularly commands the attention ...
>
> But it is of great importance, if we are to take a proper view and form a proper judgment of this matter, that we should realise that the cruelties which have occurred in this war are not confined to those which follow inevitably from aerial bombardment, that there is a long story of the most merciless cruelty carried out by the Vietcong over a long period of years.[60]

Stewart again stressed that the basis for a settlement had to involve the removal of all foreign troops and bases from Vietnam, leaving the Vietnamese free to determine their own future, although this had to take the form of a two-state solution and could not involve an "outright Communist victory". Just as Attlee had in relation to the military commitment to the defence of South Korea, so Stewart argued that the nature of the South Vietnamese regime was not important, and that if, "the proposition that because a Government is not a democracy it is, therefore, a legitimate object of aggression" were to be accepted, then "it will be extremely difficult to preserve the peace of the world".[61]

At the same time, the Government was attacked by Edward Heath, who argued that these were legitimate targeted attacks on fuel tanks that enabled the transport of reinforcements down the Ho Chi Minh Trail rather than attacks on population centres. Through dissociation, Heath maintained, Wilson had "affronted our friends and allies".[62] From the Opposition front bench Duncan Sandys argued that the bombing represented, "a counter-attack upon a perfectly legitimate military target" and that Wilson's concern over civilian casualties was misplaced since, "it is now reported that Hanoi is to be completely evacuated", in which case, "the danger of casualties will be reduced to the absolute minimum".[63]

The tactic of limited dissociation, then, clearly carried with it some risk for Wilson, opening him to attack from both sides, from his own left wing on the grounds of the illogicality of only limited dissociation. As Stan Newens argued:

> It is stupid for us to say that we are prepared to support the bombing of villages and then say that we are not prepared to support the bombing of towns. It is ridiculous to say that we are prepared to support the bombing of oil installations outside other towns but that we are not prepared to support the bombing outside Hanoi.[64]

Hence, whenever future US bombing was conducted near or over these population centres, there would be pressure for further specific or total dissociation.

From London, Ambassador David Bruce tried to explain the background to Wilson's statement for the benefit of the President, beginning with a characterisation of Wilson as, "a political animal, highly skilled, intelligent, a master at infighting, deadly in debate, and usually adept at making ambiguous public statements to serve his political aims".[65] Up until this point, Wilson's general approach to Anglo-American relations had been to:

> co-operate with the United States on major American policies in a measure that would not always be popular here. Nevertheless, to counter the charge of being a mere puppet or satellite of the US, HMG would, from time to time, assert its independence by taking exception to certain details of policies to which he is ready to give general support.[66]

Bruce believed that, for Wilson, the bombing around Hanoi and Haiphong represented a qualitatively different problem to previous Vietnam-induced problems, so much so that it had constituted a potential challenge to his leadership:

> Wilson regards the Vietnam situation as posing in acute form the problem of defining acceptable limits of Anglo-American cooperation. The military buildup apparently increased his fears of escalation and certainly cut against the grain of his belief that there could be no clear-cut military victory in Vietnam. He believed that a basis for a political settlement must be found, and he was increasingly frustrated that it could not be found. Wilson's internal party problem was not only one of

dealing with the small band of leftist militants who long ago wanted him to break unconditionally with the US. He did not have much to fear from them, despite their noise and pressures. It was when the dissidence over Vietnam widened to include a substantial number of Labor MPs in the center and on the right-wing that the problem of party management threatened to get out of hand.[67]

Why did Wilson choose this point to "disassociate" – why not earlier? As Wilson himself recognised, dissociation was something you could only do once. Thereafter, the influence you hoped to retain by association was irreparably damaged and any and every subsequent limited dissociation would register a diminishing impact on the US.[68] Proving the logic of this, Wilson's dissociation proved the final straw for Johnson, what William Bundy termed "the break point" which "established Wilson, as far as I know unchangingly, as a man not to go to the well with."[69]

The dilemma that Vietnam represented for the Wilson government by this time was summed up well in a memo by J. Gwyn Morgan, the Labour Party Overseas Secretary, sent to Foreign Secretary George Brown in May 1967, and worth quoting at length:

> If there were very convincing grounds to suppose that the US could pull it off militarily by major escalation then there might be a case for us to swallow our moral and political scruples, look the other way and just wait for the ghastly business to be over and done with. However, on the analysis of this paper it seems unlikely. In all probability the war, and serious escalations such as we have considered, will be with us in a more dangerous but inconclusive state for some time. We should, therefore, formulate our policy on this assumption.
>
> In the event of the US mining or otherwise obstructing access to the harbour in Haiphong, or bombing the dykes or extending operations to parts of Laos the action is bound to become the subject of international controversy and we shall in all probability have to make a clear-cut public statement ... if we are unable to prevent the US from further fruitless escalation even when the whole weight of our logical arguments and experience of these situations is to prevent escalation, then our influence is demonstrably illusory and we have little or nothing to lose from dissociating ourselves from American policy in the terms of the June 29th statement. As far as future diplomatic leverage goes, what we might lose with the US will be off-set to some extent by the far greater scope we shall have with the Soviet Union. Our position as Co-chairman of the Geneva Conference will ensure our participation in any negotiations that get under way ...
>
> The balance of considerations would therefore seem to point decisively in favour of a preparedness to dissociate ourselves from steps of escalation by the US. Of course we shall face a real problem in deciding at

what point to draw the line. For as they move towards escalation the US will try to do it imperceptibly without prior public announcement. However, certain actions would be of quite a new dimension – such as mining Haiphong, extending ground operations into Laos or bombing the dykes – even those that supposedly serve industrial purposes. These actions we should not support.

·. . . The history of comparable situations in our dealing with the US has shown that we stand to do best – to retain our own self-respect and exert to the maximum our limited influence on events – if we stick to our position. But it will not carry the full weight it must if President Johnson feels that we shall restrict all our disagreement to private representations. For if we encourage any such impression then we renounce in advance our most effective sanction, the prospect of a public withdrawal of our support, and thus make more likely the eventuality of escalation which, with the whole problem it poses for us of dissociation, it must be the very purpose of our policy, by working along the line we have suggested, to avoid.[70]

Backbench disquiet at the US escalation of the war continued throughout 1967, as evidenced both in meetings of the PLP and on the floor of the House of Commons.[71] In particular, there was growing backbench exasperation at the reluctance of the government to further dissociate themselves from US bombing of population centres. For example, in February 1967 Tom Driberg asked Foreign Secretary George Brown whether he viewed the, "sort of bombing which North Vietnam is being subjected to as infinitely more harmful and anti-human and destructive than what is being done in the South?", to which Brown replied:

> No, frankly I do not. I deplore both. There are horrors being inflicted in the South. Lives are being taken in the South and people are being maltreated in the South in far greater numbers compared with what is happening in the North.[72]

UN Secretary General U Thant's peace proposals were fully supported by the Left, which saw the first of these, the unconditional cessation of bombing operations over North Vietnam, as preceding the other two, a view not shared by Wilson.[73]

By 1968, Vietnam had been supplanted by Nigeria as the major international issue confronting the Wilson government,[74] although the exposure of the My Lai massacre[75] and the invasion of Cambodia would both briefly bring Vietnam back to the fore. The Wilson government distanced itself from the 1970 invasion of Cambodia in a manner similar to the 1966 dissociation. It was an event that divided the Cabinet, with Barbara Castle, Tony Benn and Richard Crossman urging a clear distancing while Michael Stewart and James Callaghan represented a more pro-US line. Once again, Wilson's House of Commons statement did withhold British support, while balancing this with the observation that the "incursion" would never have occurred had the North Vietnamese not had a presence in Cambodia.

It has been suggested by Clive Ponting that there was an explicit deal between the Wilson government and the US, "the full extent of which remained a closely guarded secret" and which the Cabinet were unaware of, to support the US in Vietnam and retain an East of Suez role in return for continued US economic aid.[76] However, a more recent body of research based on British government files and the LBJ Archives suggests that this is too simplistic an interpretation. It is true that domestic policy and foreign policy were closely inter-linked, and that the Johnson Administration took an active interest in Wilson's economic policy. It is also true that there was pressure from within the Johnson Administration to make the linkage quite explicit.[77] At the same time, it is also true that Wilson and his ministers enjoyed some leverage arising from the importance that the Johnson Administration placed on Wilson's continuation of an activist pro-American foreign policy (for example, in Malaysia, in the Middle East, and even with regard to Rhodesia), and the importance the US attached to sterling in the context of shoring up the international monetary system.[78]

Like Tony Blair's approach to the question of war in Iraq in 2002–03, Wilson's behaviour in relation to Vietnam raises questions about structure and agency in international affairs. How significant was Wilson's role in determining that no British military forces fought in Vietnam? Would the outcome have been any different if a different leader had been in post, or if a different party had been in power? If Gaitskell had not died (and had won the 1964 election), or Heath had become Prime Minister shortly thereafter, was the outcome likely to have been very different? Gaitskell's biographer talks of "the values that Britain represented to him" which were "universal values from which the whole world could benefit",[79] and of how Gaitskell "would never have made the tactical, personal and ideological mistakes that Harold Wilson made, because he had an overriding quality that Wilson lacked: integrity".[80] Yet nowhere does he confront his own characterisation of the possibility that: "His Atlanticism would have pushed Britain into a disastrous involvement in Vietnam".[81] For his part, in August 1965 George Brown confided in Richard Neustadt, then undertaking a fact-finding tour of the UK, that Gaitskell, "would have put a token force in Viet Nam last fall", an observation intended as a criticism of Wilson for delaying beyond the point where the conflict was too politically controversial for a UK commitment to be possible.[82] (During the same month, however, Brown warned Wilson, "that in no circumstances should we lead the Americans to believe that there is any prospect of a British military contingent in Vietnam."[83]) In assessing Gaitskell's legacy some 30 years after his death, Roy Jenkins argued that he would have made a better prime minister than Wilson because, "what he lacked in tactics he would have gained in sense of strategy and purpose and direction. If you live by tactics you tend to die by tactics and that was Wilson's weakness".[84] This either ignores the fact that Wilson's focus on tactics was a consequence of the tightrope he chose to walk over Vietnam in the context of the parliamentary arithmetic of the time, or supposes that Gaitskell's "sense of strategy, purpose and direction" would have negated the necessity for such a focus by an early commitment of British forces to Vietnam. For his part, Tam Dalyell, a Labour backbencher throughout these years, believes that: "if Hugh Gaitskell had lived we would have committed troops to Vietnam", and that the result would have been the same had either George Brown or Jim Callaghan prevailed in the leadership election that followed Gaitskell's death.[85] As for the Conservative Party, Vietnam does provide a clear indication that Party could matter. During the Wilson government, Heath opened up a political space to the right of Wilson by arguing consistently for fuller support of the US. This does not mean that Heath would definitely have committed British troops if the Conservative Party had won the 1966 election – in Opposition, the exploitation of an issue to create a distinctive political space is one of the few luxuries a Party can enjoy, and arguably Wilson did the same over South Africa in the months leading up to the 1964 election – but it does suggest that the likelihood would have been greater.

Whatever the primary motivation behind the Wilson government's serial efforts to mediate in the conflict (simply a response to the imperatives of party management and desire to shore up the alibi that kept British troops out of the war, or a more fundamental desire to see the war ended by diplomatic means as soon as possible), it is clear that the simple idea that Wilson supported the US war in Vietnam needs to be heavily qualified to acknowledge the degree of resistance that he demonstrated. In 1981 he himself termed his support for the US war effort, "negative support".[86] At a White House dinner in February 1968, in the immediate aftermath of the Tet Offensive, Wilson went so far as to publicly tell Johnson that,

> the problem of Vietnam, as you have always recognised, can never be settled on a durable and just basis by an imposed military solution. The events of these past days have underlined yet again that there can be no purely military solution to this problem, that there can be no solution before men meet round the conference table, determined to get peace.[87]

Such public admonishments help explain Dean Rusk's undimmed exasperation at his 1968 retirement party, recorded by journalist Louis Heren: "All we needed was one regiment. The Black Watch would have done. Just one regiment, but you wouldn't. Well, don't expect us to save you again. They can invade Sussex, and we won't do a damned thing about it".[88]

Another consideration that seems to have been of central importance to Wilson is often neglected. It is arguable that Wilson harboured fears, rooted in his own experience of the Korean War, observed from inside the Attlee government, that the US, if not restrained by a trusted ally, could be driven to use nuclear weapons in Vietnam. In his memoirs Ted Short has referred to, "behind-the-scenes efforts by Britain ... to prevent the use of nuclear weapons – which were successful".[89] At the February 1968 White House dinner mentioned above, Wilson worried about, "the danger, reinforced by the anxious words of the troubled President, that the US would lurch into policies from which there might be no easy return",[90] a clear allusion to the risk of nuclear escalation. This fear was also cited by Wilson in the House of Commons on a number of occasions.[91] Informing this was not just the spectre of Attlee's visit to Washington in 1950, but also the experience of the Cuban Missile Crisis just over five years earlier.

Is the notion that the US might have used nuclear weapons in Vietnam far-fetched? The month after Wilson's White House dinner speech, a US poll showed that twenty-seven per cent of respondents thought that the US, "should go all out to win a military victory in Vietnam, using atom bombs and weapons".[92] Moreover, it was a consideration that repeatedly arose in debates inside the Johnson Administration. In March 1964 the Joint Chiefs of Staff had discussed the use of nuclear weapons in the context of a Chinese entry into the conflict. In November 1964, a working group on Vietnam policy had advised that:

> We cannot guarantee to maintain a non-Communist South Vietnam short of committing ourselves to whatever degree of military action would be required to defeat North Vietnam and probably Communist China militarily. Such a commitment would involve high risks of a major conflict in Asia, which could not be confined to air and naval action but would almost inevitably involve a Korean-scale ground action and possibly even the use of nuclear weapons at some point.[93]

Perhaps this was the scenario Dean Rusk had in mind when, in May 1965, he told Wilson that,

> there was no discussion in Washington about the use of nuclear weapons [in Vietnam]. He would not rule out such a possibility if there were, for example, a new Korean war; but there was absolutely no discussion of it in connection with the Vietnam problem.[94]

Clearly, this was untrue. After the Christmas 1965 bombing pause ended, both General Westmoreland and the Joint Chiefs of Staff indicated that their military programme "would require mobilizing the reserves and utilizing the nation's full military capability, including the possible use of nuclear weapons".[95] In May 1967, the Joint Chiefs sent McNamara a memo arguing that, "invasions of North Vietnam, Laos, and Cambodia might become necessary, involving the deployment of US forces to Thailand and, quite possibly, the use of nuclear weapons in southern China". McNamara recalled how their, "continued willingness to risk a nuclear confrontation appalled me".[96]

Given all of this, should Wilson's approach to the Vietnam War be regarded as a success or a failure? There are clear grounds for considering it a failure, in that it failed in its stated goals. Its peace initiatives failed despite the importance Wilson appears to have personally attached to them. The influence he sought to bring to bear on the Johnson Administration was simply non-existent. Johnson tolerated Wilson, albeit with greater difficulty as time went on, but certainly did not seek him out for advice on the conduct of the war, and even became reluctant to host his visits to Washington. However, it is not at all clear that a commitment of British ground forces would have given Wilson any particular influence over US conduct of the war, something he himself would have appreciated from his own observations inside the Attlee government during the Korean War. Instead, it would have further constrained him, obliging him to support each and almost every US escalation. To take one obvious example, it would have been impossible to have dissociated over the bombings around Hanoi and Haiphong with British troops serving in Vietnam.

And yet Wilson maintained US support for Britain's global commitments, despite some pressure from within the Johnson Administration to create an explicit linkage with Vietnam, and similarly maintained US support for the pound. Most significantly, this was done while sustaining a Labour government with a reforming domestic agenda requiring the parliamentary support of Labour MPs, a number of whom felt a particular affinity with the struggle of the Vietnamese. Indeed, in the mid-1950s a group of Labour MPs including Ian Mikardo, Harold Davies, and William Warbey, had visited Hanoi and met Ho Chi Minh.[97] As a result there was a hard core of backbench rebels who could never accept the kind of premise George Brown repeatedly outlined to Parliament regarding the undesirability of a North Vietnamese victory. As Eric Heffer put it: "Without qualification, I was on the side of the North Vietnamese; they had a right to their independence and as a socialist I had to support them".[98]

Nevertheless, even some of his left-wing critics came to accept that Wilson had played a limited hand with some skill. As Heffer reflected; "Harold played a very clever game. On the one hand, the government gave verbal support to President Johnson; on the other, it took great care not to get more involved".[99] On the other hand, Peter Shore has identified Wilson's approach to Vietnam as a root cause of the Labour Party's subsequent problems, arguing that:

> Wilson's careful evasions and strictly limited assent to the American war were as nothing to the growing tide of anti-American feeling that swept not only the Labour Party but also wide swathes of British opinion outside it. British policy looked grubby and self-seeking and to a whole generation of the young ... it was morally unacceptable. The seeds of cynicism and alienation from the Labour leadership were widely sown at this time. They were to be one of the many reasons why the Labour rank and file turned to bitter left-wing policies ten years later.[100]

Perhaps, then, Wilson's greatest achievement with regard to Vietnam was a negative one – not committing British troops and withstanding considerable pressure to do so. By its very nature it is difficult to assess the scale of this achievement, because it needs to be measured in terms of things that did not happen – the bodies of dead servicemen that did not return, exacerbated balance of payments crises, Korean War-era domestic cutbacks, the impossibility of accelerated withdrawal from East of Suez and, if troops had been committed during the first term, the clear possibility of electoral defeat in view of the steadily rising tide of opposition to the war, and even greater opposition to the commitment of British troops to it.[101]

5   Labour's Falklands War

Historically, the Labour Party had been indifferent towards Latin America, the Cuban Revolution aside. Even here, under Gaitskell, the party leadership as at least as concerned about the impact on the US and the Cold War context as with the Cuban Revolution itself. In 1962 Gaitskell would argue that the US had just as much right to stop the Soviet Union establishing a base in Cuba as Britain would if it attempted to establish one in Ireland.[1] Latin America was not an area where Britain had to manage a messy post-imperial retreat, as it did in South-East Asia. Geographically remote, it was not an area whose politics attracted much interest in Labour Party circles. All of this changed, however, with the 1970 election of the socialist Salvador Allende as President of Chile at the head of the left-wing Unidad Popular coalition.

Three years later he was dead, a victim of the US-inspired military coup of 11 September 1973.[2] His death came as the presidential palace in which he was sheltering was attacked by British-supplied Hunter fighter aircraft. It marked a key moment from where human rights, debates over the internal conduct of repressive regimes, and the appropriate response by Britain and the wider international community to such repression, emerged as central concerns of Labour Party foreign policy. Although South Africa had raised similar questions during the 1960s, the experience of Chile arguably represents the emergence of the contemporary focus on human rights in foreign policy that would gather momentum in the post-Cold War environment and be used to justify war over Kosovo and, at the end of the day, Iraq.

For many on the Labour Left, the Chilean coup had a profound effect. In his memoirs Harold Wilson recalled how passions were raised over Chile, "where the socialist President Allende was murdered by the Fascist right wing".[3] In Spring 1972 Eric Heffer had led a Labour Party delegation to Chile, taking a personal message from Wilson to Allende. Heffer recalled being told by Allende that,

> socialism in Chile would be pluralist and democratic and not bureaucratic as it was in the Soviet Union 'If they let me'. That was a chilling

phrase because even then he understood that there were forces against him prepared to overthrow him.[4]

On hearing of the coup and Allende's death, Heffer, "wept unashamedly at the news, for an attempt to achieve socialism through the Parliamentary process had been murdered too. The Americans were not prepared to let socialism become a reality".[5]

This sense of the death of a shared experiment is key to understanding the depth of feeling created within the Labour Party by the coup in Chile. During the 1960s, the Wilson governments had witnessed military coups in Argentina (1966) and Peru (1968) which had not disrupted relations, and also conducted harmonious bilateral relations based around shared trade interests with the Brazilian military regime – all of which Conservative MPs gleefully pointed out in the post-coup parliamentary debates on Chile. However, for the Labour Left, the Chilean coup was different. For them, it did not arise merely out of political disorder or economic stagnation. It represented a class war in which the military and their backers were intent on the physical elimination of their left-wing opponents to a degree hitherto unseen in Latin American coups, and in which the US hand added a further dimension. Chile may have been physically far removed from Britain, but it was culturally comprehensible and, for some on the Left like Heffer, was attempting to navigate an analogous road to socialism.[6]

Within 11 days of the coup the Heath government had recognized the new military regime – two days faster than the US which had helped bring it about – and made clear its intention to continue the delivery of military equipment to Chile, despite the fact that British arms had figured so prominently in the coup. Labour's annual conference "utterly" condemned the coup and Britain's recognition of the new government, calling for the recall of the Ambassador. Consequently, the November 1973 House of Commons debate on Chile was a highly charged affair, with concerns about human rights and issues surrounding internal interference in the affairs of states to the fore. For the government, FO Minister Julian Amery argued that:

> It is not possible ... to intervene everywhere all over the world. We do our best to protect human rights in the Council of Europe and through the United Nations, but it would be unrealistic to intervene in the internal affairs of other countries ... I would go further and say that I think it would be invidious to intervene in Chile and not in other countries where there are more political prisoners and where there have been even more political executions.[7]

He concluded that the government's, "duty is to ensure the protection of British subjects and the promotion of British interests ... This is a quarrel of limited concern to the people of this country".[8] For the few months before the February 1974 general election, this effectively summarized the government's position. Labour's return to government in that election created a dilemma over how to treat arms ordered by the Chileans and approved by the Heath government, but still not delivered. The Cabinet divided between those on the Right with economic and defence-related portfolios (for example, Denis Healey and Roy Mason) and those on the Left (for example, Judith Hart, Tony Benn and Eric Heffer) with more latitude to invoke the language of human rights, internationalism, opposition to dictatorial regimes, and accountability to the conference and the NEC. The result was a period of pronounced agonising before the principle of the inviolability of existing contracts prevailed and existing orders were honoured, although no new contracts were entered into.[9]

Hence, opposition to dictatorial regimes, especially in a Latin American context, and a commitment to human rights developed as central features of Labour's approach to foreign policy during this time. As Foreign Secretary Anthony Crosland would define his foreign policy priorities as, "maintaining national security, lessening tension between east and west in Europe, reducing the risk of war elsewhere in the world, assisting with human rights and protecting British citizens abroad".[10] Alongside Chile, events in Uganda, Cambodia and Ethiopia contributed to this development. On the right wing of the party in particular, human rights also meant a focus on the internal situation in the Soviet Union and Eastern Europe, as reflected in the space devoted to them in David Owen's 1978 book *Human Rights*, written while he was Foreign Secretary.[11] As Owen explained:

> ... what is relatively new is the growing recognition, not just in the Western democracies but worldwide, that the abuse of human rights is the legitimate subject of international concern; and that the enforcement of human rights can no longer be left to national Governments alone. The basic premise of fundamental and internationally agreed documents such as the United Nations Charter, the Universal Declaration of Human Rights, the International Covenants of the United Nations, the European Convention of Human Rights essentially is that human rights stand on values which are the property of all men and which transcend national frontiers.[12]

In part, détente had created the political space within which, by the mid-1970s, a values-based foreign policy vision could be articulated, and even possibly flourish. Jim Callaghan recalled that during his time as Foreign Secretary (March 1974 to April 1976), his guiding principles were based on a recognition that a Labour Foreign Secretary, "cannot tilt at every windmill but he must seek to apply principles to foreign policy – peace, justice, human rights and human dignity, opposition to racial discrimination and support for the principles of the United Nations Charter". At the same time, in advancing these causes, Callaghan felt, "he must recognize Britain's diminished international power, and exert his influence in those areas and organizations where such principles can best be furthered, while being ready to take such other initiatives as he can construct".[13]

This is the context, then, within which the Labour Party's approach to the question of relations with military regimes in Latin America existed, a question further complicated in the case of Argentina by the existence of the Falklands problem. Here, an almost reflexive attachment to the principle of decolonisation collided with considerations of human rights (could the Islands be leased back to a 'fascist' military regime?) and the awkward principle of self-determination – awkward in this case because the Islanders did not want to be ruled from Buenos Aires. Even so, Labour government policy from the 1960s was to foster an ever closer Falklands-Argentine association, thereby making an eventual leaseback arrangement a mere formalisation of an existing reality. Indeed, shortly before his death in February 1977, Crosland had informed the House of Commons that negotiations with Argentina over the Islands had been reopened.

Complicating diplomacy aimed at relieving Britain of responsibility for the Falklands was the periodic threat of an Argentine invasion, a threat which, as was the case in 1982, tended to arise at times of acute Argentine domestic difficulty. Neither this fact nor the "fascist" nature of the regime had prevented Labour governments from selling arms to Argentina. At the same time, however, Britain had never deployed a credible armed force on the Islands, so it was essential that developments in Argentine politics were closely monitored. Preventive diplomacy, conveying to Argentina that an invasion would meet with a military response, was the order of the day. In April 1975, such preventive diplomacy by Foreign Secretary Jim Callaghan headed off a possible invasion.[14] In November 1977 indications of a possible invasion led to the dispatch of two frigates, HMS *Alacrity* and HMS *Phoebe*, together with the nuclear submarine HMS *Dreadnought*, and the drawing-up of rules of engagement within a 25-mile exclusion zone, all in complete secrecy. Callaghan, by then Prime Minister, intimated to MI6 head Maurice Oldfield that MI6 could leak this information to the Argentinian regime in order to help deter an invasion. Whether or not this happened is unclear, but the invasion never materialised.[15]

In April 1982, the first reaction from the Labour Party to the news that Argentina was about to invade the Falkland Islands was Shadow Leader of the House John Silkin's pledge of the party's, "full support for the right of the people of the Falkland Islands to stay British, as they wish", and belief that, "it is our duty to defend that right".[16] Giles Radice was one of a number of Labour MPs attending an Anglo-German Königswinter conference when news of the invasion came through. "The Germans, who are so pacifist these days, are amazed that we should be excited about these islands which are many thousands of miles away and, in any case, are a relic of our colonial past", Radice noted in his diary. "Do the British really intend to fight a war so far away? The Germans ask incredulously."[17]

The following day, 3rd April, the House of Commons was recalled on a Saturday for the first time since the Suez crisis. It quickly became apparent that the Thatcher government had been rendered vulnerable by its failure to anticipate and prevent the invasion, a consequence of the depth of back-bench Conservative feeling more than attacks from the Labour opposition. Attempting to buy political space by comparing the invasion of the South Georgia dependency with the 1976 occupation of Southern Thule ("a piece of rock in the most southerly part of the dependencies, which is completely uninhabited and which smells of large accumulations of penguin and other bird droppings", according to Ted Rowlands, the responsible Foreign Office minister of that time[18]), Mrs Thatcher immediately announced the dispatch of a large naval task force to recapture the islands, in the process creating a window of opportunity for a diplomatic settlement of the dispute, one which would close with the arrival of the task force in the South Atlantic.

Mrs Thatcher concluded her speech on a note of stirring patriotism that Labour leader Michael Foot immediately took up, telling the House that:

> The people of the Falkland Islands have the absolute right to look to us at this moment of their desperate plight, just as they have looked to us over the past 150 years. They are faced with an act of naked, unqualified aggression, carried out in the most shameful and disreputable circum-stances. Any guarantee from this invading force is utterly worthless – as worthless as any of the guarantees that are given by this same Argentine junta to its own people.[19]

MPs to both the left and right of the Labour Party were struck by the jingoism on both sides of the House.[20] The wave of patriotism stirred up in Parliament and the media placed the Labour Party in an awkward position, and left it divided over the appropriate response.[21] Foot was quick to reassure any concerned colleagues on the Labour benches that there, "is no question in the Falkland Islands of any colonial dependence or anything of that sort",[22] which might get in the way of their supporting the government. Equating the invasion with the spectre of 1930s' fascism may have been another component part of his effort to show his party the bases on which they could legitimately support the government over the crisis, but it was ill-judged and contributed to making the atmosphere a difficult one in which to sustain rational debate. For Foot the nature of the Argentinian regime was a key factor, but so too was his own political memory of earlier aggressions. As his biographer notes: "What he saw was a clear case of unprovoked aggression, and he was vividly reminded of aggressions by Hitler and Mussolini in the 1930s which were among the most emotionally powerful memories of his youth".[23] As Tam Dalyell recalled, Foot, "thought that Leopoldo Galtieri was the reincarnation of Benito Mussolini".[24] The casual equation of Latin American military regimes with fascism had been common on the Left since the events of 1973, and following Foot's lead a number of Labour MPs readily embraced this language. Only George Foulkes stood against the tide on 3rd April, opposing military action to reclaim the Islands.[25]

At the first meeting of the PLP following the invasion, Foot explained that, in his view, he had, "sought to set out the traditional views of the Labour Party on aggression and the charter of the United Nations and how we operate it".[26] While the meeting revealed divisions in the party over how to respond, it also revealed the extent to which the invasion was seen as representing something of an opportunity for the party, with the government's negligence leading up to the invasion thought likely to compound its domestic unpopularity. Hence, calls for the party to adopt a position distinct from the government's to give it room for manoeuvre and to take advantage of the situation were in part based on this calculation. Indeed, by the end of April George Robertson would be reminding Labour MPs that,

> the Party was now facing critical local government elections. He realised, of course, that world peace was paramount but the elections were also very important, and how we conducted ourselves as a Party over the Falklands issue would determine our success or failure in the local elections.[27]

Nevertheless, a fundamental tension at the root of the party's position was clear. It supported the despatch of the task force but, at the same time, did not want to be identified with the Thatcher government's policy. However, as Tony Benn pointed out, it would be impossible in practice to have supported sending it but to then withdraw support if a conflict situation arose. To a large extent, its initial support locked the party into supporting government policy as it unfolded, including the use of force, a prospect which, under the headline "Thatcher's Mad Gamble", *Tribune* termed, "complete and utter madness".[28]

These considerations dictated that the party's approach to the conflict would be dual-track, on the one hand supporting the government on the condition that it take the British case to and work through the UN to achieve a diplomatic solution; on the other critical of the policies that had contributed to the invasion and demanding an inquiry into its origins.[29] Jim Callaghan had warned the government in February 1982 about the risks of removing the British naval presence in the region, HMS *Endurance*, as part of the Nott defence review, a course that had also been urged on him as Prime Minister, but which he had rejected. Indeed, Callaghan was particularly effective in highlighting governmental negligence in the lead-up to the invasion.[30] So too was Shadow Foreign Secretary Denis Healey, who railed at this, "history of indifference to an evident threat to a people for whom we are directly responsible", with a passion that suggested that, as many initially thought, the Falklands were located somewhere off the coast of Scotland rather than eight thousand miles away, at the other end of the world. Healey called the Thatcher government's "open invitation to invasion", "one of the most disgraceful episodes in British history",[31] and warned that the government could not expect a blank cheque from the Opposition, as no "responsible Opposition in this situation could surrender their freedom of thought and action to a Prime Minister who had demonstrated such a monumental lack of judgment".[32]

Foot declined the offer of briefings on privy counsellor terms for fear this would constrain his scope for criticising the government. Nevertheless, as noted above, the Labour Party supported the dispatch of the task force, on the basis that history taught that it was impossible to negotiate with a dictator, except from a position of strength, and in support of the Islanders' right to self-determination. However, complicating the Labour position, Healey argued that the purpose of the task force was to, "give us the strength with which to negotiate", and that the government's aim had to be a diplomatic solution acceptable to the Islanders, which would avoid the "intolerable casualties" that an opposed landing on the Falklands would inflict on the very Islanders it was designed to liberate.[33] This had the advantage of carving out for Labour a position distinct from that of the government, and in many ways represented a step back from the support offered by Michael Foot four days earlier. In part, the position Healey arrived at was no doubt intended as one that the different currents in the party could unite around. However, it contained a fundamental weakness. Comparing the positions the party adopted in 1982 and 1990–91, Gerald Kaufman reflected that in the latter case:

> I gave the Labour Party a clear lead – support the UN, which is pretty easy for the Labour Party – unlike Healey in the Falklands war when he made a total mess of it. One of the problems with Denis is that he is very very very clever, but he is not as clever as he thinks he is. In a thing like the Falklands it was yes or no. The Falklands had been annexed by a fascist government in Argentina. I would have thought that was pretty straightforward, but to Denis it wasn't, because Denis always wanted to be clever, and what he didn't realise is that sometimes the cleverest thing to do is to be simple.[34]

Whether Healey's position could succeed in carrying the whole PLP was a different question. It was quickly answered by Tony Benn, who likened the dispatch of the task force to the sailing of "some armada in medieval times", and rejected the notion that MPs had an obligation to support British forces once committed to conflict, arguing that, "they did not choose to sail to the Falklands; the Prime Minister has sent them".[35] Benn also highlighted what he saw as the lack of clarity in the government's objectives, and raised the spectre of an attack on the Argentine mainland. In effect agreeing with Denis Healey that an opposed landing on the Islands would be costly, he argued that the risks involved far outweighed the potential gains. In safeguarding the Islanders, he argued, the government should be willing to discuss the sovereignty of the Islands, and meanwhile a UN peacekeeping force should be established on the Islands. "My advice", he concluded, "for what it is worth, is that the task force should be withdrawn".[36]

A vein of more qualified concern on Labour benches was well represented by John Gilbert, who supported the dispatch of the task force and use of force if that proved necessary, but who nevertheless recognised that there was, "something profoundly unattractive in the sight and sound of middle-aged men baying for brave young men to put their lives in peril – a peril that none of us is ever likely to face again".[37] Moreover, he thought the arguments presented by Benn would embolden the Argentinian regime rather than persuade them of the wisdom of a negotiated settlement. Still, Gilbert's position was not that far removed from Benn's in pointing out that:

> The biggest danger for the Prime Minister will be if the Argentines stall, make pacific noises and string the dispute out, thereby giving her no excuse immediately to use force. But there must be no use of force just to save the face of the Government or the Prime Minister. We must offer – not accept an offer – to take a United Nations force in. We must offer a condominium.[38]

The role that the UN could and should potentially play in resolving the dispute represented a clear party political difference. On 3rd April, the UNSC had passed Resolution 502, which demanded an immediate cessation of hostilities, the immediate withdrawal of all Argentine forces from the Islands, and called on Britain and Argentina to seek a diplomatic solution to the crisis. While the Thatcher government would maintain throughout that an Argentine withdrawal must precede any negotiations, there were a number of Labour MPs who felt that Resolution 502 opened the way for a diplomatic solution. As Sheffield MP Frank Hooley argued, "there is nothing in that resolution which talks about sending a battle fleet to the South Atlantic. There is nothing in that resolution to justify or encourage this country to go to war".[39] For her part Judith Hart called for a "pause for peace, so that there may be more breathing space for negotiations", in effect joining Benn in a call for the task force to be halted.[40] Betty Boothroyd also called for negotiations through the UN. Mrs Thatcher's reply to such concerns was that:

> Of course, we too want a peaceful solution, but it was not Britain that broke the peace. If the argument of no force at any price were to be adopted at this stage it would serve only to perpetuate the occupation of those very territories which have themselves been seized by force.[41]

The Thatcher government was clear in its insistence that Britain drew its right to dispatch a task force, not from specific Security Council resolutions, but from Article 51 of the UN Charter. However, Healey argued that the Argentine regime was unlikely to withdraw from the Islands prior to negotiations, "unless we can arrange for them to be replaced by some authority whose presence does not pre-empt the solution of the second stage of the diplomatic negotiation", and saw clear advantages to the UN playing this role.[42] One was that they could determine the views of the Islanders, fulfilling the Labour commitment to treating these as paramount in any settlement.

As the task force continued its southward journey, Healey would remind the government that Opposition support was conditional upon the government meeting the requirements of Resolution 502 and making meaningful efforts to find a diplomatic solution. Notwithstanding the peace efforts of US Secretary of State Alexander Haig, the chances of this being achieved narrowed when the task force arrived in the South Atlantic and British troops recaptured South Georgia on 25th April. Both Labour front and backbenches were acutely aware of this, and sceptical about the strength of Mrs Thatcher's interest in a diplomatic solution, with Tony Benn, for example, asking whether the government was aware that:

> although the House and the country are united in condemning the aggression, public opinion, so far as it can be ascertained, favours a much more serious attempt at negotiation through the United Nations than has occurred, and that a majority of people would not follow the Government into a war with the Argentine, which would threaten the loss of many lives, including Service men and Falkland Islanders, which might spread the conflict and which would isolate this country? If the Prime Minister continues to underrate the importance of negotiation and proceeds with the war, the responsibility for the loss of life will rest upon her shoulders.[43]

Indeed, from the capture of South Georgia onwards, scepticism about Mrs Thatcher's commitment to a diplomatic solution was openly voiced on the Labour front as well as backbenches. In particular, a request from the UN Secretary-General not to escalate the conflict, and for both parties to comply immediately with Resolution 502 left Mrs Thatcher unmoved, a fact that considerably agitated Michael Foot who warned that she risked inflicting a "grievous blow to our country's cause".[44] Foot wrote to the Prime Minister, telling her that, "at such a moment of international crisis, I attach the greatest importance to any statement issued by the Secretary General of the United Nations, and I am shocked that the Government does not appear to share that view".[45] Thereafter, Mrs Thatcher would deflect calls for a greater emphasis to be given to diplomacy, including the Haig peace effort, by arguing that, "it would be totally inconsistent to support the dispatch of the task force and yet to be opposed to its use"[46] – the potential dilemma that Healey's positioning of the party had created – and that Argentine withdrawal was a pre-condition for negotiations. At the same time, she voiced traditional Conservative scepticism about the capacity of the UN, which contrasted sharply with the Labour insistence on its centrality to a resolution of the conflict:

The question that we must answer is, what could further recourse to the United Nations achieve at the present stage? We certainly need mediation, but we already have the most powerful and the most suitable mediator available, Mr Haig, backed by all the authority and all the influence of the United States ... Of course, we support the United Nations and we believe that respect for the United Nations should form the basis of international conduct. But, alas, the United Nations does not have the power to enforce compliance with its resolutions, as a number of aggressors well know.[47]

This view contrasted sharply with Michael Foot's insistence that Article 51 placed obligations on the government at the same time as conferring legitimacy on its dispatch of the task force. In his view, a key obligation was to furnish the Security Council with regular reports on the actions taken, and to take account of its views. "Article 51", Foot advised, "does not give this or any other country operating under it an unlimited right to act as it wishes".[48] However, after the capture of South Georgia, Foot and Healey's continued advocacy of some form of UN trusteeship for the Islands was generally met with incredulity by Conservative MPs.

With the prospect of war imminent, brought closer by the imposition of a total exclusion zone around the Islands, Foot argued that the "paramount interest of our country and of most other countries is that we should have a peaceful settlement of this dispute".[49] Jim Callaghan, unwilling to contemplate ceding sovereignty of the Islands to Argentina, nevertheless advocated a "long naval blockade, if necessary for months" as an alternative to a military landing, which would "result in a heavy loss of life",[50] on the basis that a blockade would instead allow time for diplomacy via the UN, thereby satisfying last resort criteria. Stan Newens was another Labour MP who supported the principle of self-determination for the Islanders and the dispatch of the task force, but was reluctant to see force used except as a last resort, so that "if, in the last analysis, more force has to be used, it should be seen by everybody that we have explored every possible means of avoiding that solution".[51] The practical problem in the context of the Falklands dispute was that the principle of last resort clashed with the practicalities of maintaining a naval force in such a hostile environment so far from home shores until it was agreed all round that last-resort criteria had been satisfied.

In 1982 Robin Cook was a more reluctant warrior than he would prove to be in 1999. In 1982 he believed that military force could be applied in certain circumstances, but that there had to be a "major national interest" at stake:

Before we commit ourselves to any escalation, we must make a cool assessment of the national interests involved in the conflict over the Falkland Islands. What could that major national interest be? It is certainly not an interest of strategic significance. The Falkland Islands have not been of strategic significance to Britain since we converted our Navy from coal in the first quarter of this century. Nor is it a matter of economic significance. I am not suggesting that if there were matters of economic significance we would be justified in shedding blood. However, without any disrespect to the state of development of the Falkland Islands, there is no significant economic interest that would justify the escalation of the military conflict.[52]

Cook was not necessarily correct in his analysis,[53] but it is interesting that he saw justifications for military action as lying in such interests. Such analysis cleared the way for Cook to focus on the final consideration, the interests of the Islanders, which, he noted, had clearly become a more significant factor since the government's 1981 British Nationality Bill excluded them, against their wishes, from British citizenship. Hence, something other than the principle of self-determination had to be driving the government, namely its, "over-whelming desire to recover its reputation from the terrible humiliation that it encountered on 2 April". Given these considerations, Cook agreed with many on the Labour benches that, "not only would we not be justified in ... further military escalation, but it would be reprehensible for us to do so when we have not fully exhausted the available means of finding a diplo-matic solution".[54] However, the Galtieri regime was just as insistent that a transfer of sovereignty should precede negotiations as the Thatcher govern-ment was on the fact that an Argentinian withdrawal must come first. In view of this the grounds for negotiation seemed slim and the likelihood of the escalating naval crisis giving way to a contested landing all the greater.

The 2nd May sinking of the Argentine cruiser the *General Belgrano* with the loss of 368 lives created deep anxiety in the Labour Party, and the ensuing controversy would have a long afterlife, in particular thanks to the efforts of Tam Dalyell.[55] Concern centred on the fact that the attack seemed counter to the minimum force principle that the government had committed itself to, exemplified by the fact that the cruiser was some 35 miles outside the exclusion zone when attacked and, it transpired, moving away from the task force, raising questions about Defence Secretary John Nott's parlia-mentary defence of the sinking. This was quickly followed by an Argentinian attack on HMS *Sheffield*, generating renewed calls for a negotiated solution from some, the withdrawal of the task force beyond the reach of Argentinian aircraft from others,[56] and widely regarded in the Labour Party as a revenge attack that would not have occurred but for the sinking of the *Belgrano*.

Still, the Labour Party frontbench was caught in an increasingly precarious position largely of its own making. On the one hand it argued forcefully for a greater emphasis to be placed on peace initiatives and diplomacy, and con-tinued to pursue the government over the exact circumstances of the sinking of the *General Belgrano*. On the other, it underlined its support for the dis-patch of the task force lest it lose the political capital that its initial support generated, especially now that British service men were being killed in the

South Atlantic. Hence, in the fifth House of Commons debate on the crisis, held on 13th May, Denis Healey reiterated Labour's support for the use of the task force, explaining that:

> There would have been no point in sending the task force unless we were prepared in some circumstances to use it. To withdraw the task force now, as some have asked as part of an unconditional ceasefire, would nullify all the efforts of the Secretary-General to get the withdrawal of Argentine troops [and] encourage other Governments to use force to create a fait accompli.[57]

If this position was intended to maximise the possibility of uniting the party behind a common line, it failed. By now the Labour Party gave the impression of being increasingly divided on the issue, with a considerable range of opinions offering differing proposals and emphases. Judith Hart reiterated her opposition to the dispatch of the task force, arguing that the "principle of resolving disputes by negotiation must stand supreme".[58] Tam Dalyell spoke apocalyptically, predicting that Argentine conscripts would "fight as if they are fighting a holy war",[59] warning of massive casualties and terming the dispatch of the task force the "most unwise decision since the Duke of Buckingham left for La Rochelle in 1627".[60] The sinking of the *Belgrano* had added to the anti-war ranks, claiming previously supportive Labour MPs such as David Ennals. Michael Meacher called for a ceasefire, a phased withdrawal of Argentinian forces from the Islands and of the British task force, and the creation of a UN or other agreed international interim administration in which sovereignty would temporarily reside. David Winnick argued that sovereignty had to be negotiated, that "we cannot take the view that the Falklands will remain British forever and a day".[61] Ray Powell urged that sovereignty be treated as of secondary rather than paramount importance, and that reasonable compensation be provided for those Islanders who chose to leave, otherwise war would mean, "death to British subjects, death to our Service men and women and death to people of other countries. Wives will be made widows and children made orphans. War will mean crippled and mangled limbs and thousands of lives ruined for those who survive".[62] Andrew Faulds thought that the government had, "given foolish endorsement to the islanders' determination to insist on their British ties. We really cannot, we must not, be held to ransom by the self-determination argument".[63] Alf Dubs acknowledged that Britain had the right to recover the Islands by force, but argued that the principles at stake were not sufficiently clear-cut or important to justify the possible loss of life. Jack Ashley likened the atmosphere in Britain to the days before 1914, warned that British interests would be damaged by an invasion, and highlighted the risk that the country faced:

> all war incurs risk, but if, God forbid, either the 'Hermes' or the 'Invincible', or both, were sunk we would literally be defeated as a nation unless we

were to resort to our nuclear power, which I hope is unthinkable. We are taking this monumental risk and indulging in this crass folly for the sake of islands which, for very sensible reasons, successive Governments have been trying to give away for years ... Britain at war for islands that it has neglected and sought to abandon for two decades is an absurdity.[64]

This collection of opinion contrasted starkly with Healey's admission that further "military pressure" was inevitable because Argentine intransigence had, "shifted the balance between diplomacy and military action in the next phase of handling the dispute". Healey now made clear his party's support for the use of military force but insisted that it be, "proportionate to the issues at stake" and used in a way that would not "jeopardise the possibility of negotiation", whatever this might be.[65] At the end of a debate on 20th May, 33, overwhelmingly Labour, MPs, including Benn, Dalyell, Dubs, Faulds, Hart, Stuart Holland, Meacher, Ian Mikardo, Bob Parry, Powell, Jo Richardson, John Tilly and Dennis Skinner registered their opposition to the conduct of the war rather than follow the party line and abstain, confirming these intra-party divisions. Dalyell, Faulds and Tilly were relieved of their front-bench responsibilities as a consequence.

Four days later, British forces landed on the Falklands, at San Carlos, finally ending any slim chance of a diplomatic solution. Although John Silkin and Michael Foot still raised the question of a negotiated settlement, both Mrs Thatcher and John Nott made it plain that there was no prospect of this. In addition, Foot wrote to Thatcher arguing that Parliament should have a voice in deciding whether to prioritise force over diplomacy, arguing that:

On previous occasions in recent times when Britain has taken [the] decision to embark on full-scale military operations – say, in 1939 or in 1951, in the Korean dispute – the cause of the rupture in diplomatic exchanges was clear beyond doubt or dispute. Members of the House of Commons had no wish to demand further information. This is not the case now.

Mrs Thatcher did not share his analysis.[66] The losses of HMS *Coventry* and the merchant ship *Atlantic Conveyor* on 25th May served as a stark reminder of the human cost of the campaign and led the UN Security Council to pass Resolution 505, urging Britain and Argentina to co-operate fully with the Secretary-General with a view to ending hostilities. In practice, these losses further reduced Mrs Thatcher's interest in diplomatic initiatives, as she explained in response to Michael Foot's suggestion that she pursue them further:

Since our landings on the Islands and the losses which we have incurred it would be unthinkable to negotiate about the future of the Islands as if everything were still as it had been before. That would be a betrayal of those whom we have called upon to make such great sacrifices, even to give up their lives, because of the important principles at stake. We cannot allow the Argentines to demonstrate that they have been able to achieve progress in their attempts to impose their sovereignty over the Islands as a result of their aggression.[67]

On 15th June, 74 days after the original invasion, the Argentine forces at Port Stanley surrendered, marking the end of the war. That same day Michael Foot provoked uproar in the House of Commons when he expressed his, "hope that we shall not exclude the possibility of the trusteeship that was discussed earlier".[68] Undeterred, he continued:

Even if the Prime Minister will not give a detailed commitment now, I hope that she will say that she intends to carry out to the full, in the spirit and the letter, the resolution that she and her Government proposed at the United Nations [502] in the name of this country. I do not know whether the right. Hon. Lady is shaking her head, but it would be a breach of faith if she were to abandon that commitment. I therefore hope that she will reiterate our allegiance over these matters.[69]

Hence, even in the war's aftermath the two parties remained divided over their perception of the UN's role. Foot was not alone in resurrecting the question of a UN trusteeship, but those who raised it misjudged the mood of the country, just as Denis Healey did during the 1983 general election campaign when he accused Mrs Thatcher of "glorying in slaughter", before issuing a swift correction.[70]

Ultimately, in this case, the Labour Party was unable to overcome the dilemma the invasion of the Falkland Islands presented it with. This dilemma was compounded by leadership that risked seeming contradictory. This was especially true of Michael Foot's position. Immediately congratulated on his 3rd April speech from the Conservative backbenches by the likes of Edward du Cann, Foot was subsequently attacked by the Left for his stance (Eric Heffer considered Foot's speech, "thoroughly jingoistic and I was the only one to say so afterwards in the Shadow Cabinet"[71]). Thereafter, the different emphases within the party as to under what conditions force could be used, and whether it should be used at all, revealed a party divided over the questions of in what circumstances use of military force would be legitimate, at what point last resort had been reached.

The reality was that these divisions, with the left wing of the party opposing war and the front bench offering conditional support, were made almost inevitable both by electoral considerations and the collision of the Left's anti-colonial tradition with its pronounced hostility (the more so after the 1973 coup in Chile) towards South American military regimes. For backbenchers, this created the dilemma well articulated by Eric Heffer. One the one hand, "we could not allow a bunch of military fascist thugs to take over the island"; on the other: "there were 1,800 people on the island and approximately 600,000 sheep. It was one of the last outposts of the old empire, now largely dead and buried".[72] Of course, the contrasting fortunes of the parties during the war were not unconnected to Mrs Thatcher's good luck in the human cost of the war remaining relatively low – 255 British servicemen were killed, and 777 wounded – and hence the more apocalyptic predictions emanating from the Labour backbenches never being realised. Whether this was a price worth paying is a separate question. After all, Mrs Thatcher was later to hand over another sovereign British territory, Hong Kong, to China, despite her own personal reluctance and without according the principle of self-determination the same primacy.[73] Moreover, this does not mean that the risk to which Labour critics of the war regularly alluded was not genuinely present. As Jack Ashley correctly noted, a successful Argentinian attack on one of the two aircraft carriers had the capacity to transform the conflict, and the vulnerability of the task force was more fully apparent from the attack on HMS *Sheffield* onwards.

During the 29th April 1982 debate, Tony Benn had suggested that the Thatcher government, "see in this a diversion from the issues of unemployment and the destruction of the Welfare State" and that it was not just General Galtieri "for whom the Falklands war is a diversion from domestic failure".[74] Certainly, the "Falklands factor" was used to full effect during the 1983 general election campaign, in which the military victory in the South Atlantic allowed Ms Thatcher to drape herself in the Union Jack, and which featured footage of her January 1983 visit to the Islands. During the war itself the Labour leadership felt it was having a "good" war,[75] although there were warning signs that it was not shaping or reflecting the mood of the majority.[76] However, in an election campaign context Labour's internationalism contrasted poorly with the Thatcher government's hyper-nationalism, its commitment to working through the UN and avoiding the use of force except as a last resort, and divisions, less impressive than the government's greater unity, emphasis on the sovereignty of the Islands, and perceived greater determination to see the Union Jack fly once again over Port Stanley. During the campaign the Conservative Party was untouchable on the Falklands question. When Shadow Education spokesman Neil Kinnock responded to a heckler's observation that Mrs Thatcher had "guts", by suggesting that it was, "a pity that people had to leave theirs on Goose Green in order to prove it",[77] it was a public relations disaster. The Falklands war did not of itself secure a second victory for Mrs Thatcher, but it certainly marked the start of the revival of the government's fortunes that culminated in 1983, where the campaign itself was designed as a reminder of the victory of the previous year.

6   The Gulf War, 1990–91

The 2nd August 1990 Iraqi invasion of Kuwait represented what Margaret Thatcher rightly called, "a flagrant and blatant case of aggression" and an "outrageous breach of international law".[1] Peter Shore called it, "the first time since 1945 that an aggressor state has sought to change not just the Government of another country or rectify its borders or impose penalties but to destroy and annex the victim nation".[2] In response, the UNSC adopted Resolution 660 by 14 votes to nil, condemning the invasion and calling for immediate and unconditional Iraqi withdrawal. On 6th August, the UNSC passed Resolution 661 by 13 votes to nil, with just Cuba and Yemen abstaining, imposing comprehensive sanctions on Iraq and tellingly affirmed, "the inherent right of individual or collective self-defence in response to the armed attack by Iraq against Kuwait, in accordance with Article 51 of the Charter". The war that followed occurred on the cusp of the Cold War and post-Cold War worlds. It was the first major conflict of the post-Cold War era, although when contrasted with the type of conflicts to come, it is perhaps more accurately regarded as being the last of the Cold War era. As Foreign Secretary Douglas Hurd recalled:

> there was none of the intellectual and ethical questioning which later beset our policy on Bosnia. In that later conflict we were operating under a new and as yet unformed doctrine of humanitarian intervention in the internal affairs of a foreign country. Questions of analysis and doubts on policy cropped up at each stage. In the Gulf we were operating under the familiar necessity of resisting and reversing the aggression of one nation against another.[3]

Still, in one key respect it was the first post-Cold War conflict – the high degree of UNSC agreement on display. The response to the Iraqi invasion represented a moment when there was a definite sense that the UN had been freed to intervene in such situations and, consequently, that if it failed to rise to the challenge, it would henceforward be seriously compromised, a concern expressed repeatedly from within the Labour Party during the ensuing crisis.[4]

Yet, when Parliament was recalled on 6th September to discuss the crisis over two days, the first emergency recall of Parliament since the Falklands crisis in April 1982, it quickly became apparent that while the House was united in condemning the Iraqi invasion, the clear fact of Iraqi aggression would not of itself unite the Labour Party over the appropriate response, even though British and other foreign nationals were being used as hostages by Iraq. This reflected a more general division on the Left over the appropriate response to the Iraqi invasion and occupation of Kuwait.[5] Against the immediate post-Cold War backdrop, questions about what would emerge by the end of the decade as the doctrine of humanitarian military intervention began to be posed.

It is worth setting out the principles that the Thatcher government enunciated as forming the basis of its response to the invasion. To the fact that there could be, "no conceivable justification for one country to march in and seize another, simply because it covets its neighbour's wealth and resources" was added concern that if Iraq's invasion was not opposed, no small state could ever feel safe again. Moreover, as noted above, there was concern that the authority of the UN, just as it was emerging from the years of Cold War paralysis, would be fatally undermined. This assessment was clearly informed by what the government took to be the lesson of the 1930s, namely that "the time to stop the aggressor is at once". No post-Cold War conflict involving the UK could escape the shadow of appeasement and the "bitter memories of the consequences of failing to challenge annexation of small states in the 1930s" were regularly invoked.[6]

The root cause of much of the division within Labour Party over the 1991 war to forcibly remove Iraq from Kuwait would revolve around the question of sanctions, and whether these had been given adequate time to work, and hence whether war was the last resort that it had to be for the Labour Left. In her 6th September speech to the House of Commons Mrs Thatcher had clearly stated that the preferred method of securing complete and unconditional Iraqi withdrawal was through the application of comprehensive economic sanctions. It was thought that Iraq was particularly vulnerable to sanctions as a consequence of an economy dependent on the export of a single commodity – oil – and the import of almost everything, including food, coupled with limited reserves of currency after eight years of war with Iran. However, having outlined a preference for achieving the removal of Iraqi forces by this method, Mrs Thatcher made it clear that if this failed the government would not feel obliged to seek a further and specific UNSC resolution to justify the use of armed force to remove Iraq:

> The question has arisen whether further authority would need to be obtained from the Security Council for military action beyond that required to enforce sanctions. We have acted throughout in accordance with international law, and we shall continue to do so ... But we are not

precluded by reason of any of the Security Council resolutions from exercising the inherent right of collective self-defence in accordance with the rules of international law.[7]

The restrictionists on the Labour benches had held to a more literal interpretation of Article 51 than Mrs Thatcher during the Falklands War, so it is hardly surprising that this early indication that the government felt it could move ahead with an international response solely on the basis of Article 51 should have alarmed them. Tony Benn, by now the elder statesman of the parliamentary restrictionists, pointed out that:

> This is the nub of the whole debate. As I understand it, what the right hon. Lady has said is that the United Nations charter, and the resolutions that have been passed, have already, here and now, given her legal authority, if it comes to it and it is decided, to take military action against Iraq. I take it that, if we vote in the right hon. Lady's Lobby tomorrow night, she will claim that to be an endorsement of that view. Is that her view? She knows the real anxiety. People think that America may go to war and Britain, which is quite a minor part of the operation, will be dragged into it before the House resumes.[8]

Tam Dalyell asked why, if she was so sure about the rightness of her cause, Mrs Thatcher did not seek more specific UN authority, to be told that: "To undertake now to use no military force without the further authority of the Security Council would be to deprive ourselves of a right in international law expressly affirmed by resolution 661".[9] This reflected both her instinctive suspicion of the UN and the lower priority it was traditionally accorded in Conservative thinking on questions of war. Specifically, she was suspicious that the diplomatic process might dilute the commitment to removing Iraq from Kuwait, and warned of the risk of a Soviet veto. In a similar vein, Douglas Hurd would warn that:

> It cannot be right to put the choice entirely and wholly within the machinery of the United Nations. We know that machinery. We know that it includes vetoes and – *[Interruption.]* That reaction suggests that some hon. Members have not seriously considered the matter. We cannot leave open the possibility that necessary action against the aggressor would be blocked by such means. If we were to leave open that possibility, we would leave open the possibility that he might go away rejoicing in possession of Kuwait.[10]

Insistence on proceeding on the basis of Article 51 alone may have been unpopular with the Left of the Labour Party, but in terms of international law it was a far stronger position than the one the Labour government found itself arguing in 2002–03, when Tony Blair was unable to claim justification rooted in Article 51 and could only do so in relation to UNSC resolutions passed a decade earlier. Moreover, he could never claim, as Thatcher could, that, "our forces are part of a much wider international effort, including not only United States forces but those of our European allies, of many Arab countries and others, including members of the Commonwealth. It is a truly multinational force".[11] That Mrs Thatcher was ultimately persuaded of the wisdom of securing specific UNSC backing was a consequence of the fact that (in ascending order of importance) Gerald Kaufman had indicated that a bipartisan Labour approach was conditional on this; France and other West European states were in favour; and that in the US the Bush Administration sought one as part of its strategy for securing congressional support.

For Labour leader Neil Kinnock, the issue was clear:

> The fundamental consideration was that an infamous tyrant had invaded a peaceful neighbour. The case for armed retaliation was clear. The resistance to that argument inside the party came in two sizes. One was, this was a Tory war and we shouldn't have anything to do with it. The argument against that was that any political labelling in a British context was irrelevant because the crime against international law and against a peaceful, albeit non-democratic, neighbour was a crime of absolute prohibition. Just as you didn't, if you were the victim of crime, ask the policeman what he voted in the last election, you didn't say there's a Tory attitude and a Labour attitude to this.[12]

The second form was more rooted in Labour's pacifist tradition, and represented by MPs such as Tony Banks. As party leader, Kinnock's main focus was on the most effective ways of depriving Saddam Hussein of any military, economic, or political gain from the invasion. He also showed an acute awareness of the fact that, even if forcibly removed from Kuwait, Saddam would still pose a potential threat to the stability and security of the region. However, a secondary focus was on the need to avoid a repetition of the divisions that had characterised the party during the Falklands war. To these ends, Kinnock and his Shadow Foreign Secretary Gerald Kaufman were careful to carve out political space around Labour's greater commitment to the principle of last resort and the avoidance of war wherever possible. This they contrasted with Mrs Thatcher's always apparent lesser commitment to the UN – characterised by Kinnock as "casual and opportunistic"[13] – and the sanctions route. At the same time, however, Kinnock and Kaufman made explicit their commitment to seeing Iraq removed from Kuwait. Hence, Kinnock outlined how: "The widespread and, in our view, entirely correct approach is that sanctions should be given the fullest possible opportunity of working in order to make Saddam Hussein completely fulfill the requirements of the United Nations resolutions".[14] This did not mean that, "those considerations forbid all possibility of a strike being made at some time", but sanctions clearly had to be given adequate time to work, last resort arrived at.[15]

While the party's line, crafted principally by Kaufman, was that further explicit UNSC resolutions were necessary to legitimate the use of force, it would have been difficult to be sure of this from listening to Neil Kinnock's House of Commons speech of 6th September, reflecting the great caution with which the Labour Party approached all issues relating to war and defence after the experiences of 1982 and 1983. Kinnock told the House:

> In the public discussion that has taken place thus far on this issue, two opinions have had greatest prominence. Some assert that there is no essential need for a further specific resolution of the Security Council because, they say, the 'inherent right of individual or collective self-defence', specified in article 51 of the UN charter, gives all necessary authority for any future military action. Others say that there can be absolutely no further military action without an additional specific resolution. I believe that in the current circumstances, it is not wise to approach the matter from either of those two absolutes. Neither by itself fully addresses both the legal and the political issues at stake. It is those political issues which must unavoidably be taken into account by anyone who wants to ensure that the objectives of the United Nations and, I believe, of just about everyone in this House, are fully realised.[16]

One constant theme during the latter part of 1990 concerned whether the aims of the emerging coalition of forces should include the removal of Saddam from power. While notions of the inviolability of sovereign states would be revised by the end of the decade, at its outset a commitment to the primacy of state sovereignty held good, although facing its first post-Cold War challenge. In this case, however, there was no prospect of holding together either the military coalition, or the consensus in the UN, if the removal of Saddam became part of the equation, even if it had been a desired outcome. Moreover, on the Left of the Labour Party suspicion of US motives remained high – far higher than in relation to subsequent wars in Bosnia and Kosovo. Hence, it was logical for Kinnock, on grounds of party management if no other, to advocate limited goals for the coalition. This he did, explaining that:

> There are many who would understandably include his downfall among their list of publicly stated objectives. I think that it would be far better for them to understand that, however much we long for the ending of tyranny, we cannot include that among our motives in the case of Iraq, as that would amount to a determination to impose a form of government on what is an offending but, nonetheless, sovereign country.[17]

Reinforcing this message, at the 17th October meeting of the PLP Kaufman went so far as to condemn, "the crudity of the Prime Minister's call for

Saddam Hussein to be tried for war crimes, an action which could only be initiated if it was clear that the Geneva Convention had been breached".[18]

While the Kinnock-Kaufman line did attract some backbench criticism (discussed below) there was much that the party could unite around, in particular the emphasis on sanctions. This was not simply a case of creating a window within which a diplomatic solution could be found; there was a genuine belief within the Labour Party that sanctions could, of themselves, bring about the desired outcome. For example, Denis Healey, spoke seemingly authoritatively of his belief that:

> the blockade will be effective and will lead to Saddam's withdrawal, even if it is applied to oil alone ... The blockade is bound to take time to be economically effective. Most people believe that the minimum period will be four or five months. It might be politically effective in a shorter time, or it might take longer to be politically effective than to be economically effective.[19]

Moreover, the Kinnock-Kaufman insistence on the centrality of the UN and opposition to military action outside of that framework was something which both wings of the party could agree on. It united, for example, Healey ("it could be absolutely disastrous if it did not take place within the framework of the authority of the United Nations"[20]), on the one hand, and Benn ("I am opposed to action outside the United Nations"[21]) on the other. Finally, Kaufman had long been a critic of Israel's approach to the Palestinian question, and from an early stage joined backbenchers like Clare Short in calling for a wider regional settlement involving a resolution of the Palestinian problem once Iraq had been expelled from Kuwait, thereby neutralising it as a potential cause of intra-party friction. As he told the PLP:

> When Iraq had withdrawn from Kuwait there was need for a wider regional settlement including self-determination for the Palestinians, the settlement of refugees, a new political situation in the Lebanon and the elimination from the region of all non-conventional weapons of destruction.[22]

This is not to say that all concern, dissent or criticism was neutralised, and that which was voiced during the Autumn of 1990 was essentially focused on the role of the US. Those restrictionists who placed a high value on consistency of action, on the basis that inconsistency suggested ulterior motive, were also critical of the US record, and hence the purity of its purpose in the Gulf. The most dramatic parliamentary expression of this suspicion of US motives was sounded by Andrew Faulds, perhaps appropriately given his former career as an actor:

> In leading their great moral crusade, what hypocrisy the United States Government display! Their aggressions since the last war have been

flagrant: in Vietnam, the war they lost – America can lose wars: against Nicaragua: in Panama; and in the great military victory in one of Her Majesty's realms, Grenada. Why, when Israel invaded Lebanon, was no such stringent action, led by the United States, taken against Israel? Instead, the United States supplied Israel with its latest weapons to try out against the Lebanese civilians, who died in their thousands.[23]

Neither were the charges of US hypocrisy restricted to the backbenches. Kaufman told a meeting of the PLP that: "It was hypocritical to condemn the Iraqi regime but tolerate the authoritarian regimes of Syria and Saudi. The US had not been concerned about international law in Nicaragua, Panama and Grenada, nor had it fulfilled UN resolutions over 30 years on Israel".[24]

When expressed most thoughtfully, the question of (in)consistency of action was raised to suggest that this very inconsistency had itself encouraged actions such as the invasion of Kuwait by leading favoured allies to believe that international law may not be applied to their particular transgression, as with Ernie Ross' critique:

> The major difference in legal terms between the Israeli and Iraqi occupations lies in the reaction of the international community, and especially that of the United States and Britain and its European partners. The difference lies in the willingness and determination of the international community, and especially of the states to which I have referred, to enforce the law against the perpetrator of the offence … The enforcement of international law thus has an exceedingly practical effect, as well as a humanitarian value, but only if it is implemented consistently and without regard to the identity of the violating state. International law is assailable only if it is selectively enforced and implemented to coincide with political expediency. Past weakness, with the consequent devaluation of the law, is one factor in the context of the current crisis.[25]

The widespread suspicion on the Left, not without considerable foundation, was that the US intervention was motivated by its high dependency on oil imports from the region. This suspicion was put at its simplest by Tony Benn: "The real issue is this. Everybody knows it and nobody has mentioned it. The Americans want to protect their oil supplies". Dennis Canavan agreed, with US "double standards" confirming his, "suspicions that the United States of America and the United Kingdom are taking stronger action over the invasion of Kuwait simply because of the threat to western oil interests in the Gulf".[26]

By no means, everyone on the Labour benches had a problem with framing the conflict over Kuwait as being about the supply of oil. John Gilbert agued that if oil supplies from the region were disrupted:

> Those who will suffer will be the old-age pensioners and the single-parent families in the constituencies of every hon. Member; it is their heating

bills that will rise. Therefore, there is nothing wrong with our being in the middle east to protect our access to oil supplies.[27]

The Atlanticist wing of the Party had little difficulty in believing that the US had a legitimate interest in seeking to protect its oil supplies,[28] although it had much greater difficulty in believing that the US military build-up in Saudi Arabia could be a prologue to a permanent military presence in the region.[29]

David Winnick was one of the few Labour MPs in the autumn of 1990 willing to address the question of what would ultimately happen if sanctions failed. He made his own position clear, that force should be used, but that it had to be used with the approval of the UN, as to suggest otherwise, "would be inconsistent with what I have already said: that Kuwait should be freed from enemy occupation".[30] However, this simply begged the question of whether, in the final analysis, Article 51 would be regarded as conferring such approval in the absence of any specific authorization of force from the UNSC.

This was important in the context of Mrs Thatcher's initial ambivalence as to whether a specific UN resolution would be a necessary prelude to war. It also represented a problem for the Labour front bench. At the end of the debates of 6–7 September there was to be a vote on an adjournment motion, and there was some backbench concern that to vote with the government would allow it to subsequently claim a parliamentary mandate for any action it took – just as, some on the Left maintained, Mrs Thatcher had done in 1982. However, in its long march away from the 1983 election manifesto the Labour leadership had no option but to vote with the government if it was not to provide an easy target for the Conservative Party in the next general election, then less than two years away. Kaufman's solution was to make it clear that:

> From the day that this crisis broke, the Labour party has advocated and supported action to reverse Iraqi aggression and to deter further aggression. We have advocated throughout that such action should take place under the clear and unquestionable authority of the United Nations charter. We welcome the consistent record of the United Nations and the consistent record of the United Kingdom Government in taking action only under the clear and unquestionable authority of the United Nations. If there is a vote today, we shall vote for the Adjournment of the House to express our satisfaction that all action taken so far has been of a kind that we have advocated. We shall be voting on what has been done so far. We shall not be voting to give a blank cheque for whatever action may be taken in the future. No Government in a democracy could expect such a blank cheque and no Opposition, however loyal, could sign one.[31]

In the event, at the end of the two-day debate, 35 rebels voted against the adjournment motion. By the time the House debated the Iraqi invasion of

Kuwait again, on 11th December 1990 (once again, on an adjournment motion), it did so with a new Prime Minister, John Major, in place. The coalition military build-up in the Gulf was almost complete, and the debate took place against the background of a widespread assumption on the Left that its completion was the only thing in the way of a war to remove Iraqi forces. Hence, the atmosphere was one of heightened tension. The question of the necessary explicit authority to undertake that war was still a live one. On 29th November 1990, the UNSC had passed Resolution 678, which marked the point at which Saddam's options began to disappear. Passed by 12 votes to two (Cuba and Yemen), but with China abstaining, this arguably represented the most explicit language that would not attract a veto. It was designed to give Iraq one last chance by setting a deadline for compliance with Resolution 660 of 15th January 1991, after which Resolution 678 authorised member states to use "all necessary means" to bring about that compliance. One day later, Saddam was offered a further opportunity in the form of President Bush's announcement that he was prepared to go the "extra mile for peace" and engage in direct talks with Iraq on a peaceful resolution. By 11th December it was clear that there would be no attempt to secure a further resolution; Resolution 678 gave the coalition all the authority it required to go to war. As Douglas Hurd explained for the benefit of those Labour MPs still in doubt, "the phrase 'all necessary means' includes the use of force".[32] In this context, Tony Benn and Dennis Canavan argued within the PLP that the Party should not be asked to vote with the government, but were strongly opposed by David Winnick and Kaufman, as the leadership tried to contain a potential upsurge in intra-party dissent.[33]

Given the passage of Resolution 678, the focus shifted away from questions of consistency of behaviour, and the desirability of a wider regional settlement, to settle on the question of last resort, and specifically the question of whether sanctions should be given longer to work. "Surely", suggested Norman Godman, "even if they take more than a year to work, they are a much more effective, humane and peaceful means of bringing this man down than the sacrifice of even one British service man".[34] In this case considerations of last resort collided with the objection that the longer sanctions were given, the greater the suffering of the Kuwaitis. As Douglas Hurd put it:

> day by day Kuwait is being obliterated from the map ... There is no secret about what is happening. Whatever can be removed has been taken to Baghdad. Murder, torture and brutality have been commonplace ... With each day that passes, the likelihood that we shall be able to restore Kuwait to its former position decreases. The Iraqi aim is clear. Iraq is out to eradicate Kuwait as an independent nation. We all welcome the return of foreign hostages from Iraq, as we have just done, but we should not forget the thousands of Kuwaitis who are virtually hostages and prisoners in their own city.[35]

Concern for the fate of the Kuwaitis raised the question of whether the principle of "double effect" had been adequately taken into account. Deriving from the observations of Thomas Aquinas, double effect holds that the unintended and negative consequences of an action undertaken in pursuit of a specific end are only permissible if the desired end is in itself good and the good effect outweighs the unintended negative consequences.[36] It was a consideration raised in this context by Gavin Strang, in tandem with a concern that sanctions had not been given a sufficient opportunity:

> What is happening in Kuwait is very disturbing, but it will be disastrous for the population of Kuwait if war breaks out there. That is the choice. As the impact of sanctions was always to be on the Iraq Government's overseas earnings from oil, from which they obtain 95 per cent of their income, it is surely reasonable to allow the sanctions a proper chance to work. That will certainly not happen as a result of the months in which they have so far been applied.[37]

The reality was that the government did not believe that sanctions were working. In contrast, Denis Healey claimed that they were, but would need a further 12 months to work. "We know that by next summer", he explained, "Iraqi guns, tanks and aircraft will be running out of spares and that they have no money with which to buy more. They may also be running out of fuel".[38]

The government simply did not share Healey's confidence in the potential for sanctions to bring about a peaceful resolution. It had come to a general acceptance by December 1990 that the situation of "last resort" would be reached with the arrival of the 15th January deadline imposed by UNSC Resolution 678, by which time, coincidentally the military build-up in the Gulf would also be complete. As Conservative backbencher Ivan Lawrence argued:

> We should make clear, if we have not made clear enough before, that if economic sanctions do not work soon in securing the withdrawal of Saddam Hussein from Kuwait, we should drag him out by force. There can be no more delay and no more dithering. What should "soon" mean? It should mean 15 January 1991, a date beyond which resolution 678 says that "all necessary measures" – meaning force, because what else on earth could it mean? – can be taken to supplement economic sanctions and drive him out.[39]

While Labour backbenchers might not have agreed that last resort had been reached, the passage of Resolution 678 met the front bench's minimum requirements for being able to support the war to come. As Gerald Kaufman explained, a key Labour principle:

of paramount and overriding importance to us – is that the role of the United Nations shall be central to all actions taken to resolve the crisis and that the decisions and policies of the United Nations must at all times be upheld and supported. That is all the policies and all the decisions. That includes the authorisation, in resolution 660, of nego-tiations between Kuwait and Iraq, following unconditional withdrawal from Kuwait by Iraq, and it includes the insistence, in resolution 660 right through to resolution 678, of complete and unconditional with-drawal by Iraq from Kuwait. It is important to bear it in mind that the international coalition responsible for those resolutions is supported by the League of Arab States.[40]

Nevertheless, maintaining some small distance from the government's posi-tion and looking to maintain the party unity that had to date contrasted well with the degree to which it was achieved in 1982, Kaufman suggested that the deadline set in Resolution 678 – 15th January 1991 – was arbitrary and that if war broke out immediately thereafter, sanctions would not have been given adequate time: "We should not be hemmed in by the date of 15 January. We should not be boxed in by the compulsion of the desert time-table and the effects of the weather on the ability to wage war. If a longer haul is judged likely to achieve the effect of sanctions, we should not rely on other considerations to reject the longer haul". It was the, "overwhelming wish of the Labour party to use sanctions rather than force to oust Saddam Hussein from Kuwait", but sanctions could not be persisted with to the point where they became frayed, or to a point at which the international coalition so painstakingly constructed by the US began to fall apart.[41] In short, the Labour front bench was clearly signalling that it was resigned to and prepared to support the war to come. A motion tabled by opponents on the eve of war secured the support of just 42 MPs.

The next time the House of Commons debated the issue was 15th January 1991, the day the pause created by Resolution 678 expired. By this time there were over 35,000 British servicemen and women in the Gulf, making oppo-sition more difficult, and heightening the risk of it being labelled unpatriotic. With war inevitable, the Labour front bench was keen to be seen to support it, although a last-ditch attempt to find a diplomatic solution to the crisis revived concerns over whether last resort had been reached which, in turn, begged further questions – namely, if sanctions should be given more time, at what point and at what price would those who advocated their use be willing to concede their failure? John Major argued that more time for sanctions, "also means more time for Iraq to continue to extinguish Kuwait. It means more time for Iraq to prepare its defences against allied troops and perhaps a greater subsequent cost in the lives of allied troops. It means more time during which Kuwaitis will be tortured or killed", destroying the credibility of the international community and accentuating the risk that others would be emboldened to emulate the Iraqi action in the future.[42]

The PLP remained divided on the sanctions question until the end. For Michael Foot, for example:

> it was necessary to explore sanctions diligently, persistently and with a determination to carry them through to the end. I do not believe that our Government or any other Government can claim that they have carried out that obligation. The earlier votes at the United Nations would not have been secured, in my view, if provision had not been made for sanctions as the first major step to try to secure a settlement of the dispute.[43]

On the other hand, there were those like Peter Shore who felt that: "having pronounced a date, the authority of the United Nations is now committed and every day and every week that passes from today will lead to the erosion of United Nations' authority and to mounting tension throughout the Middle East and the world".[44] At a 16th January meeting of the PLP Gavin Strang and Dawn Primarolo moved a motion, passed virtually unanimously, that reaffirmed the Party's belief, "that the freeing of Kuwait as a result of ... international action would enhance the authority of the UN and could provide the basis for greater mutual respect of the territorial integrity of its member countries", whilst also recognizing, "the very dangerous consequences of a Gulf war" and therefore arguing that the, "UN authorized forces should not undertake military action before sanctions have been in operation long enough to have the maximum impact".[45] Strang told the meeting that this meant at least a year, but that CIA evidence "indicated that they were biting". Kinnock concluded the meeting with an appeal for unity, emphasising again that: "The Party did not support the Government we supported the United Nations and would only accept the use of force if sanctions were a definitive failure ... Unless the UN was successful on this occasion it would be condemned to perpetual impotence".[46]

Constrained by the need to carry as much of the parliamentary party with him as possible, Labour leader Neil Kinnock's position seemed somewhat contradictory by 15th January 1991. On the one hand, he recognised that Iraq had been subject to "the strictest economic sanctions in history and the most complete blockade ever".[47] Yet it remained in Kuwait, seemingly confirming the logic of the 15th January deadline giving way shortly thereafter to military force. On the other hand, he argued that 15th January, "should not be regarded as the date of ultimatum", especially if the date had been chosen on the basis of operational considerations, and that instead, "all efforts short of war should be exploited for as long as possible before force is used". When pressed on how long this should be, his answer was, "until it can be shown beyond doubt that the only means of securing the objectives of the United Nations is by resort to force".[48] This contrasted with the Liberal view that sanctions should have been given time to work, but that by 15th January they had, and "last resort" had been reached.

Kinnock's position was complex. The 1990–91 Gulf crisis was a triumph of party management for the leadership. Yet in adopting positions that helped maximise party unity, Kinnock may have suppressed his own instincts. For example, reflecting on the 15th January ultimatum, he is happy to concede that, based on his analysis of the Argentinean situation during the Falklands War (when he was a member of the Shadow Cabinet), he thought there was no real prospect of an Iraqi withdrawal, and hence that the international community had indeed arrived at last resort.[49] However, his position was more complex still. Speaking on 15th January 1991, in rejecting the last-minute French proposals, he had warned that:

> trading the immediate convening of a conference for a promise to consider withdrawal would not be the course to peace and stability; it would lead in the opposite direction. If that were to occur, Saddam Hussein would retain his current power in Iraq. He would keep intact his conventional, biological and chemical weapons. He would go on developing nuclear arms capacity. He would be a ready provider of arms to terrorists and oppressors anywhere in the world. He would have the status of a hero among parts of the population in the Middle East and elsewhere. He would therefore pose a perpetual threat to the security of the region and, indeed, of the wider world. To make concessions to Saddam Hussein before withdrawal would leave him with great strength. It would not mean war prevented; it would mean no more than war postponed, and postponed only to a time when the potential for mass destruction is even greater than it is now ... If Saddam Hussein were to accept that he should retain his power to jeopardise the region, it would light the fuse for God knows what in the future.[50]

At the time he went no further in outlining how this dilemma could be resolved. However, it is certainly possible to relate Tony Blair's subsequent approach to the dilemma to Kinnock's 1991 analysis of it. The key phrases are all there. Perhaps Kinnock played a role in shaping Blair's thinking on the post-1991 Iraq problem; he certainly had the access to Downing Street to enable him to do so. Now, looking back, Kinnock says that he: "made it clear that I thought that war should finish in Baghdad, the reason being that if it didn't on that occasion we would have to go back, because of the permanence of Saddam Hussein's threat to that region".[51] There were certainly other voices on the Labour benches voicing similar concerns in 1991.[52] However, at a time when the humanitarian military intervention paradigm was in its infancy, this was a bold position to stake out, and one that the dominant restrictionism in the party would have been unlikely to accept.[53]

Having travelled so far along the long road from 1983, the Labour front bench was unwilling to present the government and media with an opportunity to cast doubt on its patriotism or charge it with being irresponsible. To this end, Gerald Kaufman concluded his eve-of-war speech by confirming that, regardless of when it happened, "if the British armed forces are sent into action under the authority of resolution 678 and in accordance with an objective that we support, the Labour party will give its unswerving support to our armed forces".[54] Still, reflecting the deep divisions that the question of war raised for the Labour Party, at the end of this eve-of-war debate 57, overwhelmingly, Labour MPs voted to register their opposition to war commencing without allowing further time for sanctions to work.

The air war broke out in the early hours of 17th January 1991, UK time. Labour MPs were correct to point out that the passing of the 15th January deadline did not mean that it was necessary for war to begin. In practice, however, a momentum was created around this date that it would have been difficult to sustain for long thereafter in the absence of offensive operations. On 21st January, in the PLP, Gerald Kaufman explained that the whole party was united in supporting the British troops and considered the government motion for that day's parliamentary debate was acceptable to the party. Kinnock repeated again that: "The Party was not supporting military action because it was popular in the country but because this was a just war on behalf of the United Nations to which the Party had always been committed".[55] In the House of Commons Kinnock reiterated his party's reservations about the timing of the outbreak of war (notwithstanding his own personal assessment that last resort had been reached by 15th January), but emphasised his support for it. At the same time, he now moved from a focus on the *jus ad bellum* case to considerations of *jus in bello*. While rejecting calls for a ceasefire, he warned that:

> In many ways, of course, the future after this conflict will be strongly determined by the way in which the war is fought, the way in which the objectives of the use of force are adhered to by the coalition, and the way in which the conflict is concluded. I am sure that it goes without saying that, at the earliest time that the basic purpose of resolution 660 is properly fulfilled, the Security Council will want to take steps quickly to end the conflict.[56]

Gerald Kaufman highlighted how, towards this end, the war aims that Labour supported were clearly limited, although again this did not take account of the party leader's own personal preference:

> Nor for us is the war about getting rid of Saddam Hussein. We know that Saddam Hussein is a thug who has murdered men with his own hand and brought misery to millions of his own Iraqi people, to the Kurds and now to the Kuwaitis. If he were to be deposed by his fellow Iraqis, I would rejoice. Getting rid of him personally, however, is not the objective of the war.[57]

Notwithstanding the fact that the vast majority of the 34 who voted against the war on 21st January were Labour MPs, throughout the 1990–91 Gulf crisis Kinnock and Kaufman's line had proved effective in minimising division within the party and ensuring that, while the conflict did not win it many potential votes, neither did it lose it many. A number of prominent back-benchers continued to oppose the war and call for a ceasefire, a majority of these alarmed at the bombing tactics employed by the coalition forces and the fact that the UN-sanctioned war was being directed by the US rather than the UN which, in some cases, revived a dormant anti-Americanism. Some, like Terry Davies, questioned the wisdom of going to war to restore what they characterised as a feudal aristocracy. Some questioned whether the nature of the military action was consistent with the spirit or letter of Resolution 678. Ironically, in view of their leader's personal view, there was also concern lest the war aims expanded beyond those set out in Resolution 678 to embrace regime change in Baghdad, at a time when the weight accorded to the importance of state sovereignty and the strictly restrictionist reading of Resolution 678 were the dominant currents within the party.[58] Some backbenchers were openly critical of their front bench. Max Madden for one criticised the, "consensus between the Government and the official Opposition [which] amounts to a conspiracy of silence to ensure that the House will not have an opportunity to speak out in the names of the 10 million or 11 million British citizens who are totally opposed to this war".[59] More apoc-alyptically, and perhaps just a decade too early, Bob Cryer warned that:

> There will be no winners from the war. Millions of people in the middle east will feel nothing but contempt and hatred for the United States, and – alack, alas – for the United Kingdom, which has a special rela-tionship with the United States. That special relationship means that we do the bidding of the United States. We have been sucked unnecessarily into this war and we shall face vitriol and hatred from many millions of people throughout the Muslim world.[60]

Once the war ended, on 28th February, and having argued on the eve of war that "last resort" had not been reached, Kinnock spoke of the determina-tion to liberate Kuwait having been, "completely vindicated by the horrific evidence of atrocities committed there while the country was occupied by Iraq",[61] hinting at his own personal assessment at 15th January. The Labour Party, as an organisation aiming to secure electoral success and form the next government, emerged relatively unscathed from the war, aided by the short duration of the conflict, the low level of British and coalition casualties, and the failure of the more apocalyptic visions of the likes of Denis Healey to materialise. In terms of party management, 1982 and 1990–91 represent very different cases, in part a consequence of the long journey the party had embarked on after 1983. However, as Kinnock foresaw, the pro-blem of Saddam Hussein remained and, as he predicted, the international community would return to it.

7 The rise of humanitarian military intervention in the 1990s

Bosnia and Kosovo

In the aftermath of the Cold War, the nature of war itself was clearly changing, arguably necessitating a new framework within which to consider responses by the international community. Termed post-modern wars by some commentators,[1] and "New Wars" by Mary Kaldor, the conflicts that emerged in the 1990s were characterised by:

> a blurring of the distinctions between war (usually defined as violence between states or organized political groups for political motives), organized crime (violence undertaken by privately organized groups for private purposes, usually financial gain) and large-scale violations of human rights (violence undertaken by states or politically organized groups against individuals).[2]

They also involved, "a myriad of transnational connections", blurring the boundaries between "internal and external, between aggression (attacks from abroad) and repression (attacks from inside the country)".[3]

By the end of the century the type of war that had occurred in 1991 seemed to belong to a different historical era. Reflecting on the transformations of the decade, General Sir Rupert Smith observed that:

> War no longer exists. Confrontation, conflict and combat undoubtedly exist all around the world ... and states still have armed forces which they use as a symbol of power. None the less, war as cognitively known to most non-combatants, war as a massive deciding event in a dispute in international affairs: such war no longer exists.[4]

The conflicts in Bosnia and Kosovo epitomised the shift Smith identified. Moreover, they were such complex and seemingly intractable conflicts that they induced a certain nostalgia for the certainties of the Cold War, as with Labour defence specialist Bruce George:

> It might seem perverse to view the Cold War as anything other than a negative phenomenon, but in many ways it was simple. Not only did

soldiers know who the enemy was; they knew which dug-out they would be fighting in, and they probably knew the name of the tank commander who would come against them. In those days policy makers did not need to think much. The world was a simpler and stable place. All those conditions have changed, not always for the better.[5]

As George suggested, the dilemmas facing policy-makers became far more complex as, alongside this shift in the nature of war, the question of humanitarian intervention – under what circumstances it was justifiable to intervene within a sovereign state to prevent or end a humanitarian catastrophe – became highly salient. This new salience created a fundamental tension, as it clashed with the terms of Article 2 (7) of the UN Charter which maintained that:

> Nothing contained in the present Charter shall authorize the United Nations to intervene in matters which are essentially within the domestic jurisdiction of any state or shall require the Members to submit such matters to settlement under the present Charter; but this principle shall not prejudice the application of enforcement measures under Chapter VII.[6]

It would also clash with the restrictionist tradition in the Labour Party. Restrictionism privileged state sovereignty over individual human rights, seeing state sovereignty as a key safeguard protecting weaker states from interference by more powerful ones, a perspective rooted in the party's anti-colonial tradition. The corollary of this was a firm belief in the sanctity of state borders and the illegitimacy of secession.[7] However, these principles came under pressure in the post-Cold War world, with the implosion of the Soviet Union leading to the creation of Russia and a further 14 states, followed shortly thereafter by the break-up of Yugoslavia, severely challenging the Left's traditional restrictionist approach to questions of war.

Bosnia

Although in reflecting on the war in Bosnia Douglas Hurd would feel that, "one had to go back to the Spanish Civil War to find such a passionate, deep-seated distress about events in a foreign country, together with anger at the apparent passivity of the British Government",[8] in its early stages there was only isolated support for some form of intervention. Less than two years after the conclusion of the Gulf war, Europe was faced by a type of conflict it was slow to fully comprehend. Moreover, even by the end of the war over Bosnia, Labour MPs, with the exception of a small group, remained reluctant warriors, and in this the Labour and Conservative frontbenches were at one. There was a shared belief that the British public would not support the likely human costs of a military intervention.[9] Again, from Hurd's perspective:

the indignation of individuals never coalesced into a sustained national movement ... My colleagues in government and all parties in the Commons were, with individual exceptions, skeptical of the need for the even limited intervention which we undertook. They found the complicated situation in former Yugoslavia hard to understand and the characters in the drama unsympathetic. A decision to commit British troops to fight a war in Bosnia would have been deeply unpopular at all times.[10]

The first parliamentary debate on the deteriorating situation in the former Yugoslavia took place six months after Slovenia and Croatia had declared their independence, at a time when Serb-Croat skirmishes had escalated into war inside Croatia, and when the UNSC had passed Resolution 713 implementing an arms embargo on the former Yugoslavia.[11] This first debate, secured by backbench Conservative MP Patrick Cormack, took place in the middle of the night with few MPs present. The incomprehension with which the killing was met at the time was well illustrated by Labour foreign affairs spokesman and future NATO Secretary-General George Robertson's observation that:

> on our continent, on the doorstep of the most civilised part of the world, we are watching human beings killing each other for no other reason than the fact that they live next door to each other. The waste, deaths, brutality and destruction of property beggar description. All that is happening in a beautiful country which has been the holiday destination of thousands of British people over the years. Many people who have spent their holidays in that country, as I have, shake their heads in disbelief as they watch what is happening.[12]

The fact that the conflict was, as Robertson put it, on the doorstep of Europe, was a significant factor in debates about how the West should respond. Did this fact give European states a particular responsibility to intervene with peacekeeping forces? Did it have implications for European security, or was this primarily a humanitarian issue? In other words, were there British interests at stake? Both major political parties were divided on these questions, producing some strange cross-party alliances as politicians began to feel their way through fundamental issues relating to war and peace in a post-Cold War environment without any kind of map.

The arms embargo introduced as a consequence of UNSC Resolution 713 would be at the centre of much subsequent controversy over intervention in Bosnia, coming under particular challenge from proponents of what became known as "lift and strike" – lifting the embargo on the Bosnian government and undertaking air strikes against Serb targets. As Hurd reflected:

> It seemed at the outset both idealism and realism to deny weapons to the combatants in a war that the international community wished to

end. The reality, however, was rather different, as harsh argument flared up between those who saw the fighting as essentially the result of aggression (in which case the attacked party was entitled to the means of self defence) or essentially a civil war (in which case the argument for the arms embargo held).[13]

Clearly, the arms embargo affected the Bosnians more than the Serbs, who had retained the vast bulk of the former Yugoslavia's armaments, and so cemented their military advantage. However, the embargo proved highly porous and arms continued to flood into Bosnia by air, sea and road. As the Bosnian Ambassador to Washington, Sven Alkalaj, put it: "There's no problem acquiring arms. There are lots of arms sellers in the world who have access to any kind of weaponry you wish to buy". The existence of an embargo merely raised the price, making it "three or four times higher" than if openly available.[14] In addition, geopolitical interests led to states involving themselves in, or acquiescing in, serial breaches of the embargo. The Clinton Administration tacitly approved Iranian arms shipments to Bosnia. Arms or financing were also provided by a range of other states, including Saudi Arabia, Malaysia, Brunei, Turkey and Pakistan. Croatia and Bosnia also received arms via Argentina, while Germany allegedly facilitated the transfer of former East German MiG-21s to Croatia via Hungary.[15] In South Africa, allegations surfaced that the Vatican had funnelled US$40m worth of bearer bonds to Croatia to facilitate weapons purchases.[16] The ease with which Serbian forces acquired Russian arms reflected support from Moscow. However, particular attention came to focus on the supply of military equipment from Iran to the Bosnian government via Croatia. First exposed in May 1994, when an Iranian air force transport plane was observed at Zagreb airport unloading heavy crates marked "humanitarian aid" and "no smoking", this route supplied essentially small arms, but nevertheless "enabled the Bosnian government to fight the Serbs to a standstill and even, in some areas, to regain territory lost in the early years of the war".[17] It attracted attention because, although the Clinton Administration was notionally upholding the UN embargo, and although some 20,000 US troops were being deployed in the region, it was aware of and acquiesced in the Iranian arms airlifts. This stood in marked contrast with the actions of the earlier Bush Administration, which had protested over an Iranian re-supply flight in September 1992 carrying 4,000 assault rifles which was subsequently impounded by Croatia.[18] Not only did the Clinton decision raise the spectre of revenge attacks against Western forces in the area, it was also counter the Administration's declared policy of isolating Iran internationally. It was "the height of insanity", said Lawrence Eagleburger. "We are inviting Bosnian Islamic connections with a terrorist state that wishes us as much damage as they can possibly inflict upon us".[19] Hence, while the embargo was the focus of much indignation, the reality was that the scale of smuggling and range of actors involved rendered it utterly ineffective.

From the outset, it was clear that Serbia bore the greatest responsibility for the destruction being inflicted on the region. Nevertheless, during the earliest stages of the war there was a clear reluctance within the Labour Party to advocate intervention either through the insertion of peacekeeping forces or by lifting the arms embargo, while military intervention with ground forces was unthinkable.[20]

Nevertheless, Shadow Foreign Secretary Gerald Kaufman pursued Douglas Hurd over the British government's "early" recognition of Croatia and Slovenia, viewed by a number of Labour MPs as the outcome of a deal done with Germany, in return for which Britain had secured opt-outs on the Social Chapter and single currency at Maastricht.[21] That this was held to have occurred at a time when the EU was discussing a common foreign policy was taken as further proof by some Conservatives, were it needed, that national interests would and should override other considerations where they clashed. It was this act, Kaufman maintained, that had encouraged the Bosnian Serbs to declare their independence in February 1992, and hence had led to the war between Bosnian Serbs, Bosnian Muslims and Bosnian Croats (what he called "the unwise capitulation of European Community Foreign Ministers to the insistence of the German Government that every little self-declared republic in what was Yugoslavia should be given international recognition"[22]). At the same time, Kaufman was keen to demonstrate cross-party unity on the question by agreeing with Hurd that:

> The situation is far too confused for forcible intervention from outside to do any positive good. It is certain that force would lead to further unnecessary bloodshed and increase the number of people at risk. I hope that the Government will stand out inflexibly against any suggestions of forcible intervention by the European Community.[23]

To reinforce this point, Kaufman also agreed with Hurd that the Serbs were not the only guilty party, even though principally responsible. Kaufman's replacement under John Smith, Jack Cunningham, adopted the path marked out by Kaufman. Like Kaufman, he supported Hurd in ruling out the use of (British) ground forces to resolve the conflict. Crucially, both Labour and Conservative front benches continued to regard the war as a civil war. For the government, Hurd termed it, "a civil war in the sense that the huge majority – more than 90 per cent – of those fighting are Bosnian. They are Bosnian Serbs, Bosnian Croats and Bosnian Muslims".[24] Defence Secretary Malcolm Rifkind's variation was to term it, "a conflict in which all three ethnic groups have willingly engaged and which has many of the characteristics of a civil war".[25] Cunningham agreed:

> The Serbs are the principal aggressors although it does not help the case or the credibility of other political leaders in Bosnia – Croatian or Muslim – when the Croatians launch attacks on the Muslims or the

Muslims launch attacks on the Croatians. The reality is that among the political leaders as well as among the military leaders in Bosnia there are no innocents. They all bear a grave responsibility for continuing the slaughter in the way they do.[26]

Agreeing with long-standing anti-war critics on the Labour backbenches, Cunningham argued that there were limits to what could be achieved by outside intervention in a civil war, and that rather than focus on military intervention the correct solution lay in a massive increase in humanitarian aid, more rigorous enforcement of sanctions on Serbia, and the establishment of war crimes procedures through the UN. In a similar vein, Shadow Defence spokesman David Clark responded to the dispatch of British forces in a peacekeeping role by warning that:

> In no way can we give the Government a blank cheque for further escalation. To extend military participation further would be extremely dangerous, if not foolhardy. The terrain is ideal for hit-and-run attacks. The old Yugoslavian army, many of whose remnants are now fighting in Bosnia, was trained specifically for that task and we simply must not get drawn into a conflict on one of the various sides. British military involvement must not be allowed to escalate into such a quagmire, and we do not believe that escalation is inevitable.[27]

In counterpoint to the general unanimity across the frontbenches, both Labour and Conservative parties remained divided on the wisdom of intervention throughout – though, as Hurd suggests, there was never a significant number in favour of intervention. The positions that individual MPs adopted on the desirability of military intervention in Bosnia were derived from their understanding of the nature of the conflict, and whether it was a civil or an inter-state war, with those who regarded the conflict as one between states tending to favour military intervention (though not necessarily with ground troops, some proposed no more than air strikes to bring about Serb compliance), and the lifting of the arms embargo.

One difference between the Labour and Conservative parties over Bosnia lay in the evocation of the "national interest" in arguing against a British military role. The language of national interest was not used explicitly by Labour MPs as it was by Conservative backbenchers. No Labour backbencher would have asked, as Nicholas Budgen did in June 1992, "how the sad fighting in Yugoslavia affects British national interests?",[28] or again in April 1993, "what is the British national interest in Bosnia? . . . Is it not only the British national interest that can justify our intervention in any such wars?"[29] Nevertheless, the Labour Party's aversion to the commitment of British troops in a combat role was unavoidably based in part on a national interest calculus, even if not explicitly labelled as such.[30] For example, Hurd's statement in the wake of the April–May 1993 Serb assault on

Srebrenica contained arguments deployed by MPs on both sides of the House, and very much represented the general cross-party consensus of the time:

> Anger and horror are not enough as a basis for decisions. It is a British interest to make a reasoned contribution towards a more orderly and decent world. But it is not a British interest, and it would only be a pretence, to suppose that we can intervene and sort out every tragedy which captures people's attention and sympathy. I have never found the phrase "something must be done" to be a phrase which carries any conviction in places such as the House or the Government where people have to take decisions. Governments and Parliaments have to weigh and judge. Bosnia is not the same as Kuwait or the Falklands, in history or terrain or calculation of risk. Decisions cannot be based either on false analogies or on a desire to achieve better headlines tomorrow than today. That is particularly true when those decisions affect human life, and more especially still when the lives are those of British service men or civilians.[31]

This front bench bipartisanship ensured that the only parliamentary vote that would be held on Bosnia was at the instigation of the Liberal Democrats. It came in November 1992, when 37 MPs, including just 16 from the Labour Party, voted against the government, and only 206 voted at all.[32] Jack Cunningham supported Hurd's position, and would not countenance the deployment of British troops except as part of a UN force.[33] Clearly illustrating the distance that the party would travel on the question in a matter of five or six years, Cunningham did not accept the argument, "that we have a moral duty to intervene in Bosnia. No one talks about our moral duty to intervene in Angola, where nearly three times as many people have been killed in a bloody civil war. No one says that we have a moral imperative to intervene in Nagorno-Karabakh".[34]

Nevertheless, during 1992 and 1993 a small group of left-wing MPs began to put pressure on the leadership to adopt a more interventionist stance. Michael Meacher told a PLP meeting in November 1992 that, "we are now witnessing the most serious civil war in Europe since the Spanish Civil War", one that risked "creating a new Palestine of Europe".[35] What, Kate Hoey asked, was the difference between protecting fleeing Kurds and protecting fleeing Bosnians? In the face of this opposition Cunningham maintained that the only solution to the crisis was a political one facilitated by continuation of the arms embargo, sanctions against Serbia, and the Vance-Owen initiatives.[36] Invoking Labour's traditional insistence on the primacy and centrality of the UN in conflict resolution, he reminded the PLP that the party:

> could not support a position of military intervention in the states of former Yugoslavia that was not sanctioned by the United Nations. It was also the case that the UN simply did not have the resources to take

the kind of military action which some colleagues envisaged, and, in any event, there were no clear sides to intervene on behalf of over much of the terrain in this civil war situation. There is no support in the UN for increased military intervention. There are civil wars in Nagorno Karabakh, in Somalia, in Cambodia; indeed the world keeps asking more and more of an organization which does not have enough resources to carry out the tasks it has now ... We should also recognize that the UN has got 20,000 troops in former Yugoslavia even now; but the impact they are likely to have as a military force is not great. All Yugoslav males have been trained in techniques of guerrilla warfare, for the last two generations. That was Tito's defence policy against the Warsaw Pact. Taking on such an armed population is not feasible.[37]

Serb artillery attacks on Srebrenica in April 1993, killing over 50 people and injuring many more, hardened attitudes on the Labour backbenches. A letter signed by 17 backbench Labour critics was published in *The Guardian*, arguing that:

The time has come to use military force to end the systematic assaults upon Srebrenica and other civilian populations in Bosnia ... [and] if it requires active engagement of troops on the ground, we believe the crisis in Bosnia merits that scale of commitment ... We believe the left has a particular duty to stand up against the kind of pure, racially motivated fascism which the Serbian aggressors embody. We must defend the idea of pluralist, multi-cultural, multi-denominational society which Bosnia represents. The right may enquire after the economic or electoral interest involved in intervention but for the left, strong and decisive action in Bosnia is now a moral imperative.[38]

This pro-interventionist sentiment on the backbenches went beyond the signatories to the letter. For example, Dale Campbell-Savours advocated air strikes because, "it is impossible to negotiate with fascism. We believe that fascism sets its objectives and ignores its victims. Fascism is what we have in Serbia".[39] Others, such as Frank Field and Clare Short invoked self or national interest in arguing for intervention, partly on the basis that one of the consequences of the fighting was that millions of refugees were being created, partly on the basis that:

What is morally right in the former Yugoslavia is also in our self-interest, and those who have pretended that the two are in conflict are profoundly wrong. Serbia is the major aggressor in the former Yugoslavia and hon. Members who pretend either that there is a civil war or that all the parties are equally guilty are making an excuse for inaction against the major aggressor and are wrongly confusing the situation. Serbia is trying to acquire territory by force.[40]

Responding to this growing backbench pressure Labour leader John Smith now called for air strikes against Serbian lines in Bosnia unless a ceasefire could be implemented, a call that Cunningham took up, although making it clear that any intervention would have to be explicitly sanctioned by the UN and hence multinational. Even so, the party frontbench remained committed to the existing bipartisan approach on the maintenance of the arms embargo (to lift it would be to "try to douse a fire with petrol" warned David Clark[41]), and did not want to be seen to advocate military intervention on the ground. As Cunningham told the House of Commons:

> The Labour party is committed in its constitution to the United Nations. My colleagues and I support the decisions of the Security Council, and especially the arms embargo. It seems ridiculous that the people who are arguing for an end to the embargo are, in the next sentence, advocating military intervention on the ground in Bosnia. Nor do we accept that there is any sensible or legitimate argument for intervention by ground forces.[42]

Hence, in 1993–94, the Labour Party's caution about intervening in what its leadership viewed as a civil war remained intact. Air strikes against Serb supply lines would be supported in certain circumstances, but only if authorised by the UN, ruling out the possibility of bombing under NATO authority if UN authorisation was not forthcoming.

This no more than reflected the fact both that there was no overwhelming or majority public support for more direct military intervention, and the fact that the bulk of the party opposed further military intervention. This opposition was largely based on the primacy still attached to the sovereignty of states, and a belief that to intervene in a civil war would be to repeat the mistake of the US in Vietnam and be sucked into a quagmire, well articulated by Alice Mahon, who believed that:

> Experience teaches us that there are limits to external intervention in civil wars ... To be sucked into taking sides would be disastrous and would lead us into another Vietnam. That is why the United States does not want to commit any troops on the ground. The Americans have had their fingers burnt and realise that such a move would be disastrous.[43]

Linked to this was a belief that the quick military victory in the Gulf in 1991 was in danger of misleading people into underestimating the costs or likely duration of a military involvement. Still others saw air strikes against Serb targets as having been counter-productive and damaging to the humanitarian effort, which was the level of intervention that they were willing to support, as, for example, with Tony Benn's argument that:

> The air strikes were the occasion for the taking of hostages – whom the Serbs now call prisoners of war, because they say that the United Nations has

declared war on them – and the air strikes are what now prevent the resumption of the humanitarian role ... We cannot have British or French soldiers in blue berets acting as humanitarians, and pilots in blue helmets bombing: that is not a sustainable position.[44]

Finally, there were those with essentially pro-Serb sympathies, Bob Wareing in particular, who argued against intervention, pointing to the absence of consistency in responding to Croatian attacks on Serbs.

On 12th May 1994 John Smith died, to be replaced as party leader in July by Tony Blair. He came to the leadership shortly before a qualitative change in the conflict occurred with Bosnian Serb forces attacking population centres, including the infamous July 1995 siege of Srebrenica, and taking hostage members of UN forces, including British soldiers. From the outset Blair took a firm line on the conflict. When Parliament was recalled from the Whitsun recess in May 1995 for a crisis debate on the seizure of hostages and the government's decision in light of this to deploy a further 7,000 troops, including a 5,000-strong rapid deployment force, Blair argued that "talk of withdrawal in Bosnia in response to the taking of hostages is deeply unhelpful at this time. It is hardly a message of firm resolve in the face of what is effectively an act of coercive blackmail".[45] At a time when Labour MPs were unsure about the purpose of the further deployment (to help UN forces withdraw?, to enable them to continue with their mandate?) Blair was striking a bold position. Listening to Blair's speech, and that by Prime Minister John Major, Giles Radice thought that: "Both are good, Blair sounding the more prime ministerial. Both take a tough line on those doubters who want an immediate withdrawal. Curiously, more of these intervene on Blair than on Major. Blair slaps them down".[46]

Did Blair come to the leadership complete with interventionist instincts? Not necessarily. There was clear continuity with the line adopted during the Smith leadership, in terms of the continuing argument that it was correct to rule out intervening in a combat role in what Blair implicitly accepted was a civil war. Any such intervention, it was argued, would, in effect, favour one side in the conflict. Blair too emphasised the hostile nature of the terrain, which he also regarded as natural guerrilla territory. In considering the situation in Bosnia, he said, "We have to make a judgement about where our national interest lies and take humanitarian concerns into account".[47] The seeds of the Chicago speech may have been there, but no more. At the same time, he reportedly felt that the Major government had not shown sufficient moral leadership.[48] The war formally ended in November 1995 with the signing of the Dayton Peace Accords, bringing a brief period of peace. For Blair, the siege of Srebrenica would become a reference point in determining his approach to the crisis in Kosovo, which emerged as the Dayton peace unravelled during 1998.

Kosovo

Under Blair's leadership, the Labour Party, by now styling itself New Labour, won a landslide victory in the May 1997 general election, with a parliamentary majority of 187. Blair's first Foreign Secretary, Robin Cook, launched a foreign policy with an ethical dimension, with the implication that it would be proactive. Cook had already taken a strong line during the latter stages of the war in Bosnia, arguing in the wake of the 1995 siege of Srebrenica that,

> we cannot walk away from Bosnia; not only because to do so would be to abandon civilians there to humanitarian catastrophe, but because to do so would be to walk away from our own values. There must be no doubt about our commitment to those values and that is why, in Bosnia, we should take every practical step to support and defend those values.[49]

In office, Cook took an immediate interest in events in Kosovo. As a member of the International Contact group on Kosovo alongside the US, Russia, France and Italy, the Blair government had played a role in the October 1998 passage of UNSC Resolution 1203 which called on both sides, "to cooperate with international efforts to improve the humanitarian situation and to avert the impending humanitarian catastrophe". However, the situation continued to deteriorate into 1999, with 45 Kosovo Albanians being killed by Serb forces at Racak in January. In February the Rambouillet talks produced peace proposals that included autonomy for Kosovo and, highly controversially, included provision that,

> NATO personnel shall enjoy, together with their vehicles, vessels, aircraft, and equipment, free and unrestricted passage and unimpeded access throughout the FRY including associated airspace and territorial waters. This shall include, but not be limited to, the right of bivouac, maneuver, billet, and utilization of any areas or facilities as required for support, training, and operations.[50]

Arguably, this set the nationalist Serb leadership a test that they could not pass.

During February and March 1999, on the eve of NATO's 50th anniversary, the situation worsened further. Against this deteriorating background, Blair spoke out, echoing the lessons of the 1930s and drawing on his experience towards the end of the Bosnian conflict:

> Some people argue that Kosovo is a far away place that has little to do with Britain. Why should we get involved? Why there?
>
> To them I say I will not ignore war and instability in Europe. Fighting in Bosnia since 1991 has shown we cannot take our continent for

granted. Our responsibilities do not end at the English Channel. If we can prevent war, we should strive to do so. More than 200,000 people were killed in Bosnia and some 2 million forced from their homes. Fleeing ethnic cleansing and destruction in their own lands, many have ended up as refugees right across Europe, including in Britain. We do not want that repeated in Kosovo, but it could be.[51]

Clearly, then, Blair felt that the situation in Kosovo carried the potential to spiral into one comparable with Bosnia in the mid-1990s, and the lesson he took from that war, through his involvement as party leader towards its end, was that the humanitarian intervention had been well intentioned but inadequate, and should have been supported by greater military weight sooner.[52]

Fully aware that Russia would veto any UNSC resolution sanctioning military action against Serbia, it was determined to operate through NATO, hitherto a defensive rather than offensive alliance. Despite the experience of the war in Bosnia and post-war consensus that intervention had been too little and come too late, the shift to operating via NATO rather than the UN would prove inherently controversial for the restrictionists in the Labour Party, although it was one welcomed by those who had earlier advocated military intervention in Bosnia only to be disappointed by governmental caution. Supporters would argue that military intervention via NATO was consistent with international law, that international law existed before the UN, and that while the UN might have primary responsibility in these matters, it did not have sole responsibility. The precedent set by the imposition of no-fly zones and operations designed to safeguard the Kurds in the wake of the 1991 Iraq War was invoked. Moreover, by selective reference, the military action could be shown to be consistent with both the UN Charter, in particular Article 52,[53] and existing UNSC resolutions.

In Resolution 1199 of September 1998 the Security Council had expressed its grave concern over the, "excessive and indiscriminate use of force by Serbian security forces", and called on Serbia to, "cease all action by the security forces affecting the civilian population and order the withdrawal of security units used for civilian repression". However, Resolution 1199 did not authorise the use of force, instead committing the Security Council, "to consider further action and additional measures to maintain or restore peace and stability in the region". Resolution 1203 of October 1998 was also cited in support of the NATO action. This had stated that the Security Council was, "deeply alarmed and concerned at the continuing grave humanitarian situation throughout Kosovo and the impending humanitarian catastrophe" and re-emphasised the "need to prevent this from happening". The mining of old UNSC resolutions to seek justification for military action not specifically authorised by the UNSC would be taken further with Iraq. Given this dubious legal base, throughout the war Cook would be forced to confront the thorny question of whether, given that it was bombing Belgrade,

Britain was now at war with Serbia, to which his reply – perhaps inevitably, given the legal black hole in which the war was being waged – contained echoes of Anthony Eden:

> We have not declared war on Serbia ... We are not seeking a war against Belgrade, or to defeat Belgrade in war. We are seeking, through our military action, the limited – but nevertheless essential – task of enabling those dispossessed from Kosovo to return to their homes under international protection.[54]

The question of the objective legality of the war would remain controversial. It clearly did not meet the requirements of positive law, but has been characterized as "illegal but legitimate" by the Independent International Commission on Kosovo.[55] This view is consistent with the Foreign Affairs Committee's post-war judgement that, "NATO's military action, if of dubious legality in the current state of international law, was justified on moral grounds".[56] However, it also exposed the slippery legal slope that led to war in Iraq in its argument that; "faced with the threat of veto in the Security Council by Russia and China, the NATO allies did all that they could to make the military intervention in Kosovo as compliant with the tenets of international law as possible".[57]

On the basis of this authority, on 24th March 1999 NATO forces commenced air strikes of targets in the suburbs of Belgrade. The following day in Cabinet, the option of tabling a motion on Kosovo for parliamentary debate was rejected because it was recognised that this would expose intra-party divisions. While the Cabinet was in large part supportive, there was some dissenting opinion, with Frank Dobson asking: "How is it any country can take military action against a sovereign state and fellow members of the UN without the approval of the Security Council?"[58] Within the wider party he was not alone. Denis Healey argued that: "It was a terrible mistake to attack a sovereign state without even consulting the United Nations ... If you attack Yugoslavia over Kosovo why don't you attack Russia over Chechenia? Why don't you attack Turkey for its war against the Kurds?"[59] Healey and others who raised the consistency question, such as Tony Benn, were criticised for not appreciating the "moral urgency" which justified the bombings.[60]

The Labour government itself justified the launching of the air war on three separate grounds, as it did so fully expecting that the air campaign would last for just 72 hours, after which time Slobodan Milosevic would be prepared to negotiate on the basis of the Ramboullet proposals. The first was the humanitarian case presented by Blair on the eve of the bombing campaign:

> to avert what would otherwise be a humanitarian disaster in Kosovo. Let me give the House an indication of the scale of what is happening. A quarter of a million Kosovars – more than 10 per cent of the population – are now homeless as a result of repression by Serb forces; 65,000 people

have been forced from their homes in the past month, and no fewer than 25,000 in the four days since the peace talks broke down; and only yesterday, 5,000 people in the Srbica area were forcibly evicted from their villages.[61]

The government also faced the classic humanitarian intervention dilemma that the optimum time to intervene in a humanitarian crisis is at the earliest feasible moment so as to avert the impending greater disaster, but that at that moment the case for intervention may not be compellingly clear. This led it to the argument that: "If we had not acted now, we would have been obliged to act in the future when the situation had become worse".[62] As Robin Cook put it on 25th March 1999:

> Now we are seeing exactly the same pattern of ethnic violence being replayed in Kosovo. The same reports have emerged this week of masked paramilitaries, separating the men of the village from the women and children. We now know what happened next when that happened at Srebrenica – all the men were massacred. We cannot allow the same tragedy to be repeated before us again in Kosovo. That is why our service personnel were ordered to take action last night, and that is why the House should back our resolve to halt any more ethnic cleansing being imposed by President Milosevic.[63]

The lessons drawn from the Bosnian war were clear. Another lesson of Bosnia was the need to educate public opinion, to sell the war to a British public that had not regarded the Bosnia war as a compelling case for intervention, but which would view video footage of the devastation wrought by the NATO bombing campaign. Hence, Blair also emphasised that there was a national interest at stake in Kosovo:

> We act also because we know from bitter experience throughout this century, most recently in Bosnia, that instability and civil war in one part of the Balkans inevitably spills over into the whole of it, and affects the rest of Europe, too. I remind the House that there are now more than 1 million refugees from the former Yugoslavia in the European Union ... Strategic interests for the whole of Europe are at stake. We cannot contemplate, on the doorstep of the EU, a disintegration into chaos and disorder.[64]

However, there was also a more controversial justification on offer. In 1990–91 Labour politicians had argued in favour of military action against Iraq, and in favour of the notion that the 15th January 1991 deadline for Iraq to leave Kuwait represented last resort, in part on the basis that the crisis in the Gulf represented a serious test for the UN. If the UN was not, it was argued, able to act in this case, when it was freed from the paralysis that had affected it throughout most of the Cold War period, then its credibility would be seriously damaged, encouraging others to follow in the wake of Saddam Hussein and challenge the foundations of international order. Such was the party's historic and emotional attachment to the UN that the argument carried considerable weight. Now, in 1999 the Labour government sought to transfer that argument to one of NATO's credibility. For example, Cook told the House of Commons that:

> The first reason why we took action was that we were aware of the atrocities that had been carried out and we had the capacity to intervene, but that is not the only reason. Our confidence in our peace and security depends on the credibility of NATO. Last October, NATO guaranteed the ceasefire that President Milosevic signed. He has comprehensively shattered that ceasefire. What possible credibility would NATO have next time that our security was challenged if we did not honour that guarantee? The consequences of NATO inaction would be far worse than the result of NATO action.[65]

The clear implication was that Cook did not see this offensive action by a defensive organisation as exceptional, and instead seemed to present the Kosovo war as presaging a new era of NATO interventionism. This caused immediate disquiet within the restrictionist ranks of the Labour back-benches. "When I hear Ministers say that we have gone to war to prove that NATO is credible", said Tony Benn, "by God I shiver. The argument that we have to kill people to show that we are strong does not carry any weight with me or with the rest of the House".[66] What was clear was that Cook had arrived at a view of sovereignty as an instrumental value, a view that carried with it the duty to intervene inside states where they abused their citizens. As he told the House of Commons:

> Some have argued that Yugoslavia is a sovereign state and that it can do what it likes with its citizens. I totally reject that view. I would not care to explain to the Kosovo Albanians the theory that aggression against them by a neighbouring country would be unacceptable, but that the aggression that they are experiencing is acceptable because it is being carried out by their own Government.[67]

Believing that the bombing campaign would be effective in such a short time, Blair was able to reassure those concerned that there was no intention of deploying ground troops in Kosovo. When Donald Anderson, Chairman of the Foreign Affairs Committee, asked if there were, "any circumstances in which Britain would be prepared to commit ground troops in answer to the 'What then?' question?", Blair replied:

> I think that everyone shares a sense of reluctance to commit our forces. However, as my hon. Friend acknowledged, that reluctance is overcome

if circumstances dictate that it must be. We proposed committing ground troops to pursue a peace agreement. However, there is a difficulty with committing ground troops in order to fight our way in: no one should underestimate the sheer scale of what is involved in that action. We would be talking about 100,000 ground troops, and possibly even more.[68]

He subsequently confirmed that he did not, "accept that land troops are necessary to curb repression in Kosovo. Air strikes properly targeted – directed against the military capability of the oppressor – can achieve the objective that we set ourselves ... I believe that the action that we have proposed will be successful".[69] The reality, of course, was, as Donald Anderson pointed out, that "there is no consensus among our allies for ground troops to be committed to the quagmire and minefield of the Balkans".[70] Moreover, the idea that the bombing was solely affecting the "military capability of the oppressor" was misleading, it was also directed at dual-use targets such as electricity plants which also serviced hospitals and other civil facilities, and killed civilians. This naturally raised the question of double effect. However, if the purpose of the bombing was to create civilian misery so as to generate pressure on Milosevic to comply with the terms on offer at Rambouillet, then double effect could not apply because the effect was sought, and hence the bombing could not easily be reconciled with just war criteria.[71]

Nevertheless, the decision to undertake the bombing of Belgrade was widely regarded as a just one on the Labour benches, an appropriate response in a situation where the demands of positive and natural law clashed. It was seen, as the title of an article that appeared under Blair's name put it, as a case where "a new generation draws the line".[72] One important dimension of this was the shift, engendered by the experiences of Burundi and Rwanda as well as Bosnia, to a liberal cosmopolitanism which, for its adherents, involved re-casting the old just war conventions. For example, Anderson believed that the Kosovo air war was high risk but right and that:

the cause is just on humanitarian grounds. It is absolutely clear that the Government and our NATO allies had exhausted all other means. The action has limited aims and methods. International law has moved on from when we said that the integrity of sovereign states was sacrosanct. That disappeared, or was at least diminished, with the formulation of the universal declaration of human rights. The matter was taken further following the Helsinki process in 1975, and recently with the development of the doctrine – not obligation – of intervention due to an imminent or actual humanitarian catastrophe.[73]

Even so, there was a tension between the new language of liberal cosmopolitanism and the old emphasis on national interests, evident when Anderson immediately fell back on the latter when challenged as to why Britain was not already intervening in other humanitarian tragedies if this was the sole rationale for the Kosovo intervention:

> Of course there is morality in a humanitarian response. Of course we can be faulted for not intervening in other areas, such as Rwanda, where, between April and June 1994, 750,000 or 1 million people were massacred in a genocide. Perhaps we can be faulted for that, but, in the murky world of international relations, we must consider not only morality, but our interests. In this case, in our Europe, our interests are mightily involved because, as was said earlier, Hungary, which is now a member of NATO, borders Yugoslavia, and because we have the problem of more than a million refugees in our Europe already ... Therefore our interests are mightily involved. I believe that the combination of our interests and morality justifies the intervention.[74]

The cases of Bosnia and Kosovo had also created converts to the interventionist cause. Ken Livingstone, previously highly suspicious of any military intervention involving the US, was one who embraced this new liberal cosmopolitanism, drawing parallels not with Vietnam, as his colleagues on the Left did, but with the rise of Hitler:

> Hitler rose by exploiting fear of the Jews; Milosevic has risen exploiting fear of Muslims. We heard Hitler demand, 'All Germans within one state.' That is exactly the cry we hear now from Milosevic – 'Intervene in Slovenia, in Croatia, in Bosnia; seize the areas so that all Serbs come under one Serb nation.' Europe cannot be governed in that way. Nationalities are scattered across Europe, and there is no way to draw up ethnically pure communities.[75]

Nevertheless, there remained a small but hard core of anti-war rebels who retained a restrictionist approach to the war and therefore considered NATO's actions to represent a breach of the UN Charter and, moreover, an attack in which the target state was a member of the UN and so had a right to invoke Article 51 in defending itself. From within this group Tony Benn provided a classic expression of the restrictionist view of the war's legality:

> We have provided the KLA [Kosovo Liberation Army] with an air force and called it NATO. That is what it wanted all along. We are told that Kosovo is to be a protectorate. Has international law advanced to the point where, if we do not like a country we can take one of its provinces and call it a protectorate? ... This is a war of aggression, I regret to say, because the United Nations is the only body authorised to use force, but Britain and America will not go to the Security Council, because they are afraid that Russia would use its veto. Russia has a greater

geographical interest than we have. The Americans can hardly use the veto as an argument, as they have used 27 vetoes to protect Israel when the Security Council would have disciplined it for many breaches of resolutions, including when it invaded southern Lebanon.[76]

Additionally, Labour opponents voiced traditional concerns about the wisdom of intervening in a civil war, coupled with the prescient fear that the withdrawal of monitors from the ground and commencement of aerial bombing would only exacerbate the humanitarian crisis. For a number of MPs on the Left there was also a generational dimension to opposition to the war, based on Serbia's role in the Second World War. As Benn put it: "When the Serbs took on Hitler, Russia was neutral and America – the great America – had not come into the war because it had not yet been attacked at Pearl Harbour. The Serbs took on the Nazis and until the day that I die I shall be grateful for that".[77]

Key to the anti-war critique was the nature of the Rambouillet peace offer, which was seen more as an ultimatum than as a basis for genuine negotiation. "How would we feel", asked Alice Mahon:

> if events in Northern Ireland had escalated out of control and the rest of the world – some of whom thought that we were not doing too well there – had issued an ultimatum through a military alliance, telling us to accept an agreement because, if we did not accept their terms, Alder-shot would be bombed? We would be outraged and in uproar. We have to realise how Serbs think about their country.[78]

By April 1999, Blair's early assurances that a brief air war would be successful had been proved wrong. At the same time, the refugee crisis prompted by the bombing continued to get worse. Reportedly, at this time Blair confided to an aide that, "this could be the end for me", and that he was concerned that the bombing had created a "nightmare, creating human misery and death rather than saving life".[79] Under growing pressure there was a suspicion that Blair's war aims, clearly laid out and limited at the outset of the war, expanded as it dragged on to include the removal from power of Milosevic,[80] although Cook subsequently denied this.[81] However, it was clearly the assumption of a number of pro-war Labour MPs that Milosevic would not survive the war.[82] Moreover, the conduct of the war drew criticism that would carry over into its aftermath. In particular, the killing of around 70 refugees outside the town of Djakovica on 14th April when their convoy was destroyed by US military aircraft, drew fresh recruits to the anti-war ranks. Increasingly, Blair came to accept the need to plan for, or at least be able to credibly threaten, to introduce ground forces. It was in the context of the need to convince the US public of this necessity that Blair addressed the Economic Club of Chicago, offering the most comprehensive statement to date of his values-based humanitarian military interventionism, and leading to the articulation of his "five tests" (see p.10). However, he faced opposition within his own party, let alone in the US, to the idea that ground forces might be committed. Bob Wareing warned that:

> If, two months ago, my right hon. Friend the Foreign Secretary had asked me to recommend a way to bolster support for Milosevic inside Yugoslavia, I think that I would have said, 'Have you tried bombing Belgrade?' If, as a result, my right hon. Friend were to come to me and say, 'Thanks very much, it worked. What would you recommend now?', my response would be that he might consider putting in ground troops.[83]

However, by this time the anti-war Left's position was considerably weaker than it had once been. Indeed, at the end of the House of Commons debate on 19th April, just 11 Labour MPs, including Benn, Dalyell, Mahon, George Galloway, and Bob Marshall-Andrews, voted on the division to register their opposition to the war. Its weakness was a consequence of four factors in particular. First, there was the parliamentary arithmetic and the fact that, as Gerald Kaufman put it, "from 1997 to 2003 the Labour Party was basically quiescent, it would do anything that Tony Blair told it to do – not because it particularly liked Tony Blair, but because Tony Blair was a winner".[84] In this context the anti-war MPs were increasingly isolated. Second, while its key figures were largely the same, and largely drawn from the same generation, a number of previously supportive figures, such as Ken Livingstone, had by now accepted the logic of humanitarian military intervention and were supporting the war. Third, by 1999 there was a lessening of the traditional Cold War-era suspicion of US motives, with many of the 1997 Labour intake having no direct recollection of the interventions that had given rise to it. Finally, the dire warnings of anti-war MPs concerning the likely outcome of earlier wars they had opposed were by this point seen as having been ill-founded. As Dale Campbell-Savours put it:

> In my 20 years in the House, I have found that the same people oppose every war, and that they oppose each of them on the same basis. They opposed the war in the south Atlantic, which removed fascism from parts of South America. They opposed the war in Kuwait, which was about removing fascists from Kuwait. As a consequence of removing fascists from Kuwait, hundreds of thousands of lives have been saved in the Middle East ... When the public come to measure the issues of this war, I think that they should have in mind the fact that some hon. Members are simply opposed to war in all conditions, even if that war is about removing fascism. That is why the opponents of this war are, once again, just plain wrong.[85]

In the event, it was the prospect of facing significant numbers of ground troops – George Robertson had told his US counterpart that Britain was prepared to commit 50,000 – that convinced Milosevic to withdraw his forces from Kosovo, and Blair had played a key international role in arguing for this.[86] The Serb withdrawal occurred in June, and was followed by the passage of UNSC Resolution 1244, which authorised the deployment of NATO forces in Kosovo. The war had played a major role in shaping Blair's own thinking about humanitarian military intervention. In justification he drew regularly on analogies with the drift to war in Europe in the 1930s. Where the Conservative government had declined to intervene in Bosnia because of the complexity of the war, Blair increasingly saw war in moral, black and white terms.[87] Whereas David Owen, after three years of working towards an elusive peace in the Balkans, would counsel that where, "wars are in whole or in part civil wars, as is the case in the four wars fought so far in the former Yugoslavia, we delude ourselves if we think of the issues in simplistic terms, or portray the struggle as one between 'good guys' and 'bad guys'",[88] Blair argued that with regard to Kosovo: "This is no longer just a military conflict. It is a battle between good and evil; between civilization and barbarity; between democracy and dictatorship".[89]

This moral clarity, or simplicity, would be carried over into the politics of selling the 2003 war in Iraq. So too would the experience of facing down critics of the war when the going got tough, of having faith in his own moral judgements. But the war did not resolve the wider question of Kosovo's status and its viability as an independent state. It created an enormous refugee crisis – displacing some 200,000 within Kosovo and a further 850,000 beyond. Moreover, the war itself did not stop ethnic cleansing, indeed it acted as something of a spur to it and in its wake it ushered in reverse ethnic cleansing, raising key questions of whether responsibilities inherent in relation to *jus post bellum* were met, or even fully recognised.

8 New Labour goes to war (again)
Iraq 2002–03

The military intervention over Kosovo had been, in a sense, the logical culmination of the experience of the 1990s. As we have seen, the roots of the Kosovo War lay in the retrospective assessments of both Labour and Conservative politicians that military intervention should have come sooner in Bosnia.[1] Additionally, memories of the consequences of the failure to intervene to curb slaughter in Rwanda – what Paul Kennedy has termed, "the single worst decision the United Nations ever made", and the "lowest point in the UN's history" – remained fresh.[2] It was clearly possible to reconcile this humanitarian military interventionism with the Labour principles and traditions outlined in Chapter 1. After all, it was Clement Attlee, speaking at the launch of the UN General Assembly in 1946, who had told his audience that he was:

> glad that the Charter of the United Nations does not deal only with Governments and States or with politics and war, but with the simple elemental needs of human beings whatever be their race, their colour or their creed. In the Charter we reaffirm our faith in fundamental human rights. We see the freedom of the individual in the State as an essential complement to the freedom of the State in the world community of nations.[3]

However, it was just as possible to see the military intervention over Kosovo as representing a departure from the core element of the traditional Labour approach – its insistence on the centrality of the UN. While the shift over Kosovo proved controversial, it was not damagingly so. The Blair government's case for war in Iraq, however, was of a different order. This chapter begins by considering the influences that shaped Blair's interventionism and the factors that enabled it to prevail with regard to Iraq, before considering the 2002–03 case for war and the extent to which the principles Blair himself outlined as guiding interventionism were met.

The sources of Blair's military interventionism

A key factor enabling Blair to prevail over Iraq is to be found in the further development of a trend that predated his premiership – the presidentialisation of British politics. In effect, under Blair a Prime Minister's Department came to operate out of 10 Downing Street, staffed by unelected advisors, at times in apparent opposition to the departments of state. Its role and influence were most fully exposed to public scrutiny during the Hutton and Butler inquiries arising out of the suicide of MoD scientist and biological weapons expert Dr David Kelly and the failure to find weapons of mass destruction in post-war Iraq.[4] In the field of foreign policy Blair created his own prime ministerial diplomatic network, going further, in Anthony Sampson's words, "than any Prime Minister since Churchill in overriding and by-passing the advice of the Foreign Office".[5] A consequence of this presidentialism was to effectively downgrade the Cabinet as a decision-making body. Where the consent of particular ministers was required, it was sought in informal discussions away from the full Cabinet – Blair's so-called 'sofa diplomacy'. It is this alternative source of advice and bypassing of Cabinet government that Secretary of State for International Development Clare Short highlighted in her May 2003 resignation speech:

> In the second term, the problem is centralisation of power into the hands of the Prime Minister and an increasingly small number of advisers who make decisions in private without proper discussion. It is increasingly clear that the Cabinet has become ... a dignified part of the constitution, joining the Privy Council. There is no real collective, just diktats in favour of increasingly badly thought through policy initiatives that come from on high. The consequences of this are serious. Expertise in our system lies in departments. Those who dictate from the centre do not have full access to this expertise and they do not consult. This leads to bad policy ... Thus we have the powers of a presidential-type system with the automatic majority of a parliamentary system.[6]

David Owen's view is that:

> Blair is *sui generis*. All other Labour prime ministers have respected cabinet government and believed in it, and it was natural because they believed in collective arrangements – what is the Labour Party if it doesn't believe in collectivity! He doesn't believe in it. He has no understanding of what trade union negotiations are about. He wants to be President of the United Kingdom. He wanted the same machinery as Bush had and Clinton had.[7]

Blair's presidential position was further strengthened by a number of other factors, such as his large parliamentary majority,[8] his personal authority stemming from election victories in 1997 and 2001,[9] and by the absence of an effective Opposition. The Conservative Party rarely sought to create the kind of political space on key foreign policy issues of war and global order that would have allowed it scope to criticise the government, and remained incapacitated on questions relating to Europe. Moreover, Blair was less constrained by his own party than previous office-holders as a consequence of the decline in influence of Labour's National Executive Committee and the annual party conference. Finally, Neil Kinnock points to the fact that that:

> after the late 1990s the international part of Labour thinking had become reduced almost to nothing. This meant that if there was to be an argument in the wake, for example, of 9/11 it wasn't going to be conducted in very well-informed political terms, and the movement kept on being overtaken by events, and disagreement was only categorised as rebellion, not as a divergence that was based on rational consideration and open to persuasion.[10]

In explaining the rise of presidentialism, Philip Norton has identified two independent variables that make the "Blair presidency" more than simply a natural development from the Thatcher years. One of these is a lack of experience and understanding of government on the part of Blair and those around him. The second is the "particular attitude to power that shaped policy-making in Downing Street. The Labour leadership became so obsessed with power that having it became all consuming and forces that got in the way of achieving it were to be manipulated and marginalised". Norton is not alone in observing that the "attitude that brought Labour to power has been maintained in government".[11] The presidential impulse also helps explain Blair's increased interest in foreign policy during his second government. Foreign policy was an area where his expertise and exposure was severely limited prior to 1997, and about which he had shown scant interest as a backbencher. However, it was here that he found he could act with a freedom that his and Chancellor Gordon Brown's caution had made impossible in domestic policy. Spin doctor Lance Price noted in his diary as early as 1999 that: "There's a feeling about the place that TB is losing touch with ordinary people and what matters to them. He seems almost bored with the ordinary stuff and interested only in all the foreign leaders, Clinton, wars, etc".[12]

Ultimately, however, this presidentialism merely created the space within which Blair could act independently of a range of constraints. It does not of itself explain the alignment or interventionist impulse that arose out of it. Analysis of this must address the conundrum identified by McKibbin as to: "why a man usually so risk-averse was prepared to take so many risks with the unity of the Labour Party".[13] Blair's personal belief system is clearly important here.[14] There is no doubt that he is a conviction politician, in the mould of Margaret Thatcher (one of the first people he turned to for foreign policy advice following his 1997 election victory). Indeed, Roy Jenkins believed that, "far from lacking conviction, he almost has too much, particularly when dealing with the world beyond Britain".[15] This helps to explain the certainty with which Blair acted over Iraq. Additionally, Blair's religious faith seems to have played a role in reinforcing, or even driving, this conviction. Under Alistair Campbell's guidance, Blair consistently avoided questions about his faith. However, it is clearly deeply held. While preparing to record his eve-of-war address to the nation in 2003, Blair told his advisors, matter-of-factly, that he thought he would end the broadcast with the words 'God bless you', inducing a minor panic amongst those gathered. In a subsequent front-page *Times* piece, Blair announced that he was ready to "meet his Maker" and answer before God for "those who have died or have been horribly maimed as a result of my decisions".[16]

A further key influence lies in Blair and New Labour's attitude to the US. On coming to power in 1997, the links between the US Democrats and New Labour were strong. Labour opinion poll guru Philip Gould had advised Clinton during the latter part of the 1992 presidential campaign. After 1992 Clinton and his team provided something of a model for New Labour. Just three weeks into the New Labour government, journalist Larry Elliott was observing how: "Almost every idea floated since the election – operational independence for the Bank of England, a beefed-up Securities and Investment Board, Welfare to Work, hit-squads in schools, an elected mayor for London – has its origins on the other side of the Atlantic".[17] This admiration translated into a firm personal loyalty towards Clinton when the Lewinsky saga began to unravel, and into support for unilateral US foreign policy actions, even where independent commentators saw in these a diversionary tactic away from the gathering clouds of impeachment. The most notable of these was Blair's continued support in Parliament for the US cruise missile attack on the al-Shifa pharmaceutical plant in Sudan, an act he continued to defend long after US officials conceded that it had no chemical weapons function, as claimed at the time in justification of the attack.

A year after the events of 9/11, Tony Blair told the House of Commons that:

> I believed this before I became Prime Minister, but I believe it even more strongly – in fact, very strongly; it is an article of faith with me – that the American relationship and our ability to partner America in these difficult issues is of fundamental importance, not just to this country but to the wider world.[18]

Henry Kissinger once reflected that Edward Heath was the British politician, "least emotionally committed" to the US, one who "was content to enjoy no higher status in Washington than any other European leader" and indeed who, "came close to insisting on receiving no preferential treatment".[19] The contrast with Tony Blair could not be greater. The emotional attachment that a presidential-style conviction politician felt for the US drove British foreign policy in the post-9/11 period in a manner that finds its closest parallel in the Thatcher-Reagan special relationship, but which goes well beyond even this.

During the Clinton Administration, support for the enforcement of no-fly zones over northern and southern Iraq, support for the "near-war" of February 1998, and support for US strikes on Baghdad that coincided with the congressional impeachment process, were all features of Blair's foreign policy. As early as February 1998 Blair was writing of his conviction that Saddam Hussein possessed chemical and biological weapons, warning that, "our patience is not unlimited" and that "we" – by which he meant the US and Britain – "will not allow him to continue to defy the United Nations and international law".[20] Hence, Blair's support of US policy towards Iraq has been consistent, and has transferred seamlessly across two very different administrations.

The ease of this transfer, and the changed disposition towards the UN that it ultimately entailed, beg the question of the weight that should be attached to values in explaining Blair's approach to the special relationship and the question of war. Clearly, Blair did outline a values-based approach to military intervention in his 1999 Chicago Speech, but equally electoral considerations have tended to be accorded a high priority in the New Labour approach to statecraft. Hence the role played by Philip Gould's focus groups in defining what key groups of voters think in order that New Labour may, by an act of Gouldean alchemy, transform these into centre-pieces of the New Labour programme. In this respect Hugh Dalton's observation that Gaitskell thought, "too little of the Party and too much, relatively, of the general body of the electorate"[21] is one that could also be applied to Blair. In the summer of 2000 spiriting rummaging through Gould's dustbins recovered a number of memos written by Gould and Blair offering an insight into their thinking on what focus groups suggested New Labour needed to deliver, and revealing Blair's preoccupation with being seen to be strong on defence and foreign policy issues, and his belief that Labour had still not fully overcome the legacy of its 1983 defence policy. In one memo Blair is seen worrying about a range of issues where, he felt, New Labour was perceived to be weak:

> asylum and crime, where we are perceived as soft; and asserting the nation's interests where, because of the unpopularity of Europe, a constant barrage of small stories beginning to add up on defence and even issues like Zimbabwe, we are seen as insufficiently assertive ... We are in fact, taking very tough measures on asylum and crime, Kosovo should have laid to rest any doubts about our strength in defence.

Still, he worried about seeming "out of touch" and warned Gould that "On defence, we need to make the CSR [comprehensive spending review] work for defence. Big cuts and you can forget any hope of winning back ground on 'standing up for Britain'".[22]

It is hard to imagine that such considerations played no role in the process by which "strong on defence" became a central tenet of New Labour.

Blair's activist foreign policy, visibly supporting US objectives, delivered on "strength in defence", and provided clear evidence of "standing up for Britain". Moreover, Blair seemed to enjoy the role. With regard to his first experience of military conflict after becoming Prime Minister, the December 1998 US-UK air strikes on Iraq, Downing Street spin doctor Lance Price noted in his diary that he,

> couldn't help feeling TB was relishing his first blooding as PM, sending the boys into action. Despite all the necessary stuff about taking action 'with a heavy heart', I think he feels it is part of his coming of age as a leader.[23]

Already, one Cabinet member was explaining that, "supporting the Americans is part of Tony's DNA".[24]

This is not to suggest that values were of only marginal importance. From the time of the Kosovo War Blair regularly spoke of the values that shaped his approach to foreign policy and questions of war and peace. However, this appeal to values was very much a product of the experience of Kosovo, and is otherwise difficult to reconcile with his earlier unease at Foreign Secretary Robin Cook's "ethical" foreign policy. Indeed, if the parliamentary arithmetic had been different following the 1997 general election Blair may well have offered Liberal leader Paddy Ashdown the post of Foreign Secretary as the price of bringing his party into a coalition government. Moreover, Cook was not long in post before Blair wanted to replace him with Jack Straw by nominating Cook as the next NATO Secretary-General.[25] Emblematic of this unease was Blair's insistence on the continued supply of Hawk fighter aircraft to Indonesia, despite the fact that it was still in illegal occupation of East Timor at the time, and where it had killed an estimated 200,000 East Timorese since its 1975 invasion.[26]

Nevertheless, in his 1999 Doctrine of the International Community speech, Blair had set out a values-based foreign policy, based upon respect for human rights and international law but, crucially, one that carried with it the conviction that fighting for human rights could involve violating the sovereignty of states. "This is a just war", he had explained with reference to Kosovo, "based not on any territorial ambitions but on values".[27] As noted in Chapter 1, Blair set out five major considerations that should guide decisions about humanitarian military intervention (are we sure of our case? have we exhausted all diplomatic options?, are there military operations we can sensibly and prudently undertake? are we prepared for the long term? do we have national interests involved?). These criteria, taken together, represented an appropriately stiff and comprehensive test by which to measure a case for intervention, embracing considerations of last resort, certainty, prudence and *post ad bellum* commitment, and as such were consistent with the Labour tradition. With regard to Iraq, however, Blair failed to satisfy at least the first four of these criteria.

Choosing war

The immediate origins of the decision to overthrow Saddam Hussein lay in Washington, DC. While the rationales were capable of shifting – from Iraqi involvement in the 9/11 attacks, to the threat posed by his known possession of WMD, to liberating the Iraqi people from his tyranny – the determination was a constant. From the beginning of his administration, President George W. Bush was predisposed towards deposing Saddam Hussein. Terrorism expert Richard Clarke has claimed that the Bush Administration entered office "with Iraq on its agenda", and that Bush and his inner circle, a number of whom had advocated the removal of Saddam during the Clinton Administration, "must have known there was no 'imminent threat' to the US", despite their clear public message to the contrary.[28] The attacks of 9/11 made this desire more immediate. That very afternoon Defense Secretary Donald Rumsfeld told General Richard Myers to find; "[b]est info fast … judge whether good enough to hit S.H. @ same time – not only U.B.L.".[29] In the immediate aftermath Bush asked Richard Clarke three times to find a link between Saddam and the 9/11 attacks, even though Clarke told him that the intelligence community thought that al Qaeda was behind them.[30] Shortly after the attacks the Defense Department was ordered to examine the possibility of a military confrontation with Iraq.[31]

In the wake of the attacks Tony Blair visited Washington, where he was made aware of the current within the Bush Administration in favour of extending the "war on terror" to Iraq once operations in Afghanistan were complete. As British Ambassador to Washington Christopher Meyer recalled:

> Rumours were already flying that Bush would use 9/11 as a pretext to attack Iraq. On the one hand, Blair came with a very strong message – don't get distracted; the priorities were al-Qaeda, Afghanistan, the Taliban. Bush said, 'I agree with you, Tony. We must deal with this first. But when we have dealt with Afghanistan, we must come back to Iraq.'

This US commitment to removing Saddam was signalled publicly in President Bush's 29th January 2002 State of the Union address, in which he announced the existence of an "axis of evil" involving Iraq, Iran and North Korea. Hence, the Bush Administration's campaign to prepare its citizens for war in Iraq was launched well in advance of any comparable preparation of the UK electorate. "What we have found in Afghanistan", Bush explained,

> confirms that, far from ending there, our war against terror is only beginning … I will not wait on events, while dangers gather. I will not stand by as peril draws closer. The United States of America will not permit the world's most dangerous regimes to threaten us with the world's most destructive weapons.[32]

Two months later, in March 2002, Blair undertook a visit to Bush in Texas, at which his initial commitment to support the US approach to Iraq was reportedly extended. Given this, it is worth considering the state of the government's understanding of the situation in Iraq and options available at this time. As the July 2004 Butler Report shows, two options were considered to exist for achieving Iraqi disarmament: a strengthening of containment and enforced regime change. Ministers were informed that, "regime change of itself had no basis in international law; and that any offensive military action against Iraq could only be justified if Iraq were to be held in breach of its disarmament obligations".[33] They were also told that for the entire UN Security Council to take this view, "proof would need to be incontrovertible and of large-scale activity".[34] Hence, Ministers knew in March 2002 that the justification for regime change had to lie in the threat posed by an active and imminently deliverable Iraqi weapons programme. However, they were also told that "current intelligence is insufficiently robust to meet this criterion", and hence there was no legal justification for an invasion.[35] Furthermore, the best advice available to the British government was that containment was essentially working, that the Iraqi nuclear programme was effectively frozen, and that while there were indications of a continuation of chemical and biological weapons programmes, the circumstances in which Saddam could use WMD were restricted to those where his regime was threatened. At the same time, though, ministers were also informed that the US had lost confidence in containment and that the Bush Administration believed that the legal basis for an attack already existed.

In light of this assessment, it is worth reflecting on the nature of contemporaneous Cabinet discussion of Iraq. On 7th March what Robin Cook described as, "the last meeting of the Cabinet at which a large number of ministers spoke up against the war",[36] took place. Cook noted in his diary:

> I am told, not that I have witnessed it, that in the old days Prime Ministers would sum up the balance of view in the discussion. This would be simple in the present case as all contributions pointed in one direction. However, Tony does not regard the Cabinet as a place for decisions. Normally he avoids having discussions in Cabinet until decisions are taken and announced to it. Tony appeared totally unfazed that on this occasion the balance of discussion pointed strongly in the reverse direction of his intentions. Rather than attempt to sum up the discussion of this supreme body of collective government, he responded as if he was replying to a question and answer session from a party branch ... 'I tell you that we must steer close to America. If we don't we will lose our influence to shape what they do. That is understood in Europe. I have spoken to both Jospin and Schroder, and they both understand that we cannot oppose the Americans.'[37]

This portrait is consistent with Clare Short's recollection of the nature of Cabinet discussions on Iraq, wherein the Prime Minister:

raised Iraq after the summer recess of 2002 at every cabinet meeting. He would start by saying a few words, inviting [Foreign Secretary] Jack Straw or [Defence Secretary] Geoff Hoon to speak and then intervening repeatedly to inform the Cabinet of developments. Their advice was never sought. They were kept informed and most were willing to go along with the Prime Minister but there was no collective decision which was thrashed out in honest debate and to which the Cabinet then adhered.[38]

The publication of former Home Secretary David Blunkett's diaries confirms the picture provided by Cook and Short.[39] In February 2002 Blunkett (at the time Home Secretary) felt he had "blotted his copybook" simply by raising Iraq as a subject. At a Cabinet meeting a month later, he described Straw and Hoon as having, "clearly got the message to be gung ho" although everyone else was, "drawing the conclusion that we needed to go into depth with this". "Look", Blair reassured the Cabinet, "the management hasn't lost its marbles. We do know these things. We are not going to rush in". As Blunkett observed, the fear was precisely that they would. By March 2003, it seems from Blunkett's account that the Cabinet saw its role as being to support Blair uncritically, and that those who did not had "burnt their boats". Even though Britain was on the verge of engaging in its most divisive war since Suez against the prospect of which millions had marched in protest, Blunkett felt that: "It was important to be really supportive of Tony at Cabinet, and when I saw him privately afterwards he was very grateful".[40]

On Cabinet government during this period, the 2004 Butler Report concluded:

> Without papers circulated in advance, it remains possible but is obviously much more difficult for members of the Cabinet outside the small circle directly involved to bring their political judgement and experience to bear on the major decisions for which the Cabinet as a whole must carry responsibility. The absence of papers on the Cabinet agenda so that Ministers could obtain briefings in advance from the Cabinet Office, their own departments or from the intelligence agencies plainly reduced their ability to prepare properly for such discussions, while the changes to key posts at the head of the Cabinet Secretariat lessened the support of the machinery of government for the collective responsibility of the Cabinet in the vital matter of war and peace.[41]

Hence, the drift to war with Iraq during 2002–03 represents a collective failure of Cabinet, arguably, alongside the Conservative Cabinet's failure to check Eden over the Suez collusion, the gravest of the modern era.[42] As Peter Hennessy has observed; "if the full Cabinet will not take on a dominant Prime Minister in full cry – even in the last days before hostilities begin – there is no other part of the system of government that can compensate for such supineness".[43]

A week after the 7th March Cabinet meeting described by Cook, and following a trip to London by US Vice-President Dick Cheney, Blair dispatched his foreign policy adviser David Manning to Washington, in advance of his own visit to meet with Bush in Texas. Manning's report on a dinner with Bush's National Security Advisor, Condoleezza Rice, clearly suggests that Blair had already, by mid-March 2002, offered his government's support to the Bush Administration in its regime change strategy, even though his own Cabinet knew nothing of this:

> We spent a long time at dinner on Iraq. It is clear that Bush is grateful for your support and has registered that you are getting flak. I said that you would not budge in your support for regime change but you had to manage a press, a Parliament and a public opinion that was very different than anything in the States. And you would not budge on your insistence that, if we pursued regime change, it must be very carefully done and produce the right result. Failure was not an option. Condi's enthusiasm for regime change is undimmed. But there were some signs, since we last spoke, of greater awareness of the practical difficulties and political risks.[44]

Three days later, on 17th March, US Deputy Secretary of Defense Paul Wolfowitz lunched with British Ambassador Christopher Meyer at the British Embassy in Washington. As he reported back to Manning, Meyer reinforced Blair's support for regime change in advance of the Texas visit. "I opened by sticking very closely to the script that you used with Condi Rice", Meyer reported: "We backed regime change, but the plan had to be clever and failure was not an option. It would be a tough sell for us domestically and probably tougher elsewhere in Europe".[45]

Outside Downing Street and the British Embassy, however, there were clear concerns about the manner in which Blair was aligning Britain so closely to the Bush Administration over Iraq from within the Labour Party, Blair's own Cabinet (where, in addition to those voiced by Cook, Short, and Blunkett, Secretary of State for Trade and Industry Patricia Hewitt also voiced concerns), and the Foreign Office. From there, on 2nd March, Straw's policy director, Peter Ricketts, summarised his concerns. The first lay in the nature of the threat posed by Iraq. "The truth", explained Ricketts, "is that what has changed is not the pace of Saddam Hussein's WMD programmes, but our tolerance of them post-11 September".[46] Already the government was working on what would emerge, in an attempt to convince British public opinion of the necessity of war, as the September Downing Street dossier, but Ricketts warned Straw that more work was needed on it, and that, "even the best survey of Iraq's WMD programmes will not show much advance in recent years on the nuclear, missile or CW/BW fronts".[47] Getting public opinion to accept the imminence of the threat from Iraq would be problematic, especially given that other proliferators, such as Iran, were thought to be closer to achieving a nuclear capability.

Straw summarised these concerns in a memo sent to Blair less than two weeks before his visit to the US, clearly warning that he risked splitting the PLP if he supported the Bush Administration's policy of regime change:

> The rewards from your visit to Crawford will be few. The risks are high, both for you and for the Government. I judge that there is at present no majority inside the PLP for any military action against Iraq, (alongside a greater readiness in the PLP to surface their concerns). Colleagues know that Saddam and the Iraqi regime are bad. Making that case is easy. But we have a long way to go to convince them as to:
>
> (a) the scale of the threat from Iraq and why this has got worse recently;
> (b) what distinguishes the Iraqi threat from that of eg Iran and North Korea so as to justify military action;
> (c) the justification for any military action in terms of international law; and
> (d) whether the consequence of military action really would be a compliant, law abiding replacement government.[48]

Straw confirmed that from intelligence to date it was, "hard to glean whether the threat from Iraq is so significantly different from that of Iran and North Korea as to justify military action", and pointed to the Foreign Office view that if the 9/11 attacks had not occurred it was doubtful whether the US would be considering an attack on Iraq. After all, the threat from Iraq had not worsened as a result of 9/11, and there was no link between Osama bin Laden and Iraq, although members of the Bush Administration were still alluding to one. Straw then turned to the tactical approach that would have to be adopted, in light of the situation he had outlined, in order to keep PLP and public opinion on side:

> I know there are those who say that an attack on Iraq would be justified whether or not weapons inspectors were readmitted. But I believe that a demand for the unfettered readmission of weapons inspectors is essential, in terms of public explanation, and in terms of legal sanction for any subsequent military action.
>
> Legally there are two potential elephant traps:
>
> (i) regime change per se is no justification for military action; it could form part of the method of any strategy, but not a goal. Of course, we may want credibly to assert that regime change is an essential part of the strategy by which we have to achieve our ends – that of the elimination of Iraq's WMD capacity: but the latter has to be the goal;
> (ii) on whether any military action would require a fresh UNSC mandate (Desert Fox did not). The US are likely to oppose any idea of a fresh mandate. On the other side, the weight of legal advice here is

that a fresh mandate may well be required. There is no doubt that a new UNSCR would transform the climate in the PLP. Whilst that (a new mandate) is very unlikely, given the US's position, a draft resolution against military action with 13 in favour (or handsitting) and two vetoes against could play very badly here.[49]

This was the background to Blair's 5th – 7th April visit to Bush in Crawford, Texas. It is at this meeting that a number of commentators locate Blair's commitment to participate in enforced regime change in Iraq,[50] despite the advice and intelligence picture presented prior to his departure for the US. It is, then, no coincidence that, from the time of the Crawford meeting, the frequency of Blair's references to the threat posed by Iraq increased and the language used became more emphatic – more so than the intelligence warranted. Moreover, at the same time Blair continued to insist in public that no decisions had been taken on Iraq.

Whilst in Texas, Blair delivered a major foreign policy speech at the George Bush Senior Presidential Library, an update and something of a revision of his 1999 Chicago speech. Now the values he articulated in 1999 were joined by reference to the national interest, marking a move away from his earlier "Third Way"-informed rhetoric, rooted in the work of Anthony Giddens. By April 2002 this was unavoidable. For Giddens, conflicts between states were supposed to be a thing of the past; the post-Cold War liberal democratic state was, he said, "the state without enemies".[51] The problem for Giddens and the Third Way was that the US kept defining new enemies – first as Clinton National Security Adviser Anthony Lake's "Backlash States" and, by the time Blair spoke in Texas, by Bush as the "axis of evil". Consequently, while he still dipped into the vocabulary of the Third Way, national interests clearly had to assume a more prominent place in Blair's foreign policy vision, making it rather less coherent than the one he had offered in Chicago. Alongside values, Blair now revealed:

> we need a hard headed pragmatism – a realpolitik – required to give us any chance of translating those values into the practical world we live in ... I advocate an enlightened self interest that puts fighting for our values right at the heart of the policies necessary to protect our nations. Engagement in the world on the basis of these values, not isolationism from it is the hard-headed pragmatism for the 21st Century.[52]

He ended his speech by making a public commitment that was unnecessary and imprudent, as it tied his government to a course of action from which it could not easily disentangle itself thereafter:

> we don't shirk our responsibility. It means that when America is fighting for those values, then, however tough, we fight with her. No grandstanding, no offering implausible but impractical advice from the comfort of the

touchline, no wishing away the hard not the easy choices on terrorism and WMD, or making peace in the Middle East, but working together, side by side. That is the only route I know to a stable world based on prosperity and justice for all, where freedom liberates the lives of every citizen in every corner of the globe. If the world makes the right choices now – at this time of destiny – we will get there. And Britain will be at America's side in doing it.[53]

Hence, by mid-April 2002 Blair had committed his government to support the US both in secret and in public. The weakness of the case against Iraq was no barrier, but it was something of which Blair had been made aware. On 23rd July Blair met with senior Cabinet colleagues and senior officials to discuss Iraq. Here, Sir Richard Dearlove, head of MI6, reported on his recent discussions in Washington, where:

> There was a perceptible shift in attitude. Military action was now seen as inevitable. Bush wanted to remove Saddam, through military action, justified by the conjunction of terrorism and WMD. But the intelligence and facts were being fixed around the policy. The NSC had no patience with the UN route, and no enthusiasm for publishing material on the Iraqi regime's record. There was little discussion in Washington of the aftermath after military action.[54]

Defence Secretary Hoon told the meeting that the US had already begun "spikes of activity" and that the most likely time for US military action to begin was during January 2003. Straw agreed that it, "seemed clear that Bush had made up his mind to take military action", but again warned that, "the case was thin. Saddam was not threatening his neighbours, and his WMD capability was less than that of Libya, North Korea or Iran".[55] Straw also conveyed his department's advice that it would be prudent to insist that Iraq allow weapons inspectors to re-enter the country, not so as to eliminate any WMD uncovered or enable them to declare that Iraq possessed none (post-9/11, any solution that left Saddam in power was clearly unacceptable, as Blair would tell the meeting "regime change and WMD were linked in the sense that it was the regime that was producing the WMD"[56]), but because this, "would also help with the legal justification for the use of force".[57]

This was especially important because, as the Attorney-General, Lord Goldsmith, told the meeting, "the desire for regime change was not a legal base for military action". There were only three possible legal bases for an attack on Iraq – self-defence, humanitarian intervention, or UNSC authorisation based on Iraqi non-compliance with UNSC resolutions. The first two could not apply, so the only route that could confer legality on an attack involved Iraq's continued breach of UNSC resolutions. Moreover, he warned, relying for authority on UNSC resolutions passed years earlier "would be difficult".

The questions about the case and the qualified intelligence concerning the threat posed by Iraq were of less importance to Blair than being seen to perform the role of key US ally. When he flew to Camp David to meet Bush in early September 2002, according to Bob Woodward's account:

> Bush looked Blair in the eye. 'Saddam Hussein is a threat. And we must work together to deal with this threat, and the world will be better off without him.' Bush recalled that he was 'probing' and 'pushing' the Prime Minister. He said it might require – would probably entail – war. Blair might have to send British troops. 'I'm with you,' the Prime Minister replied, looking Bush back in the eye, pledging flat out to commit British military forces if necessary, the critical promise Bush had been seeking.[58]

The need to prepare the British public for the coming war led to the September 2002 publication of the Downing Street dossier, offering Downing Street's presentation of the Iraqi threat based on intelligence provided via the Joint Intelligence Committee (JIC).[59] While the public was being prepared, most of Blair's Cabinet remained in the dark about his plans. Clare Short's diary entry for 9th September recorded that: "TB gave me assurances when I asked for Iraq to be discussed at Cabinet that no decision made and not imminent".[60] However, later that day she learnt from Chancellor Gordon Brown that Blair had requested that 20,000 British troops be made available for Gulf deployment. Another Cabinet member in the dark and in need of convincing was Leader of the House and former Foreign Secretary Robin Cook. Shortly before the September dossier was published, he noted in his diary that Blair:

> attaches great importance to the forthcoming dossier ... He is particularly enthusiastic about a report they have that at a cabinet meeting Saddam has said that Iraq must get nuclear weapons to pose a threat to the West. Tony then added, 'Given the poor state of his conventional forces, it is not surprising that he wants to get his hands on nuclear weapons.' This is a curious aside. If Tony himself recognizes that Saddam's conventional forces are much weaker than they were before, it is going to be difficult for him to be convincing that Saddam is now a greater threat to his region. And in any case there is no evidence that he has got any nuclear weapons with which to threaten us.[61]

By then it was clear to Cook that Blair intended to support a US war to overthrow Saddam. Of a Cabinet meeting of 23rd September, he recorded how:

> Only Clare [Short] and I openly questioned the wisdom of military action. Clare set out a solid philosophical objection grounded in the Catholic doctrine of a Just War, and concluded that this would be an unjust one.

I said that for me the most difficult question was 'Why now?'. What has happened in the past year to make Saddam more of an imminent danger than he has been any year in the past decade? . . . There is no answer to the question 'Why now?'. Geoff Hoon made an attempt to respond to me but his answer only served to confirm the difficulty of the question. 'The key issue in answering the question 'Why now?' is September 11th,' he said. The problem with this, of course, is that no one has a shred of evidence that Saddam was involved in September 11th.[62]

Given the Labour Party's traditional insistence on the use of force only as a last resort, what Neil Kinnock termed its "retained reservation" over the use of force, and its commitment to the centrality of the UN in conflict resolution, Blair was always going to struggle to keep the PLP onside during the period that military forces were being deployed to the Gulf. This he clearly understood. Hence, as military preparations continued apace, a last minute passage was inserted into his address to the October 2002 Labour Party Conference that held out the promise of an initiative to require Israel to comply with the UNSC resolutions it had flouted since 1967, and in short time. This was clearly an insertion aimed at his own party as much as at Israel. None of his Cabinet, including his Foreign Secretary, were aware of his intention to introduce this commitment, and neither was the Foreign Office, hence no plan existed.[63] As Clare Short has noted, it was irresponsible to introduce such a commitment in this way without there being any substance to it or preparation for it.[64]

To help maximise his prospects of carrying the Labour Party with him, Blair had prevailed on the Bush Administration to pursue a UN route. Following this route would bestow a degree of legality on the coming war and so maximise international support for it. On 8th November the UNSC passed Resolution 1441. This declared that Iraq remained in breach of UNSC Resolution 687 of 1991, required Iraq to submit a "full and complete" declaration of its WMD and related programmes within 30 days, and provided for the re-entry of weapons inspectors. However, the Resolution was clearly a compromise, and consequently potentially contradictory. On the one hand, Iraqi obstruction or failure to comply would lead to an immediate convening of the UNSC which would, "consider the situation and the need for full compliance with all of the relevant Council resolutions in order to secure international peace and security", a response short of an immediate recourse to war. Hence, Resolution 1441 could clearly be interpreted as implying that a further resolution would be required, giving specific authorisation, before any military action could commence. On the other hand, Resolution 1441 recalled that, "the Council has repeatedly warned Iraq that it will face serious consequences as a result of its continued violations of its obligations", offering scope for argument that "serious consequences" extended to war. Nevertheless, at the time British ambassador to the UN Sir Jeremy Greenstock made it clear that: "There is no 'automaticity' in this

Resolution. If there is a further Iraqi breach of its disarmament obligations, the matter will return to the Council for discussion as required ... We would expect the Security Council then to meet its responsibilities".[65]

From here the die was cast and, in retrospect, it is impossible to see how Iraq could have done anything to avoid war, given that US and British intelligence were by now crediting Iraq with especial expertise in WMD concealment. Indeed, on this basis, in December Jack Straw went so far as to suggest that Iraq's weapons inventory probably included nuclear weapons, obliging the Foreign Office to issue a retraction.[66] However, this mindset helps explain Straw's swift rejection of Iraq's declaration on its WMD as required under UNSC Resolution 1441, despite the fact that it was 12,000 pages long and weighed around 10 stone. "We have not completed a full analysis of the Iraqi declaration", Straw explained:

> but it is clear, even on a preliminary assessment, that this is not the full and complete declaration requested in resolution 1441 ... It seems that Saddam Hussein has decided to continue the pretence that Iraq has had no WMD programme since UNSCOM left in 1998. This will fool nobody. If Saddam persists in this obvious falsehood, it will become clear that he has rejected the pathway to peace laid down in resolution 1441.[67]

The degree of PLP opposition to the drift to war was made clear in three highly charged parliamentary debates. The first of these, on 25th November 2002, took place on a motion of support for UNSC Resolution 1441, on the basis that Labour MPs would find it difficult to vote against a resolution affirming support for the UN. Nevertheless, 85, mainly Labour MPs voted for an amendment that opposed any war with Iraq without a further UNSC resolution and a vote in favour in the House of Commons based on a substantive motion. A further debate on 26th February was more highly charged still, given the ongoing failure to secure a further resolution, and was again framed around a motion of support for the UN. Straw opened the debate by telling MPs that, "No decision to deploy British forces in action has yet been taken",[68] while Gavin Strang offered a classic expression of the traditional Labour approach in arguing that:

> We can all agree that the most desirable outcome is full Iraqi co-operation with weapons inspectors and the peaceful dismantling of Iraq's weapons of mass destruction. That would be a victory for the United Nations and for the stance taken by the United States and our Prime Minister. A second scenario is military action that is not endorsed by the United Nations. Some may say that resolution 1441 gives authority for military action, and if Iraq is in breach, any resulting military action can be described as being authorised by the UN. However, France, China and Russia made it clear when that resolution was passed that they did not consider their support for the resolution as constituting endorsement of

future military action. Given the views of those three states, the real-politik is that an attack on Iraq will be seen by the world as authorised by the international community only if it is backed by a further resolution from the United Nations. If military action is clearly endorsed by the UN, I imagine that most Labour Members will go along with it. While many people worldwide would resent the attack, explicit authorisation by the UN would reduce the scale of opposition … A second resolution would demonstrate unequivocally to Iraq and the wider world that any military action was based on international agreement and was properly authorised by the only institution in the world that has the authority to do so: the United Nations.[69]

At the end of the debate an amendment arguing that the case for war remained "unproven" was defeated by 393 votes to 199, with a record 121 Labour MPs voting for the rebel amendment, a demonstration of the incomparability of the Kosovo and Iraq situations for many Labour MPs.[70] By the time of the final, eve-of-war, debate, Blair had been forced to abandon the diplomatic effort to secure the further UNSC resolution that would specifically authorise war against Iraq. The Blair government subsequently insisted that French President Jacques Chirac had undertaken to veto any further resolution that would have the effect of leading to war with Iraq, although this mis-represented Chirac's position, which was, in effect, that by early 2003 last resort had not been reached.[71] This erroneous characterisation gave rise to the spurious concept of the "unreasonable veto".[72] Hence, when the House of Commons debated Iraq again on 18th March Blair knew that war was imminent and that there would be no further UNSC resolution. Because of this, Blair lost a senior, albeit sidelined, member of the Cabinet, when Robin Cook resigned, explaining to the House of Commons that he could not, "support a war without international agreement or domestic support". Although he had supported military action outside the UN framework over Kosovo, for Cook that war had been legitimate because of the immediacy of the humanitarian crisis and because of the near-unanimous support within NATO. Over Iraq, there was no comparable consensus in any body that could lay claim to legitimate authority, reflecting the absence of agreement over whether last resort had been reached. As Cook explained in his resignation speech:

It is not France alone that wants more time for inspections. Germany wants more time for inspections; Russia wants more time for inspections; indeed, at no time have we signed up even the minimum necessary to carry a second resolution. We delude ourselves if we think that the degree of international hostility is all the result of President Chirac. The reality is that Britain is being asked to embark on a war without agreement in any of the international bodies of which we are a leading partner – not NATO, not the European Union and, now, not the Security Council.[73]

Nevertheless, the Blair government had conceded Parliament something that had been a demand of the Left with regard to war for many years – a vote on a substantive motion in advance of the outbreak of hostilities. This was a significant concession, because if the government had lost the vote there would have been little option but for Blair to resign. In the event, the 18th March vote saw greater opposition than in the earlier February vote, with a record 139 Labour MPs voting for an amendment stating that the case for war had still to be established constituting, according to Philip Cowley, the largest rebellion by government backbenchers in 150 years.[74] Just over 24 hours later the attack on Baghdad began.

Conclusion

In giving evidence to the Hutton Inquiry into the death of Dr David Kelly, Tony Blair had explained the case for war in Iraq in terms of the strength of intelligence on Iraqi WMD:

> What changed was really two things which came together. First of all, there was a tremendous amount of information and evidence coming across my desk as to the weapons of mass destruction and the programmes associated with it that Saddam had ... There was also a renewed sense of urgency, again, in the way that this was being publicly debated ... Why did we say it was a big problem? Because of the intelligence. And the people were naturally saying: produce that intelligence then ... So, in a sense, the 24 September dossier was an unusual – the whole business was unusual, but it was in response to an unusual set of circumstances. We were saying this issue had to be returned to by the international community and dealt with. Why were we saying this? Because of the intelligence.[1]

Unlike Hutton, however, the Butler Inquiry team that came afterwards had access to the raw intelligence on Iraqi WMD on which Blair had based his public case for war. On the basis of an analysis of this intelligence the Butler Report concluded that: "The Government's conclusion in the spring of 2002 that stronger action (although not necessarily military action) needed to be taken to enforce Iraqi disarmament was not based on any new development in the current intelligence picture on Iraq".[2] In his evidence to the Butler Inquiry, Blair "endorsed the view expressed at the time" that "what had changed was not the pace of Iraq's prohibited weapons programmes ... but tolerance of them following the attacks of 11 September 2001".[3] In other words, his answers to the Hutton Inquiry could be considered misleading. However, the Butler Inquiry's access to intelligence documents meant that Blair had little option but to retreat from his earlier emphasis on the intelligence picture. Damningly, the Butler Inquiry concluded that, "there was no recent intelligence that would itself have given rise to a conclusion that Iraq was of more immediate concern than the activities of some other countries".[4] However, in the early part of 2002, in the Foreword to the September 2002 dossier, and in presentations to Parliament as he moved the country closer to war, the intelligence, which his audience could not access for themselves, was used by Blair to justify the urgency of the case for war.

Not surprisingly, given the conclusions of the Butler Report, there is considerable evidence of Blair exaggerating the threat represented by Iraq as he made the public case for war. Moreover, the certainty with which he spoke was not reflected in the intelligence. To take just one example, on 3rd April 2002, Blair had told NBC news:

> We know that he [Saddam Hussein] has stockpiles of major amounts of chemical and biological weapons, we know that he is trying to acquire nuclear capability, we know that he is trying to develop ballistic missile capability of a greater range.[5]

However, the then most recent JIC assessment – dated 15th March – recorded that:

> Intelligence on Iraq's weapons of mass destruction (WMD) and ballistic missile programmes is sporadic and patchy ... From the evidence available to us, we believe Iraq retains some production equipment and some small stocks of CW agent precursors, and may have hidden small quantities of agents and weapons ... There is no intelligence on any BW agent production facilities but one source indicates that Iraq may have developed mobile production facilities.[6]

It would appear, as Robin Cook argued, that, "Downing Street did not worry that the intelligence was thin and inferential or that the sources were second-hand and unreliable, because intelligence did not play a big part in the real reason why we went to war".[7]

In responding to the publication of the Butler Report, Blair shifted his ground, arguing that:

> There was no conspiracy. There was no impropriety. The essential judgement and truth, as usual, does not lie in extremes. We all of us acknowledge that Saddam was evil and his regime depraved. Whether or not actual stockpiles of weapons are found, there was not and is not any doubt that Saddam used weapons of mass destruction and retained every strategic intent to carry on developing them. The judgment is this: would it have been better or more practical to have contained him through continuing sanctions and weapons inspections, or was this inevitably going to be, at some point, a policy that failed; and was removing Saddam a diversion from pursuing the global terrorist threat or part of it?[8]

The Butler Report also revealed that it was the Prime Minister himself who provided the assurances that the Attorney General, Lord Goldsmith, an expert in commercial rather than international law, required before finally judging that in the absence of specific UNSC authorisation the war was a legal one. Moreover, in a further indication of the collective failure of the Cabinet in this case, it transpired that the request for this legal opinion did not emanate from any of its members, but from the Chief of the General Staff, General Sir Michael Jackson, on the basis that he had, "spent a good deal of time recently in the Balkans making sure that Milosevic was put behind bars" and had "no intention of ending up in the next cell to him in the Hague".[9] As noted in Chapter 8, prior to the passage of UNSC Resolution 1441 the Attorney General's advice to the government had been that, "there would be no justification for the use of force against Iraq on grounds of self-defence against an imminent threat".[10] In a 7th March 2003 formal minute to the Prime Minister (not circulated to the Cabinet), the Attorney General set out his view on the legality of war. The Butler Report notes that this required the Prime Minister:

> in the absence of a further United Nations Security Council resolution, to be satisfied that there were strong factual grounds for concluding that Iraq had failed to take the final opportunity to comply with its disarmament obligations under relevant resolutions of the Security Council and that it was possible to demonstrate hard evidence of non-compliance and non-co-operation with the requirements of Security Council Resolution 1441, so as to justify the conclusion that Iraq was in further material breach of its obligations.[11]

Hence, the Prime Minister himself was the final arbiter of the legality of the coming war, ultimately it was his opinion as to Iraqi non-compliance that created the legal framework. However, this opinion was not based on any fresh JIC assessment of Iraqi compliance, but on outdated intelligence that had fed into the September 2002 Dossier, elements of which had been publicly questioned, even ridiculed, and key elements of which were subsequently withdrawn. At no point was the JIC tasked with undertaking a further assessment which could have adversely affected the case for war. Moreover, Goldsmith appeared before the Cabinet just once to present his view of the legality of war, on 17th March 2003, with no questioning being permitted.

In its disregard for the UN and international law in the absence of any consensus that last resort had been arrived at, in the deception that was an unavoidable consequence of the exaggerations involved in making the public case for war, in the absence of the WMD that were the initial *casus belli*, in the absence of any humanitarian emergency in Iraq, and given what was known of the principals' motives in the US, it is impossible to regard the Iraq War as either just or as an extension of the type of intervention undertaken by the Blair government prior to 2003.[12] It is also very difficult to reconcile it with the Labour Party tradition with regard to questions of war.

This is not to say that the 2003 war with Iraq was the first time that a Labour Prime Minister had faced criticism that he was committing British troops to a military campaign without the authorisation of the UN, simply that it was of a different order. In 1950 the Attlee government had to contend with criticism that it was committing British troops to the defence of South Korea on the basis of a vote in the Security Council that was not held in strict accordance with the letter of the UN Charter. Then, the Cabinet agreed that Attlee should:

> argue that the action which the Western Powers were taking in South Korea was fully in accordance with the spirit of the United Nations Charter and was in fact the first significant demonstration of the principle of collective security against aggression. He would proceed to develop the argument that it was the duty of peace-loving nations to make the machinery of the United Nations work effectively, despite legal quibbles, and not to allow it to be frustrated by the abstentions of a single member; and that for this purpose they were entitled to take advantage of procedures which, though they might appear to conflict with the strict letter of the Charter, had been accepted as reasonable by member States.[13]

A further milestone in the development of the Labour tradition came in 1956 with its response to the Suez crisis, and it is worth contrasting Blair's attitude towards Iraq with Gaitskell's attitude towards Nasser. Having had his resolve stiffened by Labour MPs, in August 1956 Gaitskell wrote to Anthony Eden to confirm that:

> Lest there be any doubt in your mind about my personal attitude, let me say that I could not regard an armed attack on Egypt by ourselves and the French as justified by anything which Nasser has done so far or as consistent with the Charter of the United Nations. Nor, in my opinion, would such an attack be justified in order to impose a system of international control over the Canal – desirable though this is. If, of course, the whole matter were to be taken to the United Nations and if Egypt were to be condemned by them as aggressors, then, of course, the position would be different. And if further action which amounted to obvious aggression by Egypt were taken by Nasser, then again it would be different. So far what Nasser has done amounts to a threat, a grave threat to us and to others, which certainly cannot be ignored; but it is only a threat, not in my opinion justifying retaliation by war.[14]

In 2002–3, as in 1956, there was a rush to war which stampeded over the principle of last resort. However, the greatest damage to the Labour Party tradition was undoubtedly with regard to Labour's traditional insistence on the primacy of the UN as the only vehicle through which international conflict could be legitimately resolved. As noted in Chapters 1 and 2, Labour was present at the creation of the UN. Attlee-era politicians invested the utmost faith in the capacity of this new institution to do just as the preamble to its Charter promised, and "save succeeding generations from the scourge of war, which twice in our lifetime has brought untold sorrow to mankind". The Labour Party emerged from the Suez crisis as the natural defenders of the values enshrined in the UN Charter, Gaitskell's articulate defence of these contrasting starkly with Eden's deception and dissembling. In the face of Eden's refusal to work through the UN Gaitskell had accepted its limitations, but nevertheless presented a powerful case for its primacy:

> We are members of the United Nations. I thought that we stood by the Charter. We did until six weeks ago. Why do not we take the matter to the Security Council? I do not say that the Security Council will produce an automatic solution; of course not. We are all very well aware of the veto rule. Indeed, what worries us – I must make this quite plain – is lest, even if the Government were to do that, they would be in fact from their point of view going through a mere formality. I want to emphasise with all the strength that I can that that must not be the attitude adopted. The purpose of taking this dispute to the United Nations is not just to go through formalities so that we may thereafter resort to force. It is that there may be a further period of negotiation; and negotiation is what I mean on this occasion.[15]

The Blair-Straw approach to the UN over Iraq could not have been further away from this ideal. Indeed, it resembled nothing more than Eden's approach during Suez. At the time, Kenneth Younger complained, in terms that could equally be applied to the 2002–3 period, of a government that had, "reached the conclusion that if there is any risk of a United Nations decision being unacceptable to us we are not even going to approach that organisation to see what the decision may be. Any more certain means of sabotaging an international organisation would be difficult to imagine".[16]

However, norms governing military interventions had clearly changed in the post-Cold War era, and arguments in favour of humanitarian military intervention had come to be increasingly accepted. No one, in this context, would have been able to convincingly argue, as Herbert Morrison did in July 1950 (albeit justifying Britain's military contribution to the effort to remove North Korea from South Korea), that:

> There are plenty of unpopular regimes in the world at present ... I do not think that would, in itself, justify people declaring war on all those countries in which they think the regime is unpopular ... Even if it were true as regards particular countries, and there are some where the regime is objectionable judged by British standards, it does not justify

anybody marching across their frontiers ... It is not our desire to interfere with the internal regimes of other countries. That is their busness.[17]

At the same time, as noted in Chapter 1, advocacy of pre-emption heightened the risk of humanitarian justifications for the use of military force being abused. Blair's embrace of the notion of pre-emption can be dated back to his 1999 Chicago speech ("We have learned twice before in this century that appeasement does not work. If we let an evil dictator range unchallenged, we will have to spill infinitely more blood and treasure to stop him later"[18]), but it inevitably clashed with the traditional Labour commitment to last resort. It may well be that in his enthusiastic support for pre-emption, Blair was a victim of a tendency outlined by independent MP and former war reporter Martin Bell at the time of the Kosovo campaign:

> We have lived in recent years in an age of illusion, thinking that a military operation can be a cost-free way to settle differences. That view has been reinforced by the relatively easy victory of the Allies in the Gulf war and by the incredibly light British casualties in Bosnia. Our view has been further reinforced by the actions of the television companies in self-censoring their pictures of war – I have been an accomplice in that – so that people do not understand the realities of war. That happened in Bosnia. We were invited to show the outgoing ordnance but not what happened at the other end: the maiming, the killing and the irredeemable loss of young lives, which is what warfare is about.[19]

Buoyed by the military victories over which he presided prior to 2002–3 (in the case of Kosovo in the face of considerable party and public opposition), Blair failed over Iraq to give due consideration to two key just war principles – proportionality and prudence. These were concerns that had informed the earlier caution shown by Conservative governments towards the conflict in Bosnia in the 1990s, translating into a simple test. As articulated by Douglas Hurd this was that, "we should not go down this or any other route without a reasonable judgment that it would do more good than harm".[20] Similarly, at the time of the Kosovo war, Michael Howard had maintained that: "One of the requirements of a just war is that the suffering that is an inevitable consequence of military action should be less than the suffering that that action prevents".[21] As Hurd had warned in 1993: "It is not enough to fly flags over ruined towns and villages. Worthwhile gains are not to be secured by making a desert and calling it peace".[22]

Proportionality in recourse to war, then, clearly requires that forethought be given to likely outcomes. As well as applying to the target, this forethought should extend to belligerents and the wider international community. As the sixteenth-century just war theorist Vitoria argued: "No war is just the conduct of which is manifestly more harmful to the State than it is good and advantageous; and this is true regardless of other claims or reasons advanced to make of it a just war".[23] In terms of the target, Iraq, we know that little thought was given to *jus post bellum* considerations in the US or UK, and that the absence of US planning for the post-war period was flagged up to Blair in mid-2002. This of itself raises questions about the legitimacy of the attack on Iraq on military humanitarian grounds, as *jus post bellum* planning should be a key feature of any such intervention.[24] As a consequence, the invasion has turned out to be imprudent.

It has led, both directly and indirectly, to the deaths of tens of thousands who would otherwise have lived. "What is a good life?" asks moral philosopher Ted Honderich. "For a start, a good life is one that goes on long enough. A short life may be good while it lasts ... but if it is only half the length it should have been, if it is cut down to that, it is not a good life."[25] There can be little doubt that the quality of life of the average Iraqi in 2007, measured by standard quality of life indicators, and embracing fear and likelihood of sudden violent death, had been eroded by the invasion.[26] By the end of January 2007, the Iraq Body Count database put the number of Iraqi civilians killed since the 2003 invasion at between fifty-six and sixty-two thousand,[27] with other groups offering still higher estimates.

How far did Blair's failure extended to British citizens? This is the other side of the proportionality coin. As Bellamy reminds us: "A state may not sacrifice large numbers of its citizens for uncertain humanitarian outcomes in foreign countries. Although states owe duties to foreigners, they owe their primary duty of care to their own citizens".[28] Post-Bosnia this is a dimension of debates about military intervention – another form of the traditional Conservative "national interest" test – that had been relegated to the margins. One of Blair's achievements may well be to revive it. The lessons of Iraq will certainly make it harder to make the case for future, genuine, humanitarian military interventions.[29]

Blair faced further criticism over his response to the July 2006 Israeli invasion of Lebanon where, for many in the Labour Party, he simply failed to apply the values he had earlier claimed to be guided by. Meeting at the G8 summit in St. Petersburg at the time, Britain lined up with the US in insisting that criticism of Israel be removed from a joint communiqué, delaying any response so as to allow the time in which it was thought Israel could realise its goal of incapacitating Hizbullah, and thereafter declining to condemn the Israeli action, instead insisting that two Israeli soldiers kidnapped by Hizbullah should be released. Many in the party who had suspended their earlier suspicion of US motives over Bosnia and Kosovo, such as Chris Mullin, were appalled. "Is it not just a tiny bit shameful", he asked Foreign Secretary Margaret Beckett, "that although we rightly condemn Hizbollah for what they have done, we can find nothing stronger than the word regret to describe the slaughter and misery and mayhem that Israel has unleashed on a fragile country like Lebanon?"[30] Inside the Labour Party the mood created by Blair's effective support for the Israeli invasion was described as one of "despair".[31] Joan Ruddock complained that: "I have not met any member of the Labour party who actually agrees with our strategy ... There is enormous anger, disappointment and the sense that there has to be a change of direction, but that the damage has been done".[32] It certainly had for Blair personally. His reaction to the invasion of Lebanon contributed directly to the autumn 2006 leadership crisis in which Blair was obliged to announce a timetable for his departure from office.[33]

Nevertheless, he continued to make speeches and statements and produce articles that linked Britain's role as a state prepared to deploy military force with the advancement of values. By January 2007 he seemed to be advocating nothing short of a new era of Anglo-US imperialism, telling an audience aboard HMS *Albion*:

> The frontiers of our security no longer stop at the Channel. What happens in the Middle East affects us. What happens in Pakistan; or Indonesia; or in the attenuated struggles for territory and supremacy in Africa for example, in Sudan or Somalia. The new frontiers for our security are global. Our Armed Forces will be deployed in the lands of other nations far from home, with no immediate threat to our territory, in environments and in ways unfamiliar to them. They will usually fight alongside other nations, in alliance with them; notably, but probably not exclusively with the USA.[34]

Throughout this period, the situation in Iraq continued to deteriorate. In recognition of its divisiveness, the war and anarchic aftermath featured only fleetingly in the Labour Party's 2005 election manifesto, *Britain: Forward Not Back*. This did not touch on international issues – which had defined Blair's time in office – until the seventh chapter, where it argued the New Labour case that: "The best defence of our security at home is the spread of liberty and justice overseas". On Iraq, it limited itself to explaining that:

> We mourn the loss of life of innocent civilians and coalition forces in the war in Iraq and the subsequent terrorism. But the butchery of Saddam is over and across Iraq, eight million people risked their lives to vote earlier this year. Many people disagreed with the action we took in Iraq. We respect and understand their views. But we should all now unite to support the fledgling democracy in Iraq.[35]

During the campaign itself, those Labour MPs who had supported the war chose not to emphasise it, while those who had opposed it for the most part chose not to emphasise it either for fear that any discussion at all could contribute to a protest vote that would unseat them.[36] Despite this relative silence on Iraq, the war did exact a toll at the polls, leaving the Labour Party in power, but with a majority reduced by almost 100 seats to 67.

By 2007 Blair had come full circle. In 1999 he intervened militarily in Kosovo in order to prevent further repression and murder committed on the basis of ethnic identity. On the day after NATO bombing began, Foreign Secretary Robin Cook had illustrated the urgency of the task by reference to the murder of 45 men, women and children in Racak. By 2007 Blair's military intervention in Iraq had created conditions wherein this level of killing on the basis of ethnic identity represented a quiet day in Baghdad. Meanwhile, Blair's defences of the intervention looked weaker as the security situation in Iraq continued to deteriorate throughout 2006.[37] In sum, Blair's decision to go to war in Iraq left Britain more isolated in Europe than at any time since the late Thatcher era, undermined the very foreign policy principles Blair himself had set out in 1999, set uncomfortable precedents in international law, set back the cause of humanitarian intervention, divided the Labour Party and the British public more deeply than the Vietnam War with which it became unavoidably compared, did grave damage to a hitherto principled Labour tradition with regard to questions of war, acted as a spur to suicide bombings in London, and left Iraq in a state of anarchy, with those Blair latterly spoke of liberating from Saddam's tyranny being slaughtered and maimed in a spiral of violence without apparent end. Blair was always sensitive about his political legacy. From his earliest days in office he was advising Bill Clinton to act with his in mind.[38] As a result of his 2002 commitment to the Bush Administration, Tony Blair's legacy will forever be Iraq, something that he is desperate to avoid but cannot escape.

Notes

Preface

1 Michael Howard, *War and the Liberal Conscience* (Oxford, Oxford University Press, 1981).
2 Philip Ziegler, *Wilson: The Authorised Life* (London, HarperCollins, 1995), p.222.

1 The Labour Party and the question of war

1 Cited in Paul Foot, *The Politics of Harold Wilson* (Harmondsworth, Penguin, 1968), p. 326.
2 Patrick Wintour, 'Mr Smith: Labour's New Moralist', *The Guardian*, 18 Jul. 1992.
3 Hansard, 31 May 1995, col. 1012.
4 'The Labour Party: Minutes of Parliamentary Meetings', Labour History Archive.
5 See, Kenneth O. Morgan, *Keir Hardie: Radical and Socialist* (London, Phoenix, 1997), pp. 265–68.
6 Reproduced in Peter Stansky (ed.), *The Left and War: The British Labour Party and World War I* (New York, Oxford University Press, 1969), pp. 318–19.
7 Peter Shore, *Leading the Left* (London, Weidenfeld & Nicolson, 1993), p. 8.
8 R. W. Johnson, 'Facing Both Ways: A Pacifist Ghost Still Haunts the Labour Party', *New Statesman*, 18 Jan. 1991, p. 10.
9 John F. Naylor, *Labour's International Policy: The Labour Party in the 1930s* (London, Weidenfeld & Nicolson, 1969), p. 8.
10 For example, in *Towards the Peace of Nations*, published in 1928, Dalton had warned that: "If a high moral tone is to be the League's only weapon against the material force of an aggressor, its bluff will soon be called ... To think as some sentimentalists appear to do, that we can build a new international order without any sanctions whatever, is not to think at all". Cited in Naylor, *Labour's International Policy*, p. 7.
11 Tom Buchanan, *Britain and the Spanish Civil War* (Cambridge, Cambridge University Press, 1997), p. 9.
12 Hugh Thomas, *The Spanish Civil War* (London, Hamish Hamilton, 3rd ed., 1986), p. 344.
13 Cited in Buchanan, *Britain and the Spanish Civil War*, p. 27. Similarly, in December 1936 Walter Citrine warned a meeting of the Labour Socialist International that: "It should not be assumed that in Great Britain public opinion had taken such definite sides as to the rights and wrongs of the Spanish conflict as might have been done in other countries. In Great Britain the position was that no Government would be able to secure public support for any action which the people believed would lead to war". Cited in C. Fleay & M. L. Sanders,

'The Labour Spain Committee: Labour Party Policy and the Spanish Civil War', *The Historical Journal*, Vol. 28, No. 1, 1985, p. 190.

14 Buchanan, *Britain and the Spanish Civil War*, p. 80.

15 Labour Party Annual Conference Report 1936, p. 169. Labour History Archive.

16 Fleay & Sanders, 'The Labour Spain Committee', pp. 187–97.

17 Buchanan, *Britain and the Spanish Civil War*, p. 79.

18 Archie Potts, *Zilliacus: A Life for Peace and Socialism* (London, Merlin Press, 2002), p. 35.

19 Naylor, *Labour's International Policy*, p. 200.

20 T. D. Burridge, *British Labour and Hitler's War* (London, André Deutsch, 1976), p. 18.

21 Ibid, p. 44.

22 C. R. Attlee, *As It Happened* (London, Odham's Press Ltd, 1954), p. 114.

23 Ibid.

24 Alan Bullock, *Ernest Bevin: Foreign Secretary, 1945-1951* (Oxford, Oxford University Press, 1985), p. 66. Attlee himself remarked that: "We were all united in the great task of ensuring our national survival". Attlee, *As It Happened*, p. 138.

25 Interview with Lord Kinnock, 22 Feb. 2007.

26 Ibid.

27 C. R. Attlee, *The Labour Party in Perspective* (London, Victor Gollancz, 1937), p. 226.

28 As with Donald Sassoon's comment that: "It is probably ahistorical to expect Labour leaders to have had a distinctive 'socialist' foreign policy in a field so fraught with difficulties as that of the developing Cold War, though one might have expected them to devise a foreign policy which could somehow be distinguished from that of the Conservatives". Donald Sassoon, *One Hundred Years of Socialism: The West European Left in the Twentieth Century* (London, Fontana, 1997), p. 179. Morgan considers calls for a socialist foreign policy to have been no more than "empty and unrealistic rhetoric". Kenneth O. Morgan, 'Ernest Bevin as Foreign Secretary', in Morgan, *Labour People: Leaders and Lieutenants, Hardie to Kinnock* (Oxford, Oxford University Press, 1987), p. 154.

29 Interview with Clare Short, 14 Oct. 2006.

30 Hansard, 11 Dec. 1990, col. 847.

31 Ibid, col. 872.

32 Hansard, 15 Jan. 1991, col. 792.

33 On the background and early evolution, see Paul Kennedy, *The Parliament of Man: The United Nations and the Quest for World Government* (London, Allen Lane, 2006), Ch. 1.

34 Interview with Lord Kinnock, 22 Feb. 2007.

35 Hansard, 21 Apr. 1967, col. 961.

36 For example, in the eve of Gulf War debate of 15th January 1991, Neil Kinnock argued that: "the authority of the United Nations to be the major instrument for international security in the future is now directly at stake. If, for any reason, the writ of the United Nations does not run in the Gulf, the organisation will, at best, be condemned to return to the role to which it was confined by the rigidities of the years of the cold war. The United Nations will then never achieve its full purpose and full status as a means of arresting and deterring the violence that is the cause of so much of the world's misery and so much of the world's poverty". Hansard, 15 Jan. 1991, col. 745.

37 Hansard, 29 Apr. 1993, col. 1185.

38 Hansard, 7 Sep. 1990, col. 901.

39 It reads, in full: "Nothing in the present Charter shall impair the inherent right of individual or collective self-defence if an armed attack occurs against a Member of the United Nations, until the Security Council has taken measures

necessary to maintain international peace and security. Measures taken by Members in the exercise of this right of self-defence shall be immediately reported to the Security Council and shall not in any way affect the authority and responsibility of the Security Council under the present Charter to take at any time such action as it deems necessary in order to maintain or restore international peace and security". http://www.un.org/aboutun/charter/ (accessed 5 Jan. 2007).

40 http://www.un.org/aboutun/charter/ (accessed 5 Jan. 2007).

41 Good introductions to Just War theory include: Michael Walzer, *Just and Unjust Wars: A Moral Argument with Historical Illustrations* (New York, Basic Books, 3rd ed., 2000); Alex J. Bellamy, *Just Wars: From Cicero to Iraq* (Cambridge, Polity Press, 2006); and A. J. Coates, *The Ethics of War* (Manchester, Manchester University Press, 1997).

42 Minutes of PLP meeting, 29 Apr. 1982. Labour History Archive.

43 See, for example, Ian Kershaw, *Hitler 1936-45: Nemesis* (London, Allen Lane, 2000), pp. 63–125.

44 Stuart Holland & Donald Anderson, *Kissinger's Kingdom: A Counter-Report on Central America* (Nottingham, Spokesman, 1984), p. 3.

45 In a speech at the funeral of Cubans killed during the invasion, 14th Nov. 1983, http://www1.lanic.utexas.edu/la/cb/cuba/castro/1983/19831114. Accessed 5 Jan. 2007.

46 Hansard, 25 Oct. 1983, col. 146; 26 Oct. 1983, col. 291. Geoffrey Howe's defence rested on the fact that the, "countries that have intervened are democratic countries. Their stated objective is to restore democratic and constitutional government to the island. That is an objective which we fully share". Ibid, col. 302. A few days after the invasion, the PLP sent Ioan Evans and Nigel Spearing on a fact-finding mission to Grenada. They reported that, in fact, "the majority of Grenadians welcome the invasion which is variously described as intervention or deliverance ... we believe that for Grenadians the US action is seen as a conclusion to a national terror, the magnitude and significance of which has still to be recognized by much of the outside world". Ioan Evans & Nigel Spearing, 'Report on a Visit to Grenada 2 – 7 Nov. 1983'. Labour History Archive (PLP Minutes).

47 As exemplified in Konni Zilliacus' contribution to a debate on Vietnam in July 1966: "I cannot believe that my right hon. Friends have such virginal, innocent minds on these matters that they cannot see that the whole point of the United States' pressing for so-called unconditional negotiations, with a huge force still in occupation of South Vietnam, is that they intend, when they have successfully bombed the North Vietnamese into coming to the conference table for those unconditional negotiations, to present them with demands such as the partition of Vietnam, and will threaten more bombing if the demands are rejected. That is what power politics mean. I was a League of Nations official in all the years between the wars. I hate power politics and I have fought all my life against them and for the rule of law". Hansard, 7 Jul. 1966, col. 744.

48 See, Stephen Howe, *Anticolonialism in British Politics: The Left and the End of Empire 1918-1964* (Oxford, Clarendon Press, 1993), esp. pp. 44–52, 143–75.

49 Mervyn Jones, *Michael Foot* (London, Victor Gollancz, 1994), p. 539.

50 Tony Blair, 'Doctrine of the International Community', Economic Club, Chicago', 24 Apr. 1999. http://www.pm.gov.uk/output/Page1297.asp (accessed 5 Jan. 2007).

51 Bellamy, *Just Wars*, p. 123. See also, Coates, *The Ethics of War*, pp. 189–92.

52 Hansard, 11 Dec. 1990, col. 842.

53 As, for example, with Clare Short's intervention in a July 1993 debate on the situation in Bosnia: "this is a European failure ... two nations, Britain and

France, take supreme responsibility ... they are the two European members of the United Nations Security Council and they have the armed forces capable of taking action.Those countries, of all countries, are the most guilty". Hansard, 26 Jul. 1993, col. 843.

54 Hansard, 19 Jul. 1995, col. 1748.

55 For example, Chris Brown, 'Selective Humanitarianism: In Defense of Incon-sistency', in Deen K. Chatterjee & Don E. Scheid (eds), *Ethics and Foreign Intervention* (Cambridge, Cambridge University Press, 2003), pp. 31–50.

56 Hansard, 25 Mar. 1999, col. 564.

57 On Bevan's attitude to Cold War US foreign policy, see John Campbell, *Nye Bevan and the Mirage of British Socialism* (London, Weidenfeld and Nicolson, 1987), pp. 191–5.

58 Interview with Sir Gerald Kaufman, 25 Oct. 2006.

59 *FRUS 1961-1963 Vol X Cuba 1961-1962*, p. 196. 'Reactions to Cuba in Western Europe', Memorandum From the President's Special Assistant (Schlesinger) to President Kennedy, Washington, May 3, 1961. http://www.state.gov/www/about_state/history/frusX/index.html (accessed 5 Jan. 2007).

60 Memorandum for McGeorge Bundy from Richard E. Neustadt, 'Round-up on Trip to England', 9 Aug. 1965, NSF Name File, Box 7, LBJ Library.

61 Barbara Castle, *The Castle Diaries 1964-70* (London, Weidenfeld and Nicolson, 1984), entry for 18 Jul. 1966, p. 148. Brown was, however, something of a favourite of the American political class. In September 1966, in advance of a visit by Brown to Washington, US Ambassador to Britain David Bruce offered the following characterisation: "He is intellectually gifted, forceful, courageous, able, indefatigable, mercurial in temperament, unpredictable in behaviour, frank, salty, voluble, entertaining, gregarious, a curious mixture of humility and vanity. Of a loving nature, he considers that most males merit being called 'brother' ... I heard him matched against Groucho Marx in convivial persiflage, and he convincingly bore off the laurels". Cable from London (No. 2505) 'When George Brown Comes to Washington', 26 Sep. 1966. United Kingdom Memos Vol. IX, LBJ Library.

62 National Archives, CAB 128/42, CC (67), 26 Apr. 1967, pp. 13, 16.

63 This is not, of course, to suggest that this experience was not shared by MPs from other parties.

64 See, Denis Healey, *The Time of My Life* (London, Penguin, 1990), Ch. 3.

65 Tony Benn, *Years of Hope: Diaries, Papers and Letters 1940-1962* (London, Hutchinson, 1994), pp. 53–4.

66 Tam Dalyell was notable in this regard, for example, during the war in Bosnia: "As a former member of a national service tank crew, may I ask whether the right hon. Gentleman does not think that it would be wise in the new circum-stances to provide the Welch Fusiliers with some armoured cover, because in all that we were taught, armoured cover is essential in any dangerous situation?" Hansard, 19 Jul. 1995, col. 1744.

67 Hansard, 7 Sep. 1990, col. 852.

68 Hansard, 11 Dec. 1990, col. 867.

69 Hansard, 7 Jul. 1966, col. 766.

70 Interview with Clare Short, 14 Oct. 2006.

71 The requirements of the domestic political environment did not escape the notice of, or meet with the approval of, backbench MPs on the Left of the party. As Andrew Faulds asked on the eve of the 1991 war with Iraq: "What has happened to the Labour party? We seem to be so electorally eager that every consideration must be subservient to winning the next election. Every policy, and apparently every principle, must be subject to that aim. If opposing the destruction of large areas of the middle east and avoiding the devastation

and the thousands of deaths that would ensue, together with the appalling economic damage to the countries of the third world, leads to the loss of popular support, it is a price the Labour party should be prepared to pay. Principles should still apply just occasionally in politics and, more particularly perhaps, to the Labour party". Hansard, 15 Jan. 1991, col. 782.

72 See, for example Douglas Hurd, *The Search For Peace: A Century of Peace Diplomacy* (London, Little, Brown, 1997), Ch. 1.

73 Ibid, p. 265.

74 Hansard, 6 Sep. 1990, col. 804.

75 Hansard, 7 Sep. 1990, col. 902. My emphasis.

76 Hansard, 19 Jul. 1995, col. 1755.

77 See, for example, Nicholas J. Wheeler, *Saving Strangers: Humanitarian Intervention in International Society* (Oxford, Oxford University Press, 2000).

78 Hansard, 25 Mar. 1999, col. 568.

79 Livingstone admitted that the Kosovo War represented the first question of international politics on which he had divided from Benn in his 12 years as an MP. Ibid, col. 570.

80 Hansard, 18 Jul. 1995, col. 1446.

81 A good example is provided by John Maples, the Conservative MP for Stratford-on-Avon, during the Kosovo War: "Last night, the Minister of State said on television that there was a duty, or an obligation, to intervene to prevent humanitarian disaster. I think that there must be more than that for a Government to intervene: there must be a real issue of national interest as well". Hansard, 25 Mar. 1999, col. 610.

82 Cited in Brendan Sims, *Unfinest Hour: Britain and the Destruction of Bosnia* (London, Penguin, 2002), p. 7.

83 See Blair's speech to the Economic Club, Chicago, 24 Apr. 1999, http://www.pm.gov.uk/output/Page1297.asp

84 Jim Whitman, 'Humanitarian Intervention in an Era of Pre-emptive Self-Defence', *Security Dialogue*, Vol. 36, No. 3, 2005, p. 260.

85 Walzer, *Just and Unjust Wars*, pp. 74–85; Bellamy, *Just Wars*, pp. 158–79; Coates, *The Ethics of War*, pp. 158–61.

86 Hansard, 11 Dec. 1990, col. 846.

2 Taking sides in the Cold War

1 Cited in Geoffrey Warner, 'The Impact of the Second World War Upon British Foreign Policy', in Brian Brivati & Harriet Jones (eds), *What Difference Did the War Make?* (Leicester, Leicester University Press, 1993), pp. 99–100.

2 John W. Young, *Britain and the World in the Twentieth Century* (London, Arnold, 1997), p. 145.

3 'Minute From Mr Attlee to Mr Eden (Berlin)' 18 Jul. 1945, in Rohan Butler, M. E. Pelly & H. J. Yasamee (eds), *Documents on British Policy Overseas, Series 1 Volume 1* (London, HMSO, 1984), doc. 179, pp. 363–64.

4 Raymond Smith & John Zametica, 'The Cold Warrior: Clement Attlee Reconsidered, 1945-7', *International Affairs*, Vol. 61, No. 2, Spring 1985, p. 241.

5 'Minute From Mr Attlee to Mr Churchill (Berlin)', 23 Jul. 1945, in Butler, Pelly & Yasamee (eds), *Documents on British Policy Overseas*, doc. 237, pp. 573–74.

6 'Memorandum by Mr Jebb (Berlin)' 29 Jul. 1945, in ibid, doc. 459, pp. 990–94.

7 Attlee, *As It Happened*, pp. 198–99.

8 Cited in Smith & Zametica, 'The Cold Warrior', p. 243.

9 Ibid.

10 Attlee, *As It Happened*, pp. 169–70. Nevertheless, in his memoirs, written in the immediate aftermath of the Korean War, Attlee portrayed himself as rightly

suspicious of Stalin from the first days of his premiership at Potsdam, recalling that: "The discussions were difficult, as the Russians were out to get all they could in the way of territory and reparation and insisted on the very big concessions which they had got at Teheran and Yalta. We sought to get a reasonable settlement which would allow Germany some prospect of becoming, in time, a member of the European community of nations. We were also acutely aware of the combination of Russian old-time and Communist modern Imperialism which threatened the freedom of Europe. I thought that the Americans had an insufficient appreciation of this danger and indeed of the whole European situation". He also subsequently recalled how: "Bevin at one time thought the Russians might be more friendly to a Labour Government than to a Conservative one. Personally I never believed that. I knew from experience that the Communists had always fought us more vigorously than the Tories because they thought we offered a viable alternative to Communism". Francis Williams, *A Prime Minister Remembers* (London, Heinemann, 1961), p. 71.

11 Young, *Britain and the World*, p. 149.
12 On this question, see also the discussion in Ben Pimlott, *Hugh Dalton* (London, HarperCollins, 1995), pp. 411–22.
13 Pimlott, *Hugh Dalton*, p. 500.
14 Harold Wilson, *Memoirs 1916-1964: The Making of a Prime Minister* (London, Weidenfeld & Nicolson and Michael Joseph, 1986), p. 91.
15 Kenneth O. Morgan, *Labour in Power 1945-1951* (Oxford, Oxford University Press, 1985), p. 235. In a similar vein, Ian Mikardo recalls Bevin as, "being an elemental, visceral man whose attitudes were inspired by empathies and antipathies rather than by assessments, and whose policies derived from gut reactions rather than cerebral analysis". Ian Mikardo, *Back-Bencher* (London, Weidenfeld & Nicolson, 1988), p. 97.
16 For an example of these, take the views of Christopher Warner, the Superintending Under-Secretary for the Northern and Southern Departments at the FO, characterized by his "power politics" perspective and pessimistic view of Soviet intentions and behaviour. A May 1946 memorandum from Warner to the FO's Frank Roberts worried about the resilience of ministers' belief in the official FO line about Soviet intentions and behaviour: "We have foreseen that the Russians would pretty soon realize how clumsy they have been in the last few months, and would attempt to pull a velvet glove over their iron hand; and that public opinion and many important people both here and in America might well be misled into thinking quite erroneously that the iron hand had been discarded, or even that it had been a figment of the imagination of wicked Foreign Office and Foreign Service officials". Cited in Raymond Smith, 'A Climate of Opinion: British Officials and the Development of Soviet Policy, 1945-7', *International Affairs*, Vol. 64, No. 4, Autumn 1988, p. 639. See also, Harold Wilson's account of the attitude of his Permanent Secretary at the Ministry of Works, Sir Percival Robinson, at the same time. Wilson, *Memoirs*, p. 83.
17 Bullock, *Ernest Bevin*, p. 96.
18 John Saville, 'Ernest Bevin and the Cold War1945-1950', *The Socialist Register 1984* (London, Merlin Press, 1984), p. 98. Saville considers that Bevin's, "deficiencies as Foreign Secretary were two: first, his lack of practical experience of foreign affairs, and second, the vacuum in his mind of what a Labour, let alone a socialist, foreign policy should involve". Ibid, p. 74.
19 Ben Pimlott (ed.), *The Political Diary of Hugh Dalton 1918-40, 1945-60* (London, Jonathan Cape, 1986), entry for 22 Mar. 1946, pp. 368–69.
20 Smith & Zametica, 'The Cold Warrior', p. 248. It is worth noting that on 1st March 1946, the Joint Intelligence Committee reported that: "We have practically no direct intelligence ... on conditions in the different parts of the Soviet

Union, and none at all on the intentions, immediate or ultimate, of the Russian leaders". M. E. Pelly, H. J. Yasamee & K. A. Hamilton (eds), *Documents on British Policy Overseas Series 1 Volume VI* (London, HMSO, 1991), doc. 78.

21 Smith & Zametica, 'The Cold Warrior', pp. 250–51.

22 There seems little substance to the idea that Bevin engineered the British withdrawal from Greece so as to compel the US to adopt an interventionist policy in the post-war period. On this question, see Robert Frazier, 'Did Britain Start the Cold War? Bevin and the Truman Doctrine', *Historical Journal*, Vol. 27, No. 3, 1984, pp. 715–27.

23 Field-Marshal Viscount Montgomery of Alamein, *Memoirs* (London, Collins, 1958), p. 436; Raymond Smith, 'A Climate of Opinion', p. 646.

24 Geoffrey Warner, 'From Ally to Enemy: Britain's Relations With the Soviet Union, 1941-1948', in Michael Dockrill & Brian McKercher (eds), *Diplomacy and World Power: Studies in British Foreign Policy, 1890-1950* (Cambridge, Cambridge University Press, 1996), p. 240.

25 This is also the view of biographer Francis Beckett, *Clem Attlee* (London, Politico's, 2000), pp. 219–30. In contrast, Kenneth Harris' biography, *Attlee* (London, Weidenfeld & Nicolson, 1982) presents Attlee's thinking in more traditional Cold War terms. See Ch. 18.

26 James Callaghan, *Time and Chance* (London, Fontana, 1988), pp. 89–90.

27 At the Treasury, no prior work on the possible implications of the termination of Lend Lease had been carried out. See, Pimlott, *Hugh Dalton*, pp. 428–29.

28 Callaghan, *Time and Chance*, p. 75.

29 Wilson, *Memoirs*, p. 123. Indeed, the final payment would only be made in December 2006. See, Philip Thornton, 'Britain Pays Off Final Instalment of US Loan – After 61 Years', *The Independent*, 29 Dec. 2006.

30 Attlee believed that: "Foreign Affairs are the province of the Foreign Secretary and it is, in my view, a mistake for a Prime Minister – save in exceptional circumstances – to intervene personally". Attlee, *As It Happened*, p. 196.

31 PLP Minutes, 27 Mar. 1946. Labour History Archive.

32 Peter Jones, *America and the British Labour Party: The Special Relationship at Work* (London, I. B. Tauris, 1997), pp. 43–44.

33 This amendment expressed, "the urgent hope that His Majesty's Government will so review and recast its conduct of International Affairs as so afford the utmost encouragement to, and collaboration with, all nations and groups striving to secure full Socialist planning and control of the world's resources and thus provide a democratic and constructive Socialist alternative to an otherwise inevitable conflict between American Capitalism and Soviet Communism in which all hope of World Government would be destroyed". *Hansard*, 18 Nov. 1946, col. 526. Attlee made his displeasure known at the 13th November meeting of the PLP. PLP Minutes, 13 Nov. 1946. Labour History Archive.

34 Harris, *Attlee*, pp. 302–03.

35 Cited in Jonathan Schneer, 'Hopes Deferred or Shattered: The British Labour Left and the Third Force Movement, 1945-49', *Journal of Modern History*, Vol. 56, Jun. 1984, p. 201.

36 Ibid, p. 211.

37 Additionally, Peter Weiler has suggested that the failure of the Third Force movement is attributable to the fact that, "it did not confront in any systematic way the more fundamental issue, namely, not whether the United States and the Soviet Union were wicked or good but whether Britain in its reduced economic condition could afford to continue its world commitments". Peter Weiler, 'British Labour and the Cold War: The Foreign Policy of the Labour Governments, 1945-1951', *Journal of British Studies*, Vol. 26, Jan. 1987, p. 78.

38 Cited in Morgan, *Labour in Power*, p. 261.

39 See, Francis Wheen, *Tom Driberg: His Life and Indiscretions* (London, Chatto & Windus, 1990).

40 Bernard Donoughue & G. W. Jones, *Herbert Morrison: Portrait of a Politician* (London, Phoenix Press, 2001), p. 434.

41 Both Solley and Platts-Mills went on to have successful legal careers, Platts-Mills becoming a QC. See his obituary, *The Guardian*, 27 Oct. 2001. More generally, see Darren Lilleker, *Against the Cold War: The History and Political Traditions of Pro-Sovietism in the British Labour Party, 1945-89* (London, I. B. Tauris, 2004).

42 On Zilliacus, see Potts, *Zilliacus*.

43 As recalled by Sir Michael Perrin and cited in Peter Hennessy, *Muddling Through: Power, Politics and the Quality of Government in Postwar Britain* (London, Indigo, 1997), p. 103.

44 Michael Herman, 'Threat Assessments and the Legitimation of Policy?' *Intelligence and National Security*, Vol. 18, No. 3, Autumn 2003, p. 176.

45 Morgan, *Labour in Power*, pp. 283–84.

46 Robert D. Pearce (ed.), *Patrick Gordon Walker: The Political Diaries* (London, Historian's Press, 1991), p. 299.

47 Harris, *Attlee*, p. 288.

48 Cited in Jones, *America and the British Labour Party*, p. 59.

49 Sassoon, *One Hundred Years of Socialism*, p. 172.

50 Morgan, *Labour in Power*, pp. 253–54.

51 For an indication of just how controversial, see Michael Cox & Caroline Kennedy-Pipe, 'The Tragedy of American Diplomacy? Rethinking the Marshall Plan', *Journal of Cold War Studies*, Vol. 7, No. 1, Winter 2005, pp. 97–134, and the following replies in the same issue: Marc Trachtenberg, 'The Marshall Plan as Tragedy', pp. 135–40; Günter Bischof, 'The Advent of Neo-Revisionism?', pp. 141–51; John Bledsoe Bonds, 'Looking For Love (or Tragedy) in All the Wrong Places', pp. 152–58; Lázló Borhi, 'Was American Diplomacy Really Tragic?', pp. 159–67; Charles S. Maier, 'The Marshall Plan and the Division of Europe', pp. 168–74; Michael Cox & Caroline Kennedy-Pipe, 'Rejoinder: The Tragedies of American Diplomacy – Further Reflections', pp. 175–81.

52 Cox & Kennedy-Pipe, 'The Tragedy of American Diplomacy?', p. 109.

53 See, Anne Deighton, *The Impossible Peace: Britain, the Division of Germany and the Origins of the Cold War* (Oxford, Oxford University Press, 1990), pp. 182–89.

54 Cited in Cox & Kennedy-Pipe, 'The Tragedy of American Diplomacy?', p. 120.

55 Cited in Anthony Howard, *Crossman: The Pursuit of Power* (London, Jonathan Cape, 1990), pp. 141–42. Howard also attributes this shift to the impact of a visit Crossman paid to post-coup Czechoslovakia, where he found "a very quiet, cold terror". Ibid.

56 Weiler, *British Labour and the Cold War*, p. 76.

57 Buchanan, *Britain and the Spanish Civil War*, p. 196.

58 Healey, *The Time of My Life*, p. 97.

59 Ibid, p. 96.

60 Ibid, p. 97.

61 Ibid, p. 120.

62 Ibid, pp. 122–23. On Healey, Wilson later reflected: "When he was at Oxford he was a communist. Then friends took him in hand, sent him to the Rand Corporation of America, where he was brainwashed and came back very right wing. But his method of thinking was still what it had been: in other words, the absolute certainty that he was right and everyone else was wrong … ". Wilson, *Memoirs*, p. 205.

63 Healey, *The Time of My Life*, pp. 98–99.

64 Ibid, p. 99.
65 For background, see, Christoph Frei, *Hans J. Morgenthau: An Intellectual Biography* (Baton Rouge, Louisiana State University Press, 2001).
66 Hans Morgenthau, *Scientific Man Versus Power Politics* (Chicago, University of Chicago Press, 1946), p. 66.
67 Kenneth N. Waltz, *Man, the State, and War* (New York, Columbia University Press, 1959), p. 35.
68 R. H. S. Crossman (ed.), *New Fabian Essays* (London, Turnstile Press, 1952).
69 Denis Healey, 'Power Politics and the Labour Party' (1952), reproduced in Healey, *When Shrimps Learn to Whistle*, p. 3.
70 Ibid, pp. 5, 9.
71 Ibid, p. 18.
72 Denis Healey, 'Neutralism' (1955), reproduced in Healey, *When Shrimps Learn to Whistle*, p. 124.
73 A point made by Neil Kinnock. Interview, 22 Feb. 2007.
74 Roy Mason, *Paying the Price* (London, Robert Hale, 1999), p. 70.
75 Kenneth O. Morgan, 'Hugh Gaitskell and International Affairs', *Contemporary Record*, Vol. 7, No. 2, Autumn 1993, p. 317.
76 Hugh Gaitskell, *The Challenge of Co-existence* (London, Methuen, 1956), p. 37.
77 Dan Keohane, 'Labour's International Policy: A Story of Conflict and Contention', in Brian Brivati & Richard Heffernan (eds), *The Labour Party: A Centenary History* (Houndmills, Macmillan, 2000), p. 364.

3 The Labour Party and war in the 1950s: Korea and Suez

1 Anthony Adamthwaite, 'Britain and the World, 1945-9: The View From the Foreign Office', *International Affairs*, Vol. 61, No. 2, Spring 1985, p. 229.
2 Ibid.
3 Ibid.
4 Ibid, p. 230.
5 National Archives: PREM 8/1202, PUSC (79), 'British Overseas Obligations', 27 Apr. 1950.
6 Ra Jong-yil, 'Special Relationship At War: The Anglo-American Relationship During the Korean War', *Journal of Strategic Studies*, Vol. 7, No. 3, 1984, p. 304.
7 Oliver Franks, *Britain and the Tide of World Affairs* (Oxford, Oxford University Press, 1955), pp. 5–6.
8 All UNSC resolutions are available at: http://www.un.org/documents/scres.htm. Last accessed 5 Jan. 2007.
9 David McCullough, *Truman* (New York, Simon & Schuster, 1992), pp. 781, 782.
10 UNSC Resolution 84 of 7th July sanctioned a unified military command under US leadership.
11 Michael Hickey, *The Korean War: The West Confronts Communism 1950-1953* (London, John Murray, 1999), p. 43.
12 PLP Minutes, 5 Jul. 1950, Labour History Archive.
13 Hansard, 5 Jul. 1950, col. 491.
14 My emphasis.
15 Hansard, 5 Jul. 1950, col. 494.
16 Ibid, col. 495.
17 Ibid, col. 489.
18 Pearce (ed.), *Patrick Gordon Walker: Political Diaries*, p. 189.
19 Sean Greenwood, '"A War We Don't Want": Another Look at the British Labour Government's Commitment in Korea, 1950-51', *Contemporary British History*, Vol. 17, No. 4, Winter 2003, p. 4.

20 Tony Shaw, 'The Information Research Department of the British Foreign Office and the Korean War, 1950-53', *Journal of Contemporary History*, Vol. 34, No. 2, 1999, pp. 263–81, quote on p. 265.

21 'Telegram from Ambassador Kelly, Moscow, to Kenneth Younger, FO, 30 Jun. 1950', in H. J. Yasamee & K. A. Hamilton (eds), *Documents on British Policy Overseas, Series II: Volume IV, Korea June 1950 – April 1951* (London, HMSO, 1991), p. 18.

22 On the origins of the Korean War and role of Stalin, see the work of Kathryn Weathersby available via the Cold War International History website at: http://www.wilsoncenter.org/index.cfm?topic_id = 1409&fuseaction = library.Collection&class = New%20Evidence%20on%20the%20Korean%20War particularly 'To Attack, or Not to Attack? Stalin, Kim Il Sung, and the Prelude to War', at: http://www.wilsoncenter.org/index.cfm?topic_id = 1409&fuseaction = library.document&id = 169. Accessed 5 Jan. 2007.

23 See, for example, Callaghan, *Time and Chance*, p. 77.

24 Donoghue & Jones, *Herbert Morrison*, p. 463.

25 H. J. Yasamee, 'Korea: Britain and the Korean War, 1950-51', (London, FCO Historical Branch, History Notes, No. 1, June 1990), p. 2.

26 Kenneth O. Morgan, *Labour in Power, 1945-51* (Oxford, Oxford University Press, 1984), p. 423.

27 'Minutes of a Meeting of the Defence Committee, 28 Jun. 1950', in Yasamee & Hamilton (eds), *Documents on British Policy Overseas*, p. 8.

28 Ibid, p. 28, footnote 5.

29 'Meeting in the Minister of State's Room, 15 Jul. 1950', in ibid, p.70.

30 Telegram from Sir Oliver Franks, 22 Jul. 1950, ibid, p. 76, footnote 2.

31 Telegram, Sir Oliver Franks to Kenneth Younger, 23 Jul. 1950, in ibid, p. 77. Prior to the North Korean invasion of South Korea, Franks had advocated a UK foreign policy aimed at causing; "the Americans to regard us, not as a purely European power to be lined up with the rest of the queue of supplicants for US aid, but as the third member of the 'Big Three', whose world-wide position, economic, political and military, is a vital factor in world prosperity and world peace". His advocacy over Korea was consistent with this aim. On the influence of Franks in the UK decision to commit land forces, see Michael F. Hopkins, 'The Price of Cold War Partnership: Sir Oliver Franks and the British Military Commitment in the Korean War', *Cold War History*, Vol. 1, No. 2, Jan. 2001, pp. 28–46, quote on p. 30.

32 Yasamee & Hamilton (eds), *Documents on British Policy Overseas* p. 78.

33 Pimlott (ed.), *The Political Diary of Hugh Dalton*, p. 480.

34 Cabinet meeting of 1 Aug. 1950. Cited in Morgan, *Labour in Power*, p. 424.

35 Brian Lai & Dan Reiter, 'Rally 'Round the Union Jack? Public Opinion and the Use of Force in the United Kingdom, 1948-2001', *International Studies Quarterly*, Vol. 49, No. 2, Jun. 2005, pp. 255–72.

36 William Stueck, 'The Limits of Influence: British Policy and American Expansion of the War in Korea', *Pacific Historical Review*, Vol. 55, Feb. 1986, pp. 84–85; William Stueck, *The Korean War: An International History* (Princeton, New Jersey, Princeton University Press, 1995), p. 95.

37 McCullough, *Truman*, pp. 820–21. On US consideration of the use of nuclear weapons in the conflict, see Roger Dingman, 'Atomic Diplomacy During the Korean War', *International Security*, Vol. 13, No. 3, Winter 1988/89, pp. 50–89.

38 Cited in Pimlott, *Hugh Dalton*, p. 592. Emphasis in original. See also Dalton's diary entry for 30 Nov. in Pimlott (ed.), *The Political Diary of Hugh Dalton*, p. 494.

39 Harris, *Attlee*, p. 462.

40 Attlee wrote that "the talks were useful and accomplished their object of clarifying the position". Attlee, *As It Happened*, p. 234.

41 Harris, *Attlee*, pp. 465–66.

42 Dean Acheson, *Present At the Creation: My Years in the State Department* (New York, Norton, 1987), p. 478.
43 Ibid, p. 484.
44 Ibid.
45 Ibid.
46 See the assessment by Stueck, *The Korean War*, pp. 136–38. See also, Alan P. Dobson, *Anglo-American Relations in the Twentieth Century* (London, Routledge, 1995), p. 99.
47 Healey was still deploying this argument in his memoirs some 40 years later. Healey, *The Time of My Life*, p. 125. See also the account in Morgan, *Labour in Power*, p. 429.
48 'Telegram, Attlee to Bevin, 10 Dec. 1950', in Yasamee & Hamilton (eds), *Documents on British Policy Overseas*, p. 257.
49 Ibid, pp. 256–57.
50 Pimlott (ed.), *The Political Diary of Hugh Dalton*, entry for 21 Dec. 1950, p. 495.
51 Cited in Greenwood, 'A War We Don't Want', p. 18.
52 Philip M. Williams (ed.), *The Diary of Hugh Gaitskell 1945-1956* (London, Jonathan Cape, 1983), p. 226.
53 Cited in Howard, *Crossman*, p. 154.
54 Morgan, *Labour in Power*, pp. 279, 433.
55 PLP Minutes, 31 Jan. 1951, Labour History Archive.
56 Hickey, *The Korean War*, p. 161. The government attempted to head off the inevitable protests by granting a supplementary 2d worth of corned beef.
57 Morgan, *Labour in Power*, p. 477.
58 Williams (ed.), *The Diary of Hugh Gaitskell*, p. 297.
59 See the editorial in *Tribune*, 20 Apr. 1951, pp. 3–5.
60 Wilson, *Memoirs*, pp. 115, 119. To critics, like Paul Foot, Wilson's resignation involved a Damascene conversion on the issue. However, the speeches by Wilson that Foot cites in support of this argument clearly show his concern at the domestic impact of the increased defence expenditure. Foot, *The Politics of Harold Wilson*, pp. 94–8. See also the speech by Wilson reprinted in *Tribune*, 4 May 1951, p. 11.
61 Harris, *Attlee*, p. 473.
62 To take a more recent example, Mark Hayhurst, winner of the first Ben Pimlott Essay Prize for his essay on Bevan, wrote in terms of there being: "On the one side a fundamentalist, on the other a revisionist: the constant sore between them being the running one of nationalisation. That's how it seemed at the time, and that's the way it is still viewed today". Mark Hayhurst, 'Duty Bound', *The Guardian*, 28 May 2005.
63 Kenneth O. Morgan, 'Hugh Gaitskell and International Affairs', *Contemporary Record*, Vol. 7, No. 2, Autumn 1993, pp. 315–16, 320.
64 Brian Brivati, *Hugh Gaitskell* (London, Richard Cohen Books, 1996), p. 123.
65 Brivati, *Hugh Gaitskell*, p. 99. My emphasis.
66 Philip M. Williams, *Hugh Gaitskell* (Oxford, Oxford University Press, 1982), p. 207. Jim Callaghan recalled his perspective from the right wing of the Party: "What was uppermost was that the American President was under great pressure, that the American press and public were calling on Continental Europe to do more to help itself". Callaghan, *Time and Chance*, p. 108.
67 Dalton's account of a conversation with Bevan at the height of the crisis, cited in Pimlott, *Hugh Dalton*, p. 598.
68 For example, Irving Bernstein, *Guns or Butter? The Presidency of Lyndon Johnson* (New York, Oxford University Press, 1996).
69 See, for example, the minutes of the PLP meeting of 1 Jul. 1952. Labour History Archive.

70 See his memorandum from mid-1952, 'Anti-Americanism in Britain', reproduced in Williams (ed.), *The Diary of Hugh Gaitskell 1945-1956*, pp. 316–20.
71 On the military dimension, see Ian Speller, 'A Splutter of Musketry? The British
   Military Response to the Anglo-Iranian Oil Dispute, 1951', *Contemporary
   British History*, Vol. 17, No. 1, Spring 2003, pp. 39–66.
72 Wilson, *Memoirs*, p. 129.
73 In addition to the Festival of Britain preparations, his handling of the Aberdan
   crisis was interrupted by a lengthy Scandinavian holiday and a three-week tour
   of North America.
74 Cited by Spellar, 'A Splutter of Musketry?', p. 55.
75 Donoghue & Jones, *Herbert Morrison*, pp. 503–04.
76 Ibid, p. 505.
77 Cited in Brivati, *Hugh Gaitskell*, pp. 127–28.
78 Keith Kyle, *Suez* (London, Weidenfeld & Nicolson, 1991), p. 89.
79 Williams (ed.), *The Diary of Hugh Gaitskell 1945-1956*, p. 553.
80 Herbert Morrison, *Herbert Morrison: An Autobiography* (London, Odham's
   Press, 1960), p. 281.
81 Williams (ed.), *The Diary of Hugh Gaitskell 1945-1956*, p. 553.
82 Hansard, 27 Jul. 1956, col. 777.
83 See Hansard, 2 Aug. 1956, col. 1606; Williams (ed.), *The Diary of Hugh Gaitskell*, p. 568.
84 Hansard, 2 Aug. 1956, col. 1610.
85 Ibid, cols. 1612–13.
86 Ibid, cols. 1612–14.
87 Ibid, cols. 1616–17.
88 Robert Rhodes James, *Anthony Eden* (London, Weidenfeld & Nicolson, 1986),
   p. 482.
89 Hansard, 2 Aug. 1956, col. 1626. My emphasis. See also col. 1630.
90 Ibid, cols. 1658–59.
91 Hansard (Lords), 2 Aug. 1956, cols. 617–18.
92 Harris, *Attlee*, p. 547.
93 D. R. Thorpe, *Eden: The Life and Times of Anthony Eden, First Earl of Avon,
   1897-1977* (London, Pimlico, 2004), p. 477.
94 Brivati, *Gaitskell*, p. 262.
95 Williams, *Hugh Gaitskell*, p. 279.
96 Ibid, p. 281.
97 Williams (ed.), *The Diaries of Hugh Gaitskell*, p. 569. Captain Charles Waterhouse was a leading figure in the pro-Suez faction of the Conservative Party. On
   the origins of the Suez group, see Sue Onslow, '"Battlelines for Suez": The
   Abadan Crisis of 1951 and the Formation of the Suez Group', *Contemporary
   British History*, Vol. 17, No. 2, Summer 2003, pp. 1–28.
98 Williams (ed.), p. 568.
99 Douglas Jay, *Change and Fortune* (London, Hutchinson, 1980), p. 254.
100 Williams (ed.), p. 567.
101 Ibid.
102 Ibid. Benn subsequently recalled this meeting as occurring after the 2nd August
    debate, which would add weight to the view that Gaitskell shifted position as a result
    of pressure, but the likelihood is that it was indeed held the day before and was
    a response to concern at Gaitskell's remarks of 27th July. Russell Galbraith,
    Inside Outside – The Man They Can't Gag: A Biography of Tam Dalyell (Edinburgh,
    Mainstream Publishing, 2000), p. 178; Interview with Tony Benn, 6 Feb. 2007.
103 Benn, *Years of Hope*, entry for 5 Nov. 1956, pp. 203–04.
104 Ian Mikardo, *Backbencher*, p. 158. For a flavour of *Tribune's* coverage of the
    crisis, see 'Stop this Suez Madness – Labour must not let Britain be hustled into

a shooting war', 3 Aug. 1956, p. 1; and 'Labour Must Order the Government: Halt – About Turn!', 10 Aug. 1956, p. 1.

105 James, *Anthony Eden*, p. 491. See also Benn, *Years of Hope*, p. 204.
106 Hansard, 2 Aug. 1956, col. 1626.
107 Williams, p. 279.
108 James, *Anthony Eden*, p. 493.
109 Wilson, *Memoirs*, p. 165.
110 Hansard, 12 Sep. 1956, col. 15.
111 Ibid, col. 22.
112 Ibid, col. 32.
113 Cited in Kyle, *Suez*, pp. 388–89.
114 Hansard, 1 Nov. 1956, col. 1620.
115 Ibid, col. 1640.
116 Ibid, col. 1641.
117 Ibid, 1707.
118 At the height of the crisis Gaitskell had told US Ambassador Winthrop Aldrich that: "'more than half if not three-quarters of the British nation' was opposed to this 'monstrous' policy. He called on the Americans to see that Britain and France be named as well as Israel in the UN resolution calling for the withdrawal of forces from Egyptian territory. Continuing firmness by the United States was the only way to heal the injury being inflicted by Eden on the Alliance". Aldrich reported that "without prompting and on their own initiative" a succession of Labour Party front bench figures were expressing their gratitude to Washington for its stance on the crisis. See Kyle, *Suez*, p. 387.
119 Michael Foot, *Aneurin Bevan: 1945-1960* (London, Paladin, 1975), p. 516.
120 Williams (ed.), *The Diary of Hugh Gaitskell*, pp. 619–22.
121 Hansard, 19 Apr. 1999, col. 608.

4 Harold Wilson, the Labour Party and the Vietnam War

1 Barbara Castle, *Fighting All the Way* (London, Macmillan, 1993), p. 362.
2 Charles Wheeler, 'Half the Way with LBJ', *New Statesman*, 10 Apr. 2000, p. 33.
3 On the "more flags" effort, see, Fredrik Logevall, *Choosing War: The Lost Chance for Peace and the Escalation of War in Vietnam* (Berkeley, University of California Press, 1999); Fredrik Logevall, 'America Isolated: The Western Powers and the Escalation of the War', in Andreas W. Daum, Lloyd C. Gardner & Wilfried Mausbach (eds), *America, the Vietnam War, and the World: Comparative and International Perspectives* (Cambridge, Cambridge University Press, 2003), pp. 175–96.
4 National Archives, FO371/175494. Memo from J. E. Cable, 9 Mar. 1964.
5 Pearce (ed.), *Patrick Gordon Walker: Political Diaries*, p. 299.
6 Harold Wilson, *The Labour Government 1964 – 1970: A Personal Record* (London, Weidenfeld and Nicolson/Michael Joseph, 1971), p. 48.
7 Ibid.
8 On this, see Peter Busch, 'Supporting the War: Britain's Decision to Send the Thompson Mission to Vietnam, 1960-61', *Cold War History*, Vol. 2, No.1, Oct. 2001, pp. 69–94.
9 Saki Dockrill, 'Forging the Anglo-American Global Defence Partnership: Harold Wilson, Lyndon Johnson and the Washington Summit, December 1964', *Journal of Strategic Studies*, Vol. 23, No. 4, Dec. 2000, p. 121.
10 National Archives, PREM13/692, FO Memorandum, 'Visit to Washington by Prime Minister and Foreign Secretary: Viet Nam', 3 Dec. 1964.
11 Ibid.
12 David Easter, *Britain and the Confrontation With Indonesia 1960-66* (London, I. B. Tauris, 2004), p. 1.

13 Wilson, *The Labour Government 1964-1970*, p. 48.
14 National Archives, PREM13/693, South East Asia Department Memorandum, 'US Air Attacks Against North Viet-Nam', 15 Mar. 1965.
15 Cited in Foot, *The Politics of Harold Wilson*, pp. 203–04.
16 Ibid, pp. 204–05.
17 William Warbey, *Vietnam: The Truth* (London, Merlin Press, 1965). See also, for example, the outline of the origins of the conflict provided by Philip Noel-Baker, Hansard 7 Jul. 1966, cols. 714–22.
18 Hansard, 9 Mar. 1965, col. 238.
19 Hansard, 19 Jul. 1965, col. 1131.
20 Hansard, 21 Apr. 1967, col. 960.
21 National Archives, PREM 13/692, 'Note for the Record: South Vietnam', 11 Feb. 1965.
22 Ibid; Wilson, *The Labour Government 1964 – 1970*, p. 80. When Wilson explained that: "All I want to do is to reassure the House of Commons. Do you think I can do that on the basis of a transatlantic call in the middle of the night?", Johnson replied: "You needn't say it was the middle of the night". Wheeler, 'Half the Way with LBJ'.
23 Warbey, *Vietnam: The Truth*, p. 111.
24 See, the transcript of the conversation between Johnson and George Ball, 6 Mar. 1965, G. Ball Papers, Britain III, Box 1, LBJ Library.
25 For example, see Caroline Page, *US Official Propaganda During the Vietnam War, 1965-1973: The Limits of Persuasion* (London, Leicester University Press, 1996), p. 110.
26 National Archives, PREM13/692, Letter from Warbey to Wilson, 15 Feb. 1965; Warbey to Wilson 16 Feb. 1965; Edward Short, *Whip to Wilson* (London, Macdonald, 1989), pp. 217, 235.
27 National Archives, PREM13/693, extract from record of PM's talk with Chancellor Erhard in Bonn, 8 Mar. 1965.
28 See, for example, Hansard, 17 Jun. 1965, col. 888.
29 Hansard, 5 Jul. 1965, cols. 1131-4. Michael Stewart came to Ky's defence, Hansard, 2 Aug. 1965, col. 1036.
30 National Archives, PREM13/693, Telegram, FO to Washington, 9 Mar. 1965.
31 Ibid.
32 The FO assessment was that: "Their latest attacks on North Viet-Nam are still part of a policy of drift, because the US Government have not yet, as far as we know, set themselves a specific goal or defined the means of reaching it. The attacks are intended to demonstrate American determination, but nobody knows precisely what, in concrete terms, the US Government are determined to achieve". National Archives, FO371/180580, 'Seeking a Solution in Viet-Nam', FO Memorandum, 15 Feb. 1965.
33 National Archives, PREM13/693, Minute 'Vietnam', 1 Mar. 1965.
34 National Archives, FO371/180580, Memorandum for Secretary of State, 17 Feb. 1965.
35 National Archives, PREM13/693, Record of a conversation between Wilson and Bruce, Downing Street, 12 Mar. 1965.
36 See, for example, a 22nd March letter to Wilson signed by, amongst others, Foot, Mendelson, Driberg, Zilliacus, Silverman and Eric Heffer: "We regard the present situation ... as appalling. There is little doubt ... that the Party as a whole and many many people who are not members but who are in general sympathy with the Party simply do not understand the Government's apparent determination to support the Americans in actions in conflict with accepted morality and its inflexible resolution not to say a single word in condemnation of anything the Americans do on this matter, no matter what its folly or what its peril". National Archives, PREM13/693.

37 National Archives, PREM13/693, Draft Telegram to the Foreign Secretary, no date (T.106/65). In a subsequent draft telegram (T.107/65), Wilson warned Stewart that if Johnson attempted to link British support for the US in Vietnam with US support for the pound, "I would regard this as most unfortunate … If the financial weakness we inherited and are in the process of putting right is to be used as a means of forcing us to accept unpalatable policies or developments regardless of our thoughts this will raise very wide questions indeed about Anglo-American relationships".

38 Wilson, *The Labour Government, 1964-1970*, pp. 85–6.

39 National Archives, PREM13/694, Patrick Dean, 'Condensed Record of a Meeting with President Johnson at the White House on April the 13th on Presentation of his Credentials by Sir Patrick Dean', 13 Apr. 1965.

40 National Archives, PREM13/694, 'Record of Meeting Between the Prime Minister and President of the United States at the White House on Thursday, April 15, 1965'.

41 Wilson, *The Labour Government, 1964-1970*, p. 96.

42 For example, see John W. Young, *The Labour Governments 1964-1970: International Policy* (Manchester, Manchester University Press, 2003), p. 70.

43 He reported back that US bombing (of North and South Vietnam and Laos) had helped improve the dismal morale of the South Vietnamese army. He concluded that: "We must back the Americans in their present operations in Viet-Nam. Their military effort is the only possible policy. An American defeat would be disastrous, even if a victory in the normal sense is unattainable". However, he also warned that: "In my view we should let the United States know that if they bombed Hanoi etc. they could not count on our support. If things go wrong and the choice lies between bombing Hanoi or putting in more American ground troops, the latter would be the lesser evil". National Archives, PREM13/694, 'Report by the Right Honourable Patrick Gordon Walker on His Fact-Finding Tour of South-East Asia as Special Representative of the Foreign Secretary, 14 April – 4 May 1965'.

44 For the instructions to the mission, see Wilson, *The Labour Government, 1964-1970*, p. 118.

45 See, John Young, 'The Wilson Government and the Davies Peace Mission to North Vietnam, July 1965', *Review of International Studies*, Vol. 24, No. 4, Oct. 1998, pp. 545–62.

46 Castle, *Fighting All the Way*, p. 384.

47 See John Dumbrell & Sylvia Ellis, 'British Involvement in Vietnam Peace Initiatives, 1966-1967: Marigolds, Sunflowers and 'Kosygin Week'', *Diplomatic History*, Vol. 27, No. 1, Jan. 2003, pp. 113–49.

48 John Dumbrell, *A Special Relationship: Anglo-American Relations in the Cold War and After* (London, Palgrave Macmillan, 2000), p. 152.

49 See Wilson, *The Labour Government 1964 – 1970*, pp. 357–66; Page, *US Official Propaganda*, pp. 167–68.

50 George Brown, *In My Way: The Political Memoirs of Lord George-Brown* (Harmondsworth, Penguin, 1972), p. 139.

51 Peter Paterson, *Tired and Emotional: The Life of Lord George Brown* (London, Chatto & Windus, 1993), p. 222.

52 Lyndon Baines Johnson, *The Vantage Point: Perspectives on the Presidency 1963 – 1969* (New York, Holt, Rinehart & Winston, 1971), p. 255. White House aide Chester Cooper, in London throughout this process, has also pointed to US suspicion of Wilson's motives: "There was a sense that the British Government was pushing hard, perhaps too hard, to undertake the role of mediator … some of Wilson's American cousins felt his underlying motivation was to bolster his own and England's prestige". Cited in Page, *US Official Propaganda*, p. 168.

53 Backbench disquiet was also clearly evident at the 8th December meeting of the PLP.
54 Wilson, *The Labour Government 1964-1970*, p. 187.
55 At the time, Wilson suggested that backbench MPs should have been directing their telegrams at Hanoi. Minutes of PLP meeting, 2 Feb. 1966. Labour History Archive.
56 Short, *Whip to Wilson*, p. 217.
57 Wilson, *The Labour Government 1964-1970*, pp. 205–6.
58 This was also recognized by David Bruce, who reported that: "Importance of the exchange touched off by Powell is that it shows keen awareness of political leaders in this country of public's fear of involvement in Vietnam conflict. While both government and opposition have supported US policy in Vietnam, public opinion polls have consistently reported large majority against sending British troops to Vietnam. Public draws clear distinction between British role in Malaysia and problem of Vietnam for which it has little stomach and little sense of British interest being involved". Telegram, London to Department of State, POL-14 UK, Box 2781, US National Archives.
59 'Speech by the Prime Minister, The Rt. Hon. Harold Wilson, OBE, MP, to Meeting of the Parliamentary Labour Party on Wednesday, 15th June, 1966'. Labour History Archive.
60 Hansard, 7 Jul. 1966, col. 683.
61 Ibid, col. 688.
62 Ibid, col. 711.
63 Ibid, cols. 724, 726.
64 Ibid, col. 766.
65 Telegram, London to Department of State, 11 Jul. 1966. Pol15-1 UK, Box 2782, US National Archives.
66 Ibid.
67 Telegram, London to Department of State, 11.7.66. POL 15-1 UK, Box 2782, US National Archives.
68 Page, *US Official Propaganda During the Vietnam War*, p. 109.
69 Cited in Jones, *America and the British Labour Party*, p. 173. Bruce himself reported that: "I do not conclude that Britain is going down the drain, but every sluice gate is beginning to open". Telegram, London to Department of State, 11 Jul. 1966. Pol15-1 UK, Box 2782, US National Archives.
70 J. Gwyn Morgan, 'Vietnam: The Coming Months', 16 May 1967. Lord George-Brown Papers, Bodleian Library, Ms.Eng.C.5023. Brown considered this analysis "not bad".
71 See, for example, Hansard, 18 Jan. 1967, cols. 425–38. See also the statement approved by the Foreign Affairs Group of the PLP, dated, 5 Dec. 1967, in advance of a speech to them by George Brown in Lord George-Brown Papers, Bodleian Library, Ms.Eng.C.5014.
72 Hansard, 27 Feb. 1967, cols. 80–1.
73 See the minutes of the PLP meeting, 2 Feb. 1967. Labour History Archive.
74 See, for example, the minutes of the PLP meeting of 4 Jul. 1968. Labour History Archive.
75 Wilson, *The Labour Government 1964 – 1970*, p. 730.
76 Clive Ponting, *Breach of Promise: Labour in Power 1964-1970* (London, Penguin, 1990), pp. 48–54.
77 In a July 1965 memorandum, McGeorge Bundy argued that: "We are concerned with the fact that the British are constantly trying to make narrow bargains on money while they cut back on their wider political and military responsibilities. We want to make very sure that the British get it into their heads that it makes no sense for us to rescue the Pound in a situation in which there is no British flag in Vietnam, and a threatened British thin-out in both east of Suez and in

Germany. What I would like to say to [Burke] Trend myself, is that a British Brigade in Vietnam would be worth a billion dollars at the moment of truth for Sterling. But I don't want to say it unless you want it said". 'Memorandum for the President: Your Meeting with Joe Fowler at 12.30 Tomorrow', NSF Country File, Box 215, LBJ Library. However, Johnson did not want it said. A memorandum of the following day summarized the dominant Fowler-McNamara and Ball positions as follows: "UK troops in Vietnam, while not strictly a necessary condition for us to be forthcoming on sterling, would greatly improve the odds". Memorandum, 'The UK Problem and "Thinking the Unthinkable"', 29 Jul. 1965, NSF Country Files, UK Box 215, LBJ Library.

78 Raj Roy has recently argued that: "Above all, Johnson's interest in and commitment to the defence of sterling in spite of his visible irritation with the British prime minister revealed the existence of a highly compartmentalized relationship between the two nations, which was driven by commonality of interest and an ease of dialogue born out of long-standing institutional relationships, rather than by emotions or personal feelings". Raj Roy, 'No Secrets Between "Special Friends": America's Involvement in British Economic Policy, October 1964 – April 1965', *History*, Vol. 89, No. 3, Jul. 2004, pp. 399–423. See also, John Dumbrell, 'The Johnson Administration and the British Labour Government: Vietnam, the Pound and East of Suez', *Journal of American Studies*, Vol. 30, No. 2, Aug. 1996, pp. 211–31; Glen O'Hara, 'The Limits of US Power: Transatlantic Financial Diplomacy Under the Johnson and Wilson Administrations, October 1964-November 1968', *Contemporary European History*, Vol. 12, No. 3, 2003, pp. 257–78; and Dobson, *Anglo-American Relations in the Twentieth Century*, pp. 131–38.

79 Brivati, *Hugh Gaitskell*, p. 423.

80 Ibid, p. 422.

81 Ibid, p. 420.

82 Memorandum for McGeorge Bundy from Richard E. Neustadt, 'Round-up on Trip to England', 9 Aug. 1965, NSF Name File, Box 7, LBJ Library. During the same visit, Neustadt met Anthony Crosland, who focused on the economic costs of Britain's continued world role: "Why, he asked, should Britain be the only 'middle power' carrying a world role? Hadn't they suffered enough for winning the war? Weren't they entitled now to join the happy ranks of losers and build schools?" Ibid.

83 Minute from George Brown to Harold Wilson, 26 Aug. 1965. Lord George-Brown Papers, Bodleian Library, Ms.Eng.C5002.

84 Lord Jenkins of Hillhead, 'Hugh Gaitskell (1906-63)', *Contemporary Record*, Vol. 7, No. 2, Autumn 1993, p. 311.

85 Interview with Tam Dalyell, 5 Oct. 2006.

86 Page, *US Official Propaganda*, p. 109.

87 Wilson, *The Labour Government 1964 – 1970*, p. 500.

88 Cited in Dumbrell, *A Special Relationship*, p. 154.

89 Short, *Whip to Wilson*, p. 117.

90 Wilson, *The Labour Government 1964 – 1970*, p. 500.

91 For example, Hansard 19 Jul. 1965, cols. 1124, 1128, 1134–35; 17 May 1966, col. 1121.

92 John E. Mueller, *War, Presidents and Public Opinion* (New York, John Wiley & Sons, 1973), p. 129.

93 Robert S. McNamara, *In Retrospect: The Tragedy and Lessons of Vietnam* (New York, Times Books, 1995), p. 160.

94 National Archives, PREM13/695, 'Record of a Conversation Between the Prime Minister and Mr Dean Rusk at No.10, Downing Street at 9.45am on Friday, May 14, 1965'.

95 McNamara, *In Retrospect*, p. 234.

96 Ibid, p. 275.
97 Mikardo, *Backbencher*, p. 140; Warbey, *Vietnam: The Truth*, Ch. 5.
98 Eric Heffer, *Never a Yes Man: The Life and Politics of an Adopted Liverpudlian* (London, Verso, 1991), p. 120.
99 Ibid.
100 Shore, *Leading the Left*, p. 95.
101 For a survey of polls showing domestic opposition to both the war and the commitment of British troops, see Page, *US Official Propaganda*, pp. 191–225.

5 Labour's Falklands War

1 Philip Williams, *Hugh Gaitskell: A Political Biography* (London, Jonathan Cape, 1979), p. 694.
2 The indications are that Allende took his own life during the military assault on the presidential palace. For a recent assessment of the Allende years and the forces at work, see Jonathan Haslam, *The Nixon Administration and the Death of Allende's Chile: A Case of Assisted Suicide* (London, Verso, 2005).
3 Harold Wilson, *Final Term: The Labour Government 1974-1976* (London, Weidenfeld & Nicolson and Michael Joseph, 1979), p. 4.
4 Letter from Eric Heffer to the author, 15 Feb. 1991.
5 Heffer: *Never a Yes Man*, p. 144.
6 Similarly, a number of Conservative MPs demonstrated a degree of sympathy with the coup plotters. Foreign Office Minister Julian Amery wound up a debate on Chile by arguing that: "We have accepted changes of power – Socialists or Conservatives coming into power ... But the Marxist parties do not accept this process. In a country where it is known that a Government, once in power, will never give way again, we must not be surprised if the military draw their own conclusions". *Hansard*, 28 Nov. 1973, col. 531. By 1974 the *Daily Express* was running stories to the effect that Foot, Benn, Judith Hart, Joan Lestor and Ian Mikardo were working towards an Allende-style government in Britain. Private Political Diaries and Papers of Tony Benn, 14 May 1974 in the Benn Archives.
7 Hansard, 28 Nov. 1973, col. 483.
8 Ibid, cols. 488–89.
9 See Mark Phythian, *The Politics of British Arms Sales Since 1964* (Manchester, Manchester University Press, 2000), pp. 105–13.
10 Kevin Jeffreys, *Anthony Crosland: A New Biography* (London, Politico's, 2000), p. 201.
11 David Owen, *Human Rights* (London, Jonathan Cape, 1978).
12 Ibid, p. 16.
13 Callaghan, *Time and Chance*, p. 296.
14 Ibid, p. 372.
15 See Nigel West, *The Secret War for the Falklands* (London, Little, Brown, 1997), pp. 218–20; Callaghan, *Time and Chance*, p. 375; David Owen, *Time to Declare* (Harmondsworth, Penguin, 1992), pp. 349–50; interview with Lord Owen, 2 Nov. 2006.
16 Hansard, 2 Apr. 1982, col. 571.
17 Giles Radice, *Diaries 1980-2001: From Political Disaster to Election Triumph* (London, Weidenfeld and Nicolson, 2004), p. 64.
18 Hansard, 3 Apr. 1982, col. 636.
19 Ibid, col. 639.
20 Radice, *Diaries 1980-2001*, p. 65; Heffer, *Never a Yes Man*, pp. 195–96.
21 See the account of PLP, Tribune group and NEC meetings in early April 1982 in Tony Benn's diaries. Tony Benn, *The End of an Era: Diaries 1980-90* (London, Arrow, 1994), pp. 204–11.

22 Hansard, 3 Apr. 1982, col. 638.
23 Jones, *Michael Foot*, pp. 484–85.
24 Interview with Tam Dalyell, 5 Oct. 2006.
25 Hansard, 3 Apr. 1982, cols. 660–61.
26 Minutes of PLP meeting, 7 Apr. 1982. Labour History Archive.
27 Minutes of PLP meeting, 29Apr. 1982. Labour History Archive.
28 During the conflict, Chris Mullin, subsequently a Labour MP and advocate of military intervention in Kosovo, became editor of *Tribune*, at which point its anti-war line hardened.
29 Minutes of PLP meeting, 22 Apr. 1982. Labour History Archive.
30 See, for example, Hansard, 7 Apr. 1982, cols. 972–76.
31 Ibid, col. 964.
32 Ibid, col. 965.
33 Ibid, col. 967.
34 Interview with Sir Gerald Kaufman, 25 Oct. 2006.
35 Hansard, 7 Apr. 1982, cols. 993, 990.
36 Ibid, col. 994. His speech was condemned as "disgraceful" by Antony Buck, as was the suggestion from Frank Allaun that the Islanders could be re-settled in the UK or New Zealand. Ibid, cols. 1012, 1011.
37 Hansard, 7 Apr. 1982, col. 1004.
38 Ibid, col. 1008.
39 Ibid, col. 1019.
40 Hansard, 14 Apr. 1982, col. 1162.
41 Ibid, col. 1149.
42 Ibid, cols. 1201–02.
43 Hansard, 26 Apr. 1982, col. 613.
44 Hansard, 27 Apr. 1982, col. 721.
45 Letter, Michael Foot to Margaret Thatcher, 27 Apr. 1982, Michael Foot Papers, Labour History Archive.
46 Hansard, 29 Apr. 1982, col. 982.
47 Ibid, col. 982.
48 Ibid, col. 986.
49 Ibid, col. 991.
50 Ibid, col. 996.
51 Ibid, col. 1030.
52 Ibid, col. 1033.
53 See, Klaus Dodds, *Pink Ice: Britain and the South Atlantic Empire* (London, I. B. Tauris, 2002).
54 Hansard, 29 Apr. 1982, col. 1035.
55 See, Tam Dalyell, *Misrule: How Mrs Thatcher Has Misled Parliament From the Sinking of the Belgrano to the Wright Affair* (London, Hamish Hamilton, 1987).
56 Minutes of PLP meeting, 6 May 1982. Labour History Archive.
57 Hansard, 13 May 1982, col. 959.
58 Ibid, col. 981.
59 Hansard, 20 May 1982, col. 541.
60 Hansard, 13 May 1982, col. 983.
61 Ibid, col. 1015.
62 Ibid, col. 1021.
63 Hansard, 20 May 1982, col. 512.
64 Ibid, col. 518.
65 Ibid, 20.5.82, cols. 550, 549.
66 Letter from Michael Foot to Margaret Thatcher, 17 May 1982; letter from Margaret Thatcher to Michael Foot, 18 May 1982. Michael Foot Papers, Labour History Archive.

67 Letter from Margaret Thatcher to Michael Foot, 9 Jun. 1982. Michael Foot Papers, Labour History Archive.
68 Hansard, 15 Jun. 1982, col. 732.
69 Ibid, col. 732.
70 John Campbell, *Margaret Thatcher – Volume Two: The Iron Lady* (London, Jonathan Cape, 2003), p. 199.
71 Heffer, *Never a Yes Man*, p. 195.
72 Ibid, pp. 196, 195.
73 Campbell, *Margaret Thatcher*, pp. 314–18.
74 Hansard, 29 Apr. 1982, col. 1021.
75 See, for example, Michael Foot's comments at the PLP meeting of 6 May 1982. Labour History Archive.
76 See, for example, David Winnick's comments at the PLP meeting of 10 Jun. 1982. Labour History Archive. In addition, Judith Hart's mailbag was certainly a mixed one after an appearance on BBC televsion's *Question Time* on 8th April where she queried the despatch of the task force. One correspondent complained of Hart's, "effrontery to suggest that by the Government's despatch of the Task Force to our Falkland Islands we would be seen as firing the first shot. What the hell do you think the Argentine swine did when they invaded our islands, took them over by force and raised their miserable flag". A further television appearance a month later generated further spirited correspondence, one correspondent telling of, "how disgusted I was at your TV showing the other night when you knocked and ran down our forces and country. You are only equalled by Tony Benn. In Argentina at least, despite their many differences they are pulling together in the present time … Try supporting your country for a change. Remember that in Argentina your remarks would have put you in a lime pit with a bullet hole in the back of your head. How lucky you live in Great Britain". Judith Hart Papers, Labour History Archive.
77 Campbell, *Margaret Thatcher*, p. 200.

6 The Gulf War, 1990–91

1 Hansard, 6 Sep. 1990, cols. 734–35.
2 Hansard, 15 Jan. 1991, c.798. The 1975 Indonesian invasion of East Timor, which occurred while Labour was in power in Britain, would be another example.
3 Douglas Hurd, *Memoirs* (London, Abacus, 2004), p. 431.
4 As, for example, with Peter Shore: "I do not believe that it is possible to take seriously the United Nations as an institution if we do not accept that the meaning of collective security – above all in this post-cold war age – means the willingness to use international force, economic or, if need be, military, to achieve the goals of international security and justice which many of us came out of the second world war determined to achieve". Hansard, 6 Sep. 1990, col. 795.
5 A very good guide to these issues is provided by the debate involving Fred Halliday. See, for example: Fred Halliday, 'The Left and War', *New Statesman*, 8 Mar. 1991, pp. 15–16; Letters, *New Statesman*, 15 Mar. 1991, pp. 24–5; Robin Blackburn, 'The War of Ideas', *New Statesman*, 22 Mar. 1991, pp. 30–1; Fred Halliday, 'Reply to my Critics', *New Statesman*, 22 Mar. 1991, p. 32; Norman Geras, 'The Fudge of War', *New Statesman*, 29 Mar. 1991, p. 14; Alexander Cockburn, 'The War Goes On', *New Statesman*, 5 Apr. 1991, pp. 14–15; Letters, *New Statesman*, 12 Apr. 1991, pp. 38–9; Fred Halliday, 'The War the Left Lost', *Marxism Today*, Apr. 1991, pp. 30–1.
6 Hansard, 6 Sep. 1990, col. 735.
7 Ibid, cols. 736–37.
8 Ibid, col. 737.

9 Ibid, cols. 737–38.
10 Hansard, 7 Sep. 1990, col. 901.
11 Hansard, 6 Sep. 1990, cols. 738–39.
12 Interview with Lord Kinnock, 22 Feb. 2007.
13 Ibid.
14 Hansard, 6 Sep. 1990, col. 745. This was also the Liberal position. In the same debate, Liberal leader Paddy Ashdown warned that: "Force ... must be the last option and when it is used, it must be used on behalf of the community of nations as a whole". Ibid, col. 756. In contrast, the government benches were most likely to contain those least optimistic about the potential for sanctions alone to lead to Iraq's removal from Kuwait. See, for example, Cranley Onslow's speech, Hansard, 7 Sep. 1990, cols. 857–59.
15 Hansard, 6 Sep. 1990, col. 747.
16 Ibid, col. 746.
17 Ibid, col. 750.
18 Minutes of PLP meeting, 17 Oct. 1990. Labour History Archive.
19 Hansard, 6 Sep. 1990, col. 761.
20 Ibid, col. 762.
21 Ibid, col. 776.
22 Minutes of PLP meeting, 14 Nov. 1990. Labour History Archive.
23 Hansard, 6 Sep. 1990, col. 783. Among Faulds' roles was that of the hero Jet Morgan in the 1950s' BBC radio series, *Journey Into Space*. See his obituary, *The Guardian*, 1 Jun. 2000.
24 Minutes of PLP meeting, 14 Nov. 1990. Labour History Archive.
25 Hansard, 6 Sep. 1990, col. 771.
26 Ibid, col. 807. See also Eric Heffer, col. 852.
27 Hansard, 7 Sep. 1990, col. 856.
28 For example, Giles Radice: "Naturally, the Americans want to protect their oil supplies – [Interruption.] This is a serious debate and it would be sensible for hon. Members to take it seriously ... We all want to protect our oil supplies and we are entitled to do so". Hansard, 7 Sep. 1990, col. 876.
29 Ibid.
30 Ibid, col. 881.
31 Ibid, col. 901.
32 Hansard, 11 Dec. 1990, col. 823. Some still did not appreciate this. See Dennis Canavan, col. 898.
33 See, Minutes of PLP meetings, 6 Dec. 1990 and 12 Dec. 1990. Labour History Archive.
34 Hansard, 11 Dec. 1990, col. 825.
35 Ibid, col. 825.
36 On double effect, see Coates, *The Ethics of War*, pp. 239–64; Bellamy, *Just Wars*, pp. 124–26.
37 Hansard, 11 Dec. 1990, col. 826.
38 Ibid, cols. 857–58.
39 Ibid, col. 864.
40 Ibid, col. 830, see also col. 834.
41 Ibid, cols. 835–36.
42 Hansard, 15 Jan. 1991, col. 739. There were also MPs on the government benches who did not think that "last resort" had been reached, albeit many fewer than on the opposition benches. See, for example, Edward Heath's speech, ibid, cols. 751–55.
43 Ibid, col. 765.
44 Ibid, col. 798.
45 Minutes of PLP meeting, 16 Jan. 1991. Labour History Archive.

46 Ibid.
47 Hansard, 15 Jan. 1991, col. 744.
48 Ibid, col. 749.
49 Interview with Lord Kinnock, 22 Feb. 2007.
50 Hansard, 15 Jan. 1991, cols. 744–45.
51 Interview with Lord Kinnock, 22 Feb. 2007.
52 For example, Leicester MP Greville Janner, who reminded the House that: "Some hon. Members may remember that, in 1981, I ventured to suggest that Israel was right to take out Iraq's nuclear potential. I do not believe that anyone agreed with me. This place rose up and shouted. But today I am grateful for Israel's action. I hope that other hon. Members will realise what a catastrophe it would be if Saddam Hussein now had a nuclear potential. I believe that if we must act, we must do so today, before he gets nuclear potential tomorrow". Hansard, 15 Jan. 1991, col. 776.
53 For example, on the eve of war in 1991, Tony Benn expressed concern that: "Hon. Members on both sides of the House have said, 'We must topple Saddam before he gets nuclear weapons.' Where is the UN resolution about toppling Saddam before he gets nuclear weapons? What emerges from debates of this character is that there is a major difference between the UN agenda, which is to restore legality, and the other agenda". Ibid, col. 778.
54 Ibid, col. 813.
55 Minutes of PLP meeting, 21 Jan. 1991. Labour History Archive.
56 Ibid, col. 32.
57 Ibid, col. 98.
58 These views were also expressed at the PLP meeting of 6 Feb. 1991. Labour History Archive.
59 Hansard, 12 Feb. 1991, col. 822.
60 Ibid, col. 826.
61 Hansard, 28 Feb. 1991, col. 1119.

7 The rise of humanitarian military intervention in the 1990s: Bosnia and Kosovo

1 For example, Charles Hables Gray, *Post-Modern War: The New Politics of Conflicts* (Routledge, London, 1997); Mark Duffield, 'Post-Modern Conflict: Warlords, Post-Adjustment States and Private Protection', *Civil Wars*, Vol. 1, No.1, Apr. 1998, pp. 65–102.
2 Mary Kaldor, *New and Old Wars: Organized Violence in a Global Era* (Cambridge, Polity Press, 1999), p. 2.
3 Ibid.
4 Rupert Smith, *The Utility of Force: The Art of War in the Modern World* (London, Penguin, 2006), p. 1.
5 Hansard, 25 Sep. 1992, col. 164.
6 http://www.un.org/aboutun/charter/index.html
7 For a good overview, see Thomas G. Weiss, *Humanitarian Intervention* (Cambridge, Polity, 2007).
8 Hurd, *Memoirs*, p. 492.
9 On this question, see Paul Dixon, 'Britain's Vietnam Syndrome? Public Opinion and British Military Intervention – From Palestine to the Former Yugoslavia', *Review of International Studies*, Vol. 26, No. 1, Jan. 2000, pp. 99–121.
10 Hurd, *Memoirs*, p. 492.
11 On the break-up of Yugoslavia and the background to war, see, Laura Silber & Allan Little, *The Death of Yugoslavia* (London, Penguin, 2nd ed., 1996); Sabrina P. Ramet, *Thinking About Yugoslavia: Scholarly Debates About the Yugoslav Break-up and the Wars in Bosnia and Kosovo* (Cambridge, Cambridge University

Press, 2005); Tom Gallagher, *The Balkans After the Cold War: From Tyranny to Tragedy* (London, Routledge, 2003).

12 Hansard, 12 Dec. 1991, col. 1162–63.
13 Hurd, *The Search for Peace*, p. 136.
14 Quoted in Michael T. Klare, 'The Guns of Bosnia', *The Nation*, 22 Jan. 1996, p. 23.
15 Tim Judah, 'German Spies Accused of Arming Bosnian Muslims', *Sunday Telegraph*, 20 Apr. 1997.
16 Chris McGreal & Philip Willan, 'Vatican "Secretly Armed Croatia"', *The Guardian*, 19 Nov. 1999.
17 Klare, 'The Guns of Bosnia', p. 24.
18 John Pomfret & David B. Ottaway, 'Balkan Arms Smuggling: Wider Than US Acknowledged', *International Herald Tribune*, 13 May 1996.
19 Tom Rhodes, 'Clinton Approved Iran's Secret Arms Deals with Bosnia', *Times*, 6 Apr. 1996.
20 Hansard, 12 Dec. 1991, col. 1164.
21 For Hurd's account, see Hurd, *Memoirs*, pp. 495–99. The belief carried over into the Kosovo War. In March 1999, for example, Harry Barnes, argued that: "the former Yugoslavia was destroyed from outside by the German-inspired recognition of the secession of two of the richest republics in Yugoslavia: Slovenia and Croatia. The recognition of Slovenia and Croatia and the conflicts that followed led to the crisis in Bosnia. We must recognise the background to the present situation for which the world community has a serious responsibility". Hansard, 25 Mar. 1999, col. 555. However, see Sims, *Unfinest Hour*, pp. 18–19.
22 Hansard, 2 Jun. 1992, col. 715.
23 Ibid, col. 715.
24 Hansard, 29 Apr. 1993, col. 1170. Similarly: "We know that all, or almost all, those who are fighting in Bosnia have homes in Bosnia because they are Bosnian Serbs or Bosnian Croats or Bosnian Muslims ... we are dealing with, essentially, a harsh civil war, originally supported from outside, with confused fighting lines, in which cruelties and lies abound". Hansard, 19 Jul. 1995, col. 1753.
25 Hansard, 14 Apr. 1993, col. 829.
26 Hansard, 29 Apr. 1993, col. 1178. Cunningham characterised the civil war as being a product of "the aggressive nationalism that is now so rampant". Ibid, col. 1179.
27 Hansard, 25 Sep. 1992, col. 180.
28 Hansard, 2 Jun. 1992, col. 718.
29 Hansard, 19 Apr. 1993, col. 30.
30 There were odd exceptions as, for example, from Dennis Skinner: "Let me tell people like those on the Liberal Democrat Benches, who want to fight the war with the blood of other people's kids: do it yourselves. If they do not have the guts to put on their own flak jackets, they should not ask me to call on other kids to spill their blood to resolve what is a civil conflict in Yugoslavia as a result of the efforts of the Common Market". Ibid, col. 31.
31 Hansard, 29 Apr. 1993, col. 1176.
32 Hansard, 16 Nov. 1992, cols. 105–06.
33 For example, Hansard, 25 Sep. 1992, col. 132.
34 Hansard, 29 Apr. 1993, col. 1180.
35 Minutes of PLP meeting, 18 Nov. 1992. Labour History Archive.
36 The ultimately unsuccessful attempt by David Owen and former US Secretary of State Cyrus Vance to impose a peace plan on the warring parties. See, David Owen, *Balkan Odyssey* (London, Victor Gollancz, 1995).
37 Minutes of PLP meeting, 18 Nov. 1992. Labour History Archive.
38 *The Guardian*, 17 Apr. 1993. The 17 were: Calum Macdonald, Malcolm Wicks, Peter Mandelson, Frank Field, Angela Eagle, Max Madden, Chris Mullin, John

Austin Walker, Hugh Bayley, Clive Betts, Mike Watson, Nick Raynsford, Tony Wright, Michael Connarty, John Gunnell, Peter Hain and John Denham.

39 Hansard, 14 Apr. 1993, col. 835.
40 Clare Short, Hansard, 29 Apr. 1993, col. 1235.
41 Hansard, 14 Apr. 1993, col. 831.
42 Hansard, 19 Apr. 1993, col. 24.
43 Hansard, 31 May 1995, col. 1081.
44 Ibid, col. 1021. Similarly, Tam Dalyell asked: "If the air option were used, what would happen to those of our fellow countrymen in uniform who are pursuing a humanitarian role? As soon as those aircraft began to drop bombs, what would happen to the men in blue berets on the ground? Slit throats?" Hansard, 19 Jul. 1995, col. 1777.
45 Hansard, 31 May 1995, col. 1007.
46 Radice, *Diaries, 1980-2001*, p. 335.
47 Hansard, 31 May 1995, col. 1009.
48 Anthony Seldon, *Blair* (London, Free Press, 2005), p. 392.
49 Hansard, 19 Jul. 1995, col. 1752.
50 http://www.state.gov/www/regions/eur/ksvo_rambouillet_text.html. Last accessed 5 Jan. 2007.
51 Tony Blair, 'Our Responsibilities Do Not End at the Channel', *Independent on Sunday*, 14 Feb. 1999.
52 Ibid.
53 Which states, in part: "Nothing in the Present Charter precludes the existence of regional arrangements or agencies for dealing with such matters relating to the maintenance of international peace and security as are appropriate for regional action provided that such arrangements or agencies and their activities are consistent with the Purposes and Principles of the United Nations".
54 Hansard, 1 Apr. 1999, col. 574.
55 Bellamy, *Just Wars*, p. 215. On the question of legality, Labour MP Bob Marshall-Andrews would ask: "Why are we embarked on an air war rather than on an invasion? I suggest that nation states are naturally inhibited from invading other nation states because they know that it is an act of wanton illegality. That is the box in which we are caught. Does legality matter? Of course it does, because acting legally gives one's actions coherence. Legality is not merely a question of the right to intervene: it is also the duty to intervene. If there is a legal duty to intervene, there is no debate about whether to commit ground troops because one's duty is to intervene to the maximum extent". Hansard, 18 May 1999, col. 912.
56 Foreign Affairs Committee, *Kosovo* (Fourth Report, Session 1999–2000, HC 28-I, London, The Stationery Office), para. 138.
57 Ibid, para. 134.
58 Seldon, *Blair*, p. 395.
59 Denis Healey, 'Wrong Move', *The Guardian*, 26 Mar. 1999.
60 Jonathan Freedland, 'The Left Needs to Wake Up to the Real World. This War is a Just One', *The Guardian*, 26 Mar. 1999.
61 Hansard, 23 Mar. 1999, col. 161.
62 Robin Cook, Hansard, 25 Mar. 1999, col. 540.
63 Ibid, col. 541.
64 Hansard, 23 Mar. 1999, col. 161.
65 Hansard, 25 Mar. 1999, col. 539.
66 Ibid, col. 564.
67 Hansard, 18 May 1999, col. 886.
68 Hansard, 23 Mar. 1999, col. 166.
69 Ibid, col. 173. See also, Tony Blair, 'We Must Keep Bombing to Save the Refugees', *Sunday Telegraph*, 4 Apr. 1999.

70 Hansard, 25 Mar. 1999, col. 549.
71 Henry Shue, 'Bombing to Rescue? NATO's 1999 Bombing of Serbia', in Chatterjee & Scheid (eds), *Ethics and Foreign Intervention*, pp. 97–117.
72 Tony Blair, 'A New Generation Draws the Line', *Newsweek*, 19 Apr. 1999.
73 Hansard, 25 Mar. 1999, col. 550.
74 Ibid, col. 551.
75 Ibid, cols. 572–73.
76 Ibid, cols. 565–66. See also, Tony Benn, 'Fighting for Democracy While Kosovo Burns', *The Observer*, 18 Apr. 1999.
77 Hansard, 25 Mar. 1999, col. 565.
78 Ibid, col. 578.
79 Seldon, *Blair*, p. 395.
80 Andrew Sparrow & Ben Fenton, 'Milosevic Must Go, Says Blair', *Daily Telegraph*, 19 Apr. 1999.
81 Hansard, 18 May 1999, col. 887.
82 For example, Bruce George. See, Hansard, 18 May 1999, col. 898.
83 Hansard, 19 Apr. 1999, col. 599.
84 Interview with Sir Gerald Kaufman, 25 Oct. 2006.
85 Hansard, 18 May 1999, cols. 941–42.
86 Adam LeBor, *Milosevic: A Biography* (London, Bloomsbury, 2003), p. 293.
87 See, Tony Blair, 'A New Moral Crusade', *Newsweek*, 14 Jun. 1999, p. 38.
88 Owen, *Balkan Odyssey*, p. 374.
89 Blair, 'We Must Keep Bombing to Save the Refugees'.

8 New Labour goes to war (again): Iraq 2002–03

1 Even Douglas Hurd, reluctant to commit British ground forces to Bosnia in a military capacity in the mid-1990s, was conceding by 1997 that, "we are all interventionists now" – although this was still not true of the strict restrictionists in both the Labour and Conservative parties. Hurd, *The Search for Peace*, p. 242; *Memoirs*, p. 493.
2 Kennedy, *The Parliament of Man*, p. 103.
3 Attlee, *As It Happened*, p. 199.
4 Lord Hutton, *Report of the Inquiry into the Circumstances Surrounding the Death of Dr. David Kelly CMG* (HC 247, London, HMSO, 2004); Lord Butler, *Review of Intelligence on Weapons of Mass Destruction: Report of a Committee of Privy Counsellors*, HC898, (London, The Stationery Office, July 2004).
5 Anthony Sampson, 'Hijacked by that Mob at No.10', *The Observer*, 8 Jun. 2003.
6 *The Independent*, 13 May 2003.
7 Interview with Lord Owen, 2 Nov. 2006.
8 Clare Short believes that: "Blair would have been a different Blair if he had only had the majorities Wilson had, because then he would have been using his charm, which is his distinctive feature, to keep his majority together and get things through Parliament. He would have been a completely different political creature, Labour's tradition would have constrained him more". Interview with Clare Short, 14 Oct. 2006.
9 As per Gerald Kaufman's observation quoted in Chapter 7, p. 127.
10 Interview with Lord Kinnock, 22 Feb. 2007.
11 Norton, 'The Presidentialization of British Politics', p. 277. In addition to this, see Lance Price, *The Spin Doctor's Diary: Inside Number 10 With New Labour* (London, Hodder & Stoughton, 2005); Nicholas Jones, *Sultans of Spin* (London, Victor Gollancz, 1999); Peter Oborne & Simon Walters, *Alastair Campbell* (London, Aurum Press, 2004).
12 Price, *The Spin Doctor's Diary*, p. 69.

13 Ross McKibbin, 'Why Did He Risk It?', *London Review of Books*, 3 Apr. 2003, www.lrb.co.uk/v25/n07/mcki01_.html. Last accessed 5 Jan. 2007.

14 On the importance of Blair's background, see Inderjeet Parmar, '"I'm Proud of the British Empire": Why Tony Blair Backs George W. Bush', *The Political Quarterly*, Vol. 76, No. 2, Apr. 2005, pp. 218–31.

15 Cited in Peter Riddell, *Hug Them Close: Blair, Clinton, Bush and the 'Special Relationship'* (London, Politico's, 2003), p. 8.

16 Colin Brown, 'Campbell Interrupted Blair as he Spoke of his Faith: "We Don't do God"', *Daily Telegraph*, 4 May 2003.

17 Cited in Dumbrell, *A Special Relationship*, p. 120.

18 Hansard, 24 Sep. 2002, col. 21.

19 Henry Kissinger, *White House Years* (Boston, Little, Brown, 1979), p. 933.

20 Tony Blair, 'For Once, There Is No Third Way', *The Observer*, 15 Feb. 1998.

21 Pimlott (ed.), *The Political Diary of Hugh Dalton*, entry for 5 Apr. 1951, p. 518.

22 Patrick Wintour, 'What the Memo Tells us About Tony Blair's Style of Leadership', *The Guardian*, 18 Jul. 2000.

23 Melissa Kite, 'Tony Blair "Relished" Sending British Soldiers Off to War', *Daily Telegraph*, 18 Sep. 2005. http://www.telegraph.co.uk/news/main.jhtml?xml = / news/2005/09/18/nblur18.xml. In the published version, this entry was altered to: "I couldn't help feeling TB had mixed emotions about sending the boys into action". Price, *The Spin Doctor's Diary*, p. 62.

24 John Kampfner, *Blair's Wars* (London, Free Press, 2004), p. 33.

25 Price, *The Spin Doctor's Diary*, p. 130.

26 Phythian, *The Politics of British Arms Sales Since 1964*, Ch. 7. In June 1998 Downing Street spin doctor Lance Price noted in his diary that on: "the 'ethical foreign policy'. TB clearly thinks Cook has been grandstanding too much." Price, *The Spin Doctor's Diary*, p. 13.

27 'Doctrine of the International Community', 22 Apr. 1999.

28 Richard A. Clarke, *Against All Enemies* (New York, Free Press, 2004), pp. 264, 268. On this pre-history, see also James Mann, *Rise of the Vulcans: The History of Bush's War Cabinet* (New York, Viking, 2004).

29 Andrew Cockburn, *Rumsfeld: His Rise, Fall, and Catastrophic Legacy* (New York, Scribner, 2007), p. 9.

30 Clarke, *Against All Enemies*, p. 32.

31 Glenn Kessler, 'U.S. Decision On Iraq Has Puzzling Past', *Washington Post*, 12 Jan. 2003.

32 George W. Bush, State of the Union Address, 29.1.02. http://www.whitehouse.-gov/news/releases/2002/01/20020129-11.html. Last accessed 5 Jan. 2007.

33 Butler Report, para. 266.

34 Ibid, para. 267.

35 Ibid.

36 Robin Cook, *The Point of Departure* (London, Simon & Schuster, 2003), p. 116.

37 Ibid, pp. 115–16.

38 Clare Short, 'There Was Never An Honest Debate in Cabinet', *The Independent*, 19 Jul. 2004. See also, Clare Short, *An Honourable Deception? New Labour, Iraq, and the Misuse of Power* (London, Free Press, 2004), pp. 150–51.

39 Additionally, Lance Price records sitting in on a Cabinet meeting in October 1999: "TB said at the beginning that he hoped they would be able to have a good discussion and when somebody made an aside about making a decision he said, 'Oh, I don't think we should go that far.' His disarming manner allows him to get away with murder like that". Price, *The Spin Doctor's Diary*, p. 156.

40 David Blunkett, *The Blunkett Tapes: My Life in the Bear Pit* (London, Bloomsbury, 2006) pp. 355, 359, 460.

41 Butler Report, para. 610.

42 Peter Hennessy, *Having It So Good: Britain in the Fifties* (London, Allen Lane, 2006), p. 437.

43 Peter Hennessy, 'Informality and Circumscription: The Blair Style of Government in War and Peace', *The Political Quarterly*, Vol. 76, No. 1, Jan.–Mar. 2005, pp. 3–11.

44 'Your Trip to the US'. Memo from David Manning to Tony Blair, 14 Mar. 2002. http://www.downingstreetmemo.com/docs/manning.pdf. Last accessed 5 Jan. 2007.

45 Memo from Christopher Meyer to Sir David Manning, 18 Mar. 2002. http://www.downingstreetmemo.com/docs/meyermemo.pdf. Last accessed 5 Jan. 2007.

46 'IRAQ: Advice for the Prime Minister'. Memo from P. F. Ricketts to Jack Straw, 22 Mar. 2002. http://www.downingstreetmemo.com/docs/ricketts.pdf. Last accessed 5 Jan. 2007.

47 Ibid.

48 'Crawford/Iraq'. Memo from Jack Straw to Tony Blair, 25 Mar. 2002. http://www.downingstreetmemo.com/docs/straw.pdf. Last accessed 5 Jan. 2007.

49 Ibid.

50 For example, Kampfner, *Blair's Wars*, p. 168.

51 Anthony Giddens, *The Third Way: The Renewal of Social Democracy* (Cambridge, Polity Press, 1998), p. 70. Earlier, Giddens had argued that: "States without enemies, and marked by a concomitant decline in militarism, are in quite a different situation from either the Cold War or pre-existing systems of military alliance and national antagonism. Although border disputes may remain, and invasions sometimes occur, most states no longer have any incentive to wage offensive war". Anthony Giddens, *Beyond Left and Right* (Cambridge, Polity, 1994), p. 235.

52 Prime Minister's speech at the George Bush Senior Presidential Library, 7 Apr. 2002. http://www.pm.gov.uk/output/Page1712.asp. Last accessed 5 Jan. 2007.

53 Ibid.

54 'Iraq: Prime Minister's Meeting, 23 July'. Memo from Matthew Rycroft to David Manning, 23 Jul. 2002. http://www.downingstreetmemo.com/memos.html#originalmemo. Last accessed 5 Jan. 2007.

55 Ibid.

56 Ibid.

57 Ibid.

58 Bob Woodward, *Plan of Attack* (London, Simon & Schuster, 2004), p. 178.

59 Available at: http://www.pm.gov.uk/output/Page271.asp. Last accessed 5 Jan. 2007. See also, Mark Phythian, 'Hutton and Scott: A Tale of Two Inquiries', *Parliamentary Affairs*, Vol. 58, No. 1, January 2005, pp. 124–37.

60 Bryan Burrough, Evgenia Peretz, David Rose & David Wise, 'The Path to War', *Vanity Fair*, May 2004, p. 172.

61 Cook, *The Point of Departure*, p. 203.

62 Ibid, pp. 212–13.

63 Kampfner, *Blair's Wars*, p. 214.

64 Short, *An Honourable Deception?*, pp. 152–53; Interview with Clare Short, 14 Oct. 2006.

65 Mark Danner, 'The Secret Way to War', *New York Review of Books*, 9 Jun. 2005, p. 72.

66 Straw had said that: "He's got these weapons of mass destruction, chemical, biological and, probably, nuclear weapons which he has used in the past against his own people as well as his neighbours and could almost certainly use again in the future". Ewen MacAskill & Nick Watt, 'Anger Over Straw's Dossier on Iraqi Human Rights', *The Guardian*, 3 Dec. 2002

67 'Saddam Lied About Weapons Says Straw', 18 Dec. 2002. http://www.guardian.co.uk/Iraq/Story/0,2763,862304,00.html. Last accessed 5 Jan. 2007.

68 Hansard, 26 Feb. 2003, col. 265.
69 Ibid, col. 317.
70 Philip Cowley, *The Rebels: How Blair Mislaid His Majority* (London, Politico's, 2005), pp. 114–16.
71 See the letter from the French Ambassador to the US, Jean-David Levitte, in *Foreign Affairs*, Vol. 85, No. 5, Sep.–Oct. 2006, p. 182. See also, Kampfner, *Blair's Wars*, pp. 286–89.
72 Blair attempted to define this for the benefit of MPs, see Hansard, 18 Mar. 2003, col. 765.
73 Hansard, 17 Mar. 2003, col. 726.
74 Cowley, *The Rebels*, p. 123.

Conclusion

1 Phythian, 'Hutton and Scott', pp. 128–29.
2 Butler Report, para. 427.
3 Ibid.
4 Ibid.
5 Glen Rangwala & Dan Plesch, 'A Case to Answer: A First Report on the Potential Impeachment of the Prime Minister for High Crimes and Misdemeanours in Relation to the Invasion of Iraq', Aug. 2004, para. 1.1.16. http://www.impeach-blair.org/downloads/A_Case_To_Answer.pdf. Last accessed 5 Jan. 2007.
6 Ibid, para. 1.1.19.
7 Robin Cook, 'The Die Was Cast: The Dossiers Were Irrelevant', *The Independent on Sunday*, 18 Jul. 2004.
8 Hansard, 14 Jul. 2004, col. 1436.
9 Cited in Hennessy, 'Informality and Circumscription', p. 8.
10 Butler Report, para. 374.
11 Ibid, para. 379.
12 See also the assessment by Bellamy, *Just Wars*, pp. 219–21.
13 Yasamee & Hamilton (eds), *Documents on British Policy Overseas*, pp. 27–28.
14 Williams, *The Diary of Hugh Gaitskell 1945–1956*, p. 575. In his November 1956 televised address, Gaitskell highlighted the fact that: "We're doing all this alone, except for France. Opposed by the world, in defiance of the world. It is not a police action; there is no law behind it. We have taken the law into our own hands". Ibid, p. 620.
15 Hansard, 12 Sep. 1956, col. 27.
16 Ibid, cols. 138–39.
17 Hansard, 5 Jul. 1950, cols. 594–96.
18 Tony Blair, Doctrine of the International Community, 24 Apr. 1999.
19 Hansard, 19 Apr. 1999, col. 606.
20 Hansard, 19 Apr. 1993, col. 23.
21 Hansard, 25 Mar. 1999, col. 54.
22 Hansard, 29 Apr. 1993, col. 1169.
23 Cited in Coates, *The Ethics of War*, p. 167.
24 Bellamy, *Just Wars*, p. 214. See also, Michael Walzer, *Arguing About War* (New Haven, Yale University Press, 204), pp. 162–68.
25 Ted Honderich, *After the Terror* (Edinburgh, Edinburgh University Press, revised ed., 2003), p. 1.
26 See Patrick Cockburn, *The Occupation: War and Resistance in Iraq* (London, Verso, 2006).
27 http://www.iraqbodycount.org/database/
28 Bellamy, *Just Wars*, p. 213.
29 Weiss, *Humanitarian Intervention*, Ch. 5.

30 Ben Russell & Colin Brown, 'Ministers Accused of Giving Israel Green Light to Bomb', *The Independent*, 21 Jul. 2006.
31 Patrick Wintour & Ewen MacAskill, 'Blair: You've Misunderstood Me Over the Middle East', *The Guardian*, 3 Aug. 2006.
32 Ibid.
33 This was subsequently confirmed by Jack Straw. Tania Branigan, 'Blair's Pro-Israel Stance "Trigger for Coup Bid"', *The Guardian*, 6 Mar. 2007.
34 Tony Blair, 'The Role of the UK's Armed Forces in the 21st Century', 12 Jan. 2007. http://www.number10.gov.uk/output/Page10735.asp. Last accessed 16 Jan. 2007.
35 http://a4.g.akamai.net/7/4/15010/1/labourparty1.download.akamai.com/15010/manifesto_13042005_a3/flash/manifesto_2005.swf. Last acessed 5 Jan. 2007.
36 Jonathan Freedland, 'War: The Great Unknown Among Election Issues'; Audrey Gillan, Steven Morris & Helen Carter, 'Why Rake Up the War?', *The Guardian*, 18 Apr. 2005.
37 As with an article for *Foreign Affairs*, in which he argued that: "The debate over the wisdom of the original decisions, especially about Iraq, will continue. Opponents will say that Iraq was never a threat, that there were no weapons of mass destruction, that the drug trade in Afghanistan continues. I will point out that Iraq was indeed a threat, as two regional wars, 14 UN resolutions, and the final report of the Iraq Survey Group showed. I will remind people that in the aftermath of the Iraq war, we secured major advances in tackling the proliferation of weapons of mass destruction, not least a new relationship with Libya and the shutting down of A. Q. Khan's nuclear weapons network. I will recall that it was the Taliban who manipulated the drug trade and housed al Qaeda and its training camps". Tony Blair, 'A Battle for Global Values', *Foreign Affairs*, Jan/Feb 2007. http://www.foreignaffairs.org/20070101faessay86106-p30/tony-blair/a-battle-for-global-values.html. Last accessed 1 Feb. 2007.
38 Kampfner, *Blair's Wars*, p. 48.

Index